Reforming Public Institutions and Strengthening Governance

A World Bank Strategy
November 2000

Public Sector Group

Poverty Reduction and Economic Management (PREM) Network

Copyright © 2000 The International Bank for Reconstruction
and Development / THE WORLD BANK
1818 H Street, N.W.
Washington, D.C. 20433, USA

The findings, interpretations, and conclusions expressed in this book are entirely those of the authors
and should not be attributed in any manner to the World Bank, to its affiliated organizations, or to
members of its Board of Executive Directors or the countries they represent. The World Bank does
not guarantee the accuracy of the data included in this publication and accepts no responsibility for
any consequence of their use. The boundaries, colors, denominations, and other information shown
on any map in this volume do not imply on the part of the World Bank Group any judgment on the
legal status of any territory or the endorsement or acceptance of such boundaries.

The material in this publication is copyrighted. The World Bank encourages dissemination of its
work and will normally grant permission to reproduce portions of the work promptly.

Permission to photocopy items for internal or personal use, for the internal or personal use of
specific clients, or for educational classroom use is granted by the World Bank, provided that the
appropriate fee is paid directly to the Copyright Clearance Center, Inc., 222 Rosewood Drive, Danvers,
MA 01923, USA; telephone 978-750-8400, fax 978-750-4470. Please contact the Copyright Clearance
Center before photocopying items.

For permission to reprint individual articles or chapters, please fax a request with complete information to the Republication Department, Copyright Clearance Center, fax 978-750-4470.

All other queries on rights and licenses should be addressed to the Office of the Publisher, World
Bank, at the address above or faxed to 202-522-2422.

Library of Congress Cataloging-in-Publication Data has been applied for.

CONTENTS

Figures

Tables

FOREWORD

The critical importance of well-performing public institutions and good governance for development and poverty reduction has come to the forefront in the 1990s. Just as it was increasingly recognized in the 1980s that individual investment projects are less likely to succeed in a distorted policy environment, so it has become obvious in the 1990s that neither good policies nor good investments are likely to emerge and be sustainable in an environment with dysfunctional institutions and poor governance.

At the same time, it is also clear that reforming public institutions is a complex and difficult task, both technically and politically. "First-generation" reforms, such as exchange rate unification and trade liberalization, could often be undertaken through the actions of a relatively small number of policymakers and public managers. Institutional reform typically involves fundamental changes in the "rules of the game" for a large number of civil servants and private citizens. Such changes are likely to require long-term high-level commitment, in-depth knowledge, and extensive support and assistance.

The World Bank is deeply committed to helping its client countries build well-functioning and accountable governments. As a result, both our lending and nonlending support for core public sector reform have expanded rapidly in the past four years. *Reforming Public Institutions and Strengthening Governance* is part of a broader World Bank effort to delineate sector and thematic strategies. While it is intended primarily as a guide for our own work, we hope that the lessons of experience and the goals and approaches for the future that it lays out will serve the broader development community.

Kemal Dervis
Vice President
Poverty Reduction and Economic Management Network

Acknowledgments

This strategy paper was prepared by the Public Sector Board of the Poverty Reduction and Economic Management (PREM) Network, under the direction of Public Sector Director Cheryl Gray. Current or past members of the Board who contributed to the report and were primarily responsible for the individual VPU strategies in Part II include Shanta Devarajan (Development Research Group), Ali Khadr (Middle East and North Africa), Daniel Kaufmann (World Bank Institute), Brian Levy (Africa), Helga Muller and Sanjay Pradhan (Europe and Central Asia), Barbara Nunberg (East Asia and the Pacific), Shekhar Shah (South Asia), and Geoffrey Shepherd (Latin America and the Caribbean). Melissa Thomas and Tripti Thomas had major roles in editing parts of the document. Anna Hansson was primarily responsible for compiling the data on the public sector portfolio. Nick Manning contributed to the annex on analytic tools, and Steve Knack had a major role in updating the annexes on governance indicators and on the links between poverty and governance. Vinaya Swaroop contributed to the annex on Bank-IMF relations. In addition, many useful contributions were received from other Bank staff and external advisors, including Paul Bermingham, Isabelle Bleas, Colin Bruce, Monali Chowdhurie-Aziz, Mamadou Dia, John Heilbrunn, Malcolm Holmes, Arturo Israel, Phil Keefer, Jennie Litvack, Yasuhiko Matsuda, Robert Picciotto, Allen Schick, Miguel Schloss, Graham Scott, Anwar Shah, Rick Stapenhurst, Mike Stevens, Eric Swanson, John Todd, and Ulrich Zachau. We also benefited from extensive comments from members of the Executive Board during discussions with the Committee on Development Effectiveness (CODE) in December 1999 and January 2000 and discussions with the full Board in July 2000, and from comments received from numerous external partners during consultations (most between January and May 2000) in Abidjan, Copenhagen, Harare, London, Maastricht, Manila, New York, Paris, Stockholm, Warsaw, and Washington. We are grateful to the many other people inside and outside the Bank who also provided valuable comments on previous drafts.

The strategy and extensive related and supporting material on various aspects of public sector reform and governance are available through the World Bank's website at *www.worldbank.org/publicsector*. Extensive governance-related information is also available through WBI's website at *www.worldbank.org/wbi/governance*.

Acronyms and Abbreviations

ACBF	Africa Capacity Building Foundation
ADB	Asian Development Bank
AfDB	Africa Development Bank
AFR	Africa Regional Vice-Presidency
AMF/	Arab Monetary Fund/Arab Fund for
AFSED	Social and Economic Development
APL/C	Adaptable Program Loan/Credit
ASA	Association for Social Advancement
ASEM	Asia-Europe Meeting
AU	Anti-bribery Undertaking
BERI	Business Environmental Risk Intelligence
BRAC	Bangladesh Rural Advancement Committee
CAPAM	Commonwealth Association for Public Management
CAS	Country Assistance Strategy
CCCE	Caisse Centrale de Coopération Economique
CDF	Comprehensive Development Framework
CEE	Central and Eastern Europe
CEM	Country Economic Memorandum
CFAA	Country Financial Accountability Assessment
CIDA	Canadian International Development Agency
CIS	Commonwealth of Independent States
CLAD	Centro Latinoamericano de Administracion para el Desarrollo
CMU	Country Management Unit
CPAR	Country Procurement Assessment Report
CPI	Corruption Perception Index
CPIA	Country Performance and Institutional Assessment
CSR	Civil Service Reform
DAC	Development Assistance Committee
DANIDA	Danish International Assistance Agency
DEC	Development Economics Vice-Presidency
DECDG	Development Data Group
DRG	Development Research Group
DFID	Department for International Development, U.K.
DL	Distance Learning
EA5	East Asia 5 (Indonesia, Korea, Malaysia, Philippines, Thailand)
EAP	East Asia and Pacific Regional Vice-Presidency
EASPR	Poverty Reduction and Economic Management Sector Unit, EAP
EBRD	European Bank for Reconstruction and Development
ECA	Europe and Central Asia Regional Vice Presidency
ECSPE	Poverty Reduction and Economic Management Sector Unit, ECA
EDI	Economic Development Institute (now WBI)
ERF	Economic Research Forum
ESSD	Environmentally and Socially Sustainable Development Network
ESW	Economic and Sector Work
EU	European Union
EUROMED	Euro-Mediterranean Partnership
FIAS	Foreign Investment Advisory Service
FPSI	Finance, Private Sector and Infrastructure Network
GCA	Global Coalition for Africa
GDP	Gross Domestic Product
GNP	Gross National Product
GR	Institutional and Governance Review
GTZ	German Association for Technical Cooperation
IBRD	International Bank for Reconstruction and Development
HD	Human Development Network
HNP	Health Nutrition and Population
HIPC	Heavily Indebted Poor Country
IBTA	Institution-Building/Technical Assistance
ICITAP	International Criminal Investigation Training Assistance Program
ICRG	International Consulting Resources Group
IDA	International Development Association
IDB	Inter-American Development Bank
IDF	Institutional Development Facility
IGR	Institutional and Governance Review
INFID	International NGO Forum on Indonesian Development
IFI	International Financial Institutions
IMF	International Monetary Fund
INDECOPI	Instituto Nacional de Defensa de la Competencia y de la Protección de la Propiedad Intelectual, Peruvian Competition Agency
INTOSAI	International Organization of Supreme Audit Institutions
IRIS	Center for Institutional Reform and the Informal Sector, University of Maryland
IRMT	International Records Management Trust

JICA	Japan International Cooperation Agency	PRD	Prefecture Development Council
KMS	Knowledge Management System	PREM	Poverty Reduction and Economic Management Network
LCR	Latin America and Caribbean Regional Vice-Presidency	PRMPS	Public Sector Group, PREM
LCSHD	Human Development Sector Unit, LCR	PRR	Policy Research Report
LCSPR	Poverty Reduction and Economic Management Sector Unit, LCR	PRSP	Poverty Reduction Strategy Paper
		PSB	Public Sector Board
LEG	Legal Vice-Presidency	PSI	Private Sector Development and Infrastructure Vice Presidency
LEGLR	Legal and Judicial Reform Unit		
LIL	Learning and Innovations Loan	PSM	Public Sector Management
LLC	Learning and Leadership Center (WBI)	PSMAC	Public Sector Management Adjustment Credit
LTPS	Long-Term Perspectives Study for Sub-Saharan Africa	PSAL/C	Programmatic Structural Adjustment Loan/Credit
MDB	Multilateral Development Bank	PSR	Public Sector Reform
MDF	Mediterranean Development Forum	PSRL	Public Sector Reform Loan
MIS	Management Information Systems	PUMA	Public Management Committee and Public Management Service
MNA	Middle East and North Africa Regional Vice-Presidency		
		QAG	Quality Assurance Group
MOJ	Ministry of Justice	SAC	Structural Adjustment Credit
MTEF	Medium Term Expenditure Framework	SAL	Structural Adjustment Loan
NGO	Nongovernmental Organization	SAR	South Asia Regional Vice-Presidency
NMAD	National-Municipal Accountability Diagnostics	SAS	South Asia Sector Units
NORAD	Norwegian Agency for Development Cooperation	SES	Senior Executive Service
		SEWA	Self-Employed Women's Association, India
NPM	New Public Management	SFO	Special Financial Operations Unit
O&M	Operations & Maintenance	SIDA	Swedish International Development Agency
OAS	Organization of American States	SIGMA	Support for Improvement in Governance and Management in Central and Eastern European Countries
OCS	Operational Core Services Network		
OECD	Organization for Economic Co-operation and Development		
		SIP	Sectoral Investment Program
OED	Operations Evaluation Department	SSR	Social and Structural Review
ONEP	Oficina Nacional de Etica Publica	TA	Technical Assistance
OP	Operational Policy	TACIS	Technical Assistance for Commonwealth of Independent States
OPE	Office of Professional Ethics		
OSCE	Organization for Security and Co-operation in Europe	TAL	Technical Assistance Loan
		TI	Transparency International
OSG	Operations Support Group	UNCTAD	United Nations Conference on Trade and Development
OVP	Operational Vice President		
PACT	Partnership for Capacity Building in Africa	UNDP	United Nations Development Programme
PER	Public Expenditure Review	UNICEF	United Nations Children's Fund
PHARE	Poland and Hungary: Action for Restructuring the Economy	USAID	U.S. Agency for International Development
		VAT	Value Added Tax
PHRD	Policy and Human Resource Development Fund	WBER	World Bank Economic Review
		WBES	World Business Environment Survey
PIU	Project Implementation Unit	WBI	World Bank Institute
PNG	Papua New Guinea	WDR97	World Development Report, 1997
PPI	Private Provision of Infrastructure		

Reforming Public Institutions and Strengthening Governance

As the World Bank confronts the challenge of reducing poverty, it must address the root causes of poverty and focus on necessary conditions for sustainable development. Poorly functioning public sector institutions and weak governance[1] are major constraints to growth and equitable development in many developing countries. The *World Development Report (WDR) 2000/2001: Attacking Poverty*, contains a rich discussion of the importance of good governance and effective public sector institutions for poverty reduction. The *World Development Report 1997: The State in a Changing World*, lays out an agenda for action to improve the performance of governments. This strategy paper takes stock of the Bank's recent work on governance, public sector institutional reform, and capacity building (particularly in core public institutions) and addresses what the World Bank can do to enhance its ability to help client countries implement this agenda.

The topic is important not only because of its centrality to development, but also because of the mixed track record the Bank has traditionally had in this line of work. Until recently, evaluations by the Operations

Evaluation Department (OED) and the Quality Assurance Group (QAG) consistently indicated weak performance in the Bank's portfolio of public sector management (PSM) projects and in the institution-building components of projects in other sectors, although recent OED and QAG data indicate a marked improvement over the past three years. Bank and other donor efforts at technical assistance have been criticized for over a decade, and questions more recently have been raised about the quality and impact of analytic work, in particular Public Expenditure Reviews (PERs).

Given the complexity and depth of the challenge, this strategy envisions significant changes in the focus of the Bank's work and the way it does business in this area. These changes are fully in line with the themes underpinning the Comprehensive Development Framework (CDF), and many are already well underway as a result of the Bank's enhanced focus on governance, capacity building, and anticorruption. The agenda for the next three years is to continue to foster these changes through the advancement of analytic tools, new approaches to the design of lending operations, expanded emphasis on partnership with clients and other donors, and progressive shifts in staffing, incentives, and evaluation techniques.

The conditions for governance reform in the developing world are better now than they have been in decades. *We have a real chance to make a difference, and we must do all we can to build on that opportunity.*

Moving Institutional Development and Capacity Building to Center Stage

As highlighted in President Wolfensohn's speech to the 1999 Annual Meetings, capacity building—that is, building effective and accountable institutions to address development issues and reduce poverty in borrowing countries—should be at the core of World Bank activity. As highlighted in *WDR97*, helping the public sector work better in developing countries is a two-fold challenge: it involves (a) helping it define its role in line with economic rationale and with its own capacity, and (b) helping it enhance performance within that role. Providing good policy advice is not enough; the Bank needs to focus even more than it has in the past on helping governments develop the processes and incentives to design and implement good policies themselves. Only through such institution-building will countries be able to achieve the ultimate goals of poverty reduction, inclusion, environmental sustainability, and private sector development.

Institutions are broadly defined in this strategy: they are the "rules of the game" that emerge from formal laws, informal norms and practices, and organizational structures in a given setting. The incentives they create shape the actions of public officials. Institutions overlap with but are not synonymous with organizations; they are affected by policy design but are broader in scope and less subject to frequent change than most policy frameworks.

Institutional development is not a sector (as "public sector management" has traditionally been treated in the past) but rather cuts across all sectors.[2] The many economic functions of the public sector can be classified into three broad categories—policymaking, service delivery, and oversight and accountability. Most Bank activities deal with public institutions in at least one of these categories. Indeed, institution-building components exist in almost all Bank loans. Some loans focus on the reform of core institutions in the public sector (such as the civil service, institutions for public expenditure and financial management, systems of revenue collection, or legal and judicial institutions), while others focus on reform of institutions in specific sectors. The lack of systematic and integrated treatment of institutional issues at the country level has meant that these individual efforts are often fragmented, and in many cases they have been sacrificed to a shorter-term emphasis on policy change or the direct provision of outputs.

An emphasis on institution-building has already increased significantly in some areas of Bank work (such as public expenditure and infrastructure work), and it needs to continue. For example, rather than advising countries exclusively on the content of annual budget allocations, as was the focus of early Public Expenditure Reviews, the Bank is increasingly helping countries build effective budgeting and expenditure management systems. Rather than focusing on layoffs of a certain number of civil servants, as was common in early adjustment lending, it is increasingly helping build long-term systems for efficient employment and career incentives in the civil service. And rather than focusing on the direct supply of physical infrastructure or social services, it is increasingly helping build the institutions that allow public and private actors to enter the market and that encourage them to provide services efficiently and equitably.

This strategy paper focuses primarily on reforms of core public sector institutions (such as administrative and civil service reform, public expenditure management, tax administration, public enterprise reform, and legal and judicial reform) and their *interface* with sectoral institutions. It touches only lightly on institutional concerns within specific sectors (for example, in health, education, and rural infrastructure), and it does so primarily to point out generic issues that concern many sectors. But institutional issues are clearly important in all sectors, and indeed span the full range of Bank work. All of the sector families need to work together to mainstream institutional concerns in Bank work and integrate them in country settings as much as possible.

Learning from Experience: Four Strategic Changes for the Future

The World Bank has had a mixed record in public sector reform to date. Analysis by OED and QAG, as well as the experience gained during the past decade by the Bank's operational staff, show the extensive breadth and depth of Bank involvement and effort, with both successes and failures as outcomes. They also point to several systemic shortcomings of past Bank work in this area:

- The Bank has sometimes taken a rather narrow and "technocratic" view of what is needed for public sector reform, interacting exclusively with government interlocutors and funding consulting services, computers, and other inputs in the absence of deep and sustainable demand for institutional reform on the part of the borrower and society. Because it has not been sensitive enough to underlying demand and potential for change, the Bank has not always been good at focusing its resources where they might have had the greatest long-term impact. This critique is not unique to the Bank, but applies to much of the donor community.

- It has sometimes relied on models of "best practice" that have not been feasible in the particular country setting, given variations in human and institutional capacity.

- Traditional applications of the Bank's lending instruments—Structural Adjustment Loans (SALs), Technical Assistance (TA) loans, and investment loans—have not always allowed the long-term commitment and systemic viewpoint needed to achieve lasting results. Short-term demands (for example, for quick disbursements or "enclaved" project administration) have sometimes compromised longer-term goals of institutional-building, with negative long-term impacts.

- There has traditionally been a shortage of staff skills in certain specialized areas related to governance, institutional reform, and capacity building, in part reflecting the lower demand for these skills in the past given the limited emphasis placed on institution-building goals.

The publication of *WDR97*, the approval and initial implementation of the Bank's anticorruption agenda, the piloting of the CDF (with its stress on comprehensiveness and partnerships), and the renewed emphasis on capacity building in the Bank together have provided an excellent opportunity to rethink the Bank's strategy in this critical area. This strategy supports four broad changes in the way the Bank does its work to address the shortfalls in our experience.

(1) Approach. Reform will proceed only when a country's leaders are committed and in the driver's seat. But changing the internal rules of government is usually not enough to achieve reform. To be effective, we need to work with our partners to understand and address the broad range of incentives and pressures— both inside and outside of government—that affect public sector performance.

There is no question that reforms must be supported and driven at the highest levels of government to be effective. But changing internal rules of government is not enough to foster ownership and promote sustainable reform. *WDR97* highlighted the importance of three mechanisms that promote public sector effectiveness and good governance (see Figure A below):

- *Internal rules and restraints*—for example, internal accounting and auditing systems, independence of the judiciary and the central bank, civil service and budgeting rules, and rules governing ombudsmen and other internal watchdog bodies (that often report to Parliaments);

- *"Voice" and partnership*—for example, decentralization to empower communities, service delivery surveys to solicit client feedback, and "notice and comment" regulatory rulemaking; and

- *Competition*—for example, competitive social service delivery, private participation in infrastructure, alternative dispute resolution mechanisms, and pri-

vatization of certain market-driven activities. These may involve a fundamental rethinking of the role of the state, often a key component of reform.

Until the 1990s the Bank generally limited its scope of concern primarily to internal rules and restraints, although greater concern for "voice" and competition has emerged in recent years. Such a broader framework is essential for supporting improvements in public sector performance through a combination of Bank activities tailored to specific country situations. Although the Bank's mandate requires a focus on economic issues (of which public sector performance is clearly one), work on institutional reform also inevitably involves social and political issues to which the Bank must be sensitive.

The expanding body of anticorruption work[3] in the Bank provides a good example of the growing emphasis on "voice," participation, and country ownership. In addition to working with governments to streamline the role of the state and reform the internal rules of public sector functioning, the Bank is helping clients to develop and implement surveys of citizens, private firms, and public officials. The survey results, often disseminated through workshops, help to set priorities for further action and to involve civil society in the monitoring of public sector performance. Decentralizing more decisionmaking power to communities and enhancing competition in the delivery of public services can also increase transparency and accountability. They are key components of any anticorruption strategy and are increasingly emphasized in the Bank's lending and policy work.

Mainstreaming governance concerns should lead to greater selectivity in the Bank's lending program. As laid out in the 1997 anticorruption strate-

FIGURE A Mechanisms to Enhance State Capability: Three Drivers of Public Sector Reform

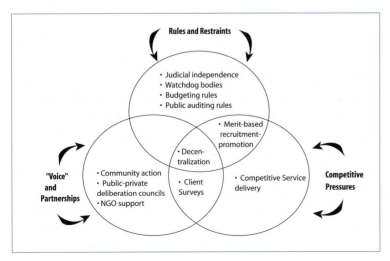

gy, *Helping Countries Combat Corruption: The Role of the World Bank*, "Corruption should be explicitly taken into account in country risk analysis, lending decisions, and portfolio supervision if it affects project or country performance and the government's commitment to deal with it is in question." Both for development goals and for fiduciary reasons, the Bank should reduce lending or take extra steps to promote accountability and sound financial management (or both) in situations where it cannot otherwise be confident that its funds will be used to promote economic development and poverty reduction. Both IDA and IBRD lending have increasingly taken governance concerns into account in lending allocations in recent years, and general guidelines are now being developed in the Bank (outlined in Box 12 in the main report) to help guide these decisions on selectivity.

(2) Analytic Work. We need to start with a thorough understanding of what exists on the ground and emphasize "good fit" rather than any one-size-fits-all notion of "best practice." And we need to work with our clients and other partners to develop and apply analytic tools to do this effectively.

The Bank's unique advantage is its ability to combine expert cross-country knowledge with in-depth understanding of specific situations in client countries. Too often, however, the Bank's efforts at reform have relied on foreign or "best practice" models that do not necessarily fit well with country circumstances and capabilities. Although broad end-goals (such as efficiency, equity, accountability and poverty reduction) are likely to be similar everywhere, specific means to achieve them will differ. This strategy emphasizes the need to start with what exists on the ground and to clarify which reform options "fit" well in specific settings.

In virtually all sectors where the Bank is active, a variety of institutional options exist for achieving results on the ground. Should a country use an inde-

pendent agency to regulate utilities or the environment, or should more emphasis be given to offshore enforcement of fixed rules for utilities or to public information and citizen "voice" for environmental protection? Should efforts to improve the quality of education focus on reforming education ministries, or are more far-reaching measures to involve parents and communities in school governance or to stimulate non-governmental provision of education services called for? Should money supply growth be constrained by independent central banks, by currency boards, or by transnational monetary unions? A key message of this strategy (following *WDR97*) is that questions such as these have no answer that is right under all circumstances. Rather, the key to success is the "fit" between the institutional prerequisites of each option and the institutional capabilities of individual countries.

This emphasis on "good fit" has two implications for Bank work. First, it means that we need to work harder across all sectors to identify reform options that are feasible and can be readily implemented on the ground. That "the perfect is the enemy of the good" is often true in this complex area of work. Institutional assessments to understand realities on the ground (including, for example, the capacity of local institutions and the extent of political support for reform) should be part of the design of every Bank project, and we need to work with our clients to develop and apply specific tools for assessing these institutional realities. Second, it means that we need to be more attuned to how the range of public institutions fit together and reinforce (or undermine) each other in any particular setting. Sector institutions (such as public health providers, transportation ministries, and schools) and institutions at the core of government (such as cabinets, finance ministries, and parliaments) do not operate separately but rather interrelate in complex ways.

The need for a good fit applies to the Bank's role also. In some settings, where leadership is strong and capacity is adequate, the Bank's optimal contribution is likely to be the provision of policy advice or technical assistance for further capacity building. In other settings, where conditions are less favorable, the Bank's optimal role may be more in stimulating dialogue, sharing knowledge, empowering communities, or fostering greater transparency.

In sum, we need to work with our clients and other partners to understand thoroughly the settings in which we work, beginning with problems on the ground (in policymaking, accountability, or service delivery) and tracing those problems to their institutional roots. This strategy proposes that we move upstream where possible and work with our clients to try to understand institutional systems—through country-specific variants of Institutional and Governance Reviews (IGRs) and Public Expenditure Reviews (PERs)—and integrate this knowledge into country strategy formulation. A growing number of country strategies (such as those for Albania, Armenia, Azerbaijan, Bangladesh, Bolivia, Bulgaria, Kenya, Mexico, Papua New Guinea, Philippines, and Thailand) are designed around a core goal of improving public sector performance and governance. Given the Bank's current direction and the findings of the aid-effectiveness literature, more are likely to be designed this way in the future.

(3) Lending instruments. We need to ensure our lending enhances institution-building (in addition to addressing relevant policy, physical investment, and resource transfer objectives). Both investment and adjustment loans have important roles to play, and it is important that lending approaches be tailored to country conditions. Longer-term programmatic lending approaches can help in some settings—both by emphasizing a longer-term institutional focus and by reducing the fragmentation often caused by uncoordinated donor activities.

Traditional applications of the Bank's lending instruments have sometimes been inadequate to support effective public sector reform, especially in countries with high levels of foreign aid. Long-term institutional concerns can fit awkwardly into investment projects, given the projects' limited scope and their need to disburse against actual project expenditures. Furthermore, projects typically "enclave" government functions (including budgets, personnel, procurement, and financial oversight); in countries with high aid inflows, donors' activities can fragment governments and undermine their ability to function effectively and in an integrated way. Traditional adjustment lending may focus more readily than investment projects on systemic institutional concerns, particularly those at the core of government, but its typically short time frame and irregular disbursement patterns can be inadequate for sustained efforts at institution-building. Learning and Innovation Loans (LILs) and Institutional Development Fund (IDF) grants have added flexibility and can be very useful in certain cases but have their own limitations.

The strategy paper supports current trends in the Bank to complement these traditional approaches with broader, longer-term variants to support institution-building in countries committed to reform. Programmatic lending instruments—such as sector-wide approaches (SIM/SIP), the Adaptable Program Loan (APL), and the Programmatic SAL or SAC (PSAL/C)—can be useful to encourage a longer-term and more systemic approach to public sector reform. APLs for Ghana, Bolivia, Tanzania, and Zambia and PSALs in Latvia, Thailand, Uganda, and Uttar Pradesh are among those that have been approved or are under consideration. These types of loans are specifically designed to facilitate a longer-term focus on institution-building and to link disbursements more closely with governments' needs and with improvements in monitorable indicators of institutional performance, outputs, and outcomes (most notably poverty reduction). They are typically underpinned by sound analytic and advisory work, such as PERs or IGRs (including service delivery, governance, or public expenditure tracking surveys). They can encourage greater donor coordination and help to reduce the fragmentation often caused by multiple uncoordinated aid initiatives.

Program-based lending, like project lending, must be careful to address fiduciary concerns and incorporate adequate safeguards to ensure that the Bank's resources are devoted to development goals. The Bank has made major efforts to increase safeguards in project lending. However, individual donor projects typically constitute only a small share of total public spending in client countries. Moreover, there is growing evidence that money lent for individual projects is to some extent fungible, because it frees up government resources to be allocated elsewhere, and that foreign aid tends to have limited impact in environments with weak policies and institutions. Sustainable poverty reduction requires that core public sector institutions, including essential systems of public expenditure management and governance, be developed and nurtured. For these reasons, the key to addressing both long-term development goals and the Bank's own fiduciary concerns is to focus Bank efforts on institutional reform to improve financial management and increase accountability in the system as a whole. This focus is key both to the use of programmatic lending to support long-term public sector reform and to much of the Bank's recent work in the areas of procurement and financial management.

(4) Staffing, organization, and partnerships. We need to continue to develop the skills to do better institutional, governance, and capacity building work in the Bank and fine-tune our organizational setup as needed to enhance responsibility, accountability, and quality assurance. Collaborating closely with partners is critical in this area of work.

Our understanding of how institutions work and how they can be strengthened is at a less developed stage than our understanding of many "first-generation" economic reforms, such as exchange rate reform or trade liberalization. However, the body of knowledge and experience on which to draw has grown rapidly in recent years. The strategy paper identifies three types of skills that are needed for the Bank's work in governance, public sector institutional reform, and capacity building: task management skills, broad skills in institutional analysis and assessment, and substantive expertise in specific areas (such as budgeting, civil service reform, decentralization, tax administration, alternative modes of service delivery, judicial systems, etc.). While the Bank has traditionally had the first in abundance, it has recently needed to expand its expertise in the other two through a combination of new hiring and redeployment of existing staff. Given the complexity and interdisciplinary nature of this work, a heavy reliance on teamwork and extensive partnerships (in both knowledge sharing and operational work) with other donors, nongovernmental organizations (NGOs), the private sector, and local experts in client countries is required.

We must prioritize our activities in order to staff effectively under current resource constraints. We aim for the Bank to be considered one of a very few *leading* authorities worldwide in several core areas where we have a track record or a comparative advantage, including (a) the role of the public sector, (b) the broad structure of government (including decentralization and intergovernmental fiscal relations), (c) core system-wide administrative and civil service reform and capacity building, (d) public expenditure analysis and management, and (e) sectoral institution-building (including regulation of private service delivery). We aim for the Bank to be considered an expert along with other partner organizations in several other areas, including (a) revenue policy and administration, (b) legal and judicial reform, and (c) other accountability and law enforcement institutions (such as ombuds-men, audit institutions, and parliamentary oversight bodies). For reasons of either limited mandate or limited expertise, we do not envision the Bank becoming involved in some other areas of public sector reform, such as (a) police reform, (b) criminal justice systems (including prosecutorial and prison reform), (c) general parliamentary processes, or (d) political governance (including election processes or the structure and financing of political parties). Many of our partners, including UNDP, bilateral donors, and NGOs, have clearer mandates or a likely comparative advantage in these areas of work.

The Bank's matrix structure has clearly enhanced the incentives and ability of staff working on reform of core public sector institutions to cooperate and share knowledge, and ongoing efforts to strengthen the matrix should help further. The experience of the past three years points to the importance of having sector board members who are clearly accountable in their regions or central units for delivering effective programs of support across the range of relevant topics to country directors or other clients, and whose accountability is matched by the authority and resources to hire and manage the staff needed to do the job. The network family should then be jointly accountable to the whole of the Bank to set strategy and priorities, recruit and train staff, and oversee quality.

Plan of Action

The last section of Part I of the strategy paper summarizes our specific goals—both outcome objectives in client countries and output objectives within the Bank—for the next three years and a set of specific actions to be taken to help achieve them. Part II includes strategies and short descriptions of innovative initiatives prepared by each of the Bank's six regional

vice-presidencies and by the Development Research Group (DRG) and the World Bank Institute (WBI). While aggregate lending volumes and in-country Bank activities are determined largely by country demand, the overall strategy and the strategies for individual Regions, DRG, and WBI propose specific proactive measures to enhance the quality and impact of Bank analytic work, partnerships, in-country training initiatives, and lending for institutional reform and governance in the public sector.

Strategic goals and performance indicators *by substantive area* are summarized in Table 3 (main text), and the proactive steps we plan to take to address *past issues and problems* are laid out in Table 4. The strategy seeks to expand our approach, deepen our analytic work, and focus our energies to help achieve demonstrable results on the ground. To this end the strategy includes efforts to:

- establish clear criteria to ensure that institutional and governance concerns are reflected in country assistance strategies and lending programs,

- develop toolkits and survey techniques for governance analysis and assessment and work with our clients and other partners to apply them,

- pilot new analytic approaches (including variants of Institutional and Governance Reviews and governance/anticorruption surveys) in at least 10 countries where we want to focus strong efforts and catalyze attention and ownership,

- expand the institutional content, more clearly define the scope and function, enhance relevance and client ownership, and improve the quality of Public Expenditure Reviews,

- organize and disseminate existing knowledge through the Bank's Knowledge Management System, and

- build new knowledge—including more reliable indicators of governance and institutional performance—through experimentation and research.

To orient our lending more toward long-term institution–building, the strategy includes proactive efforts to:

- develop and implement longer-term programmatic lending approaches with a focus on governance and public sector institution-building in 10 or more countries,

- work with sector colleagues to mainstream institutional concerns in Bank projects (through, among other things, joint piloting of an Operational Policy on institutional assessment), and

- work with OED and QAG to refine evaluation techniques and enhance our focus on performance and outcomes.

To enhance our internal capacity, the strategy includes efforts to:

- expand our staff capabilities through training and recruitment,

- ensure a clear focus of managerial authority and accountability for core public sector institutional reform work in all regions,

- deepen our partnerships with other donors, NGOs, and our clients, and

- enhance our selectivity and focus our efforts where they can have the biggest impact.

To keep a firm eye on portfolio quality, this strategy includes efforts to:

- reinforce responsibilities for monitoring and quality assurance across networks and across units in the matrix,

- give careful attention to the selection and training of task teams and leaders,

- identify potential problem areas within the public sector portfolio (whether lending or nonlending services) and address them collectively at an early stage, and

- enhance monitoring and review processes, through both stronger peer review mechanisms and Quality Enhancement Reviews.

Just as institutional issues cut across almost all Bank work, so the implementation of this ambitious agenda will need to involve many parts of the Bank. Furthermore, there are still many difficult and unanswered questions in the complex areas of institutional reform, governance, and capacity building, and we intend to work closely with our many partners outside the Bank to draw lessons from ongoing experience.[4] Enhancing the Bank's role and success in facilitating long-term institution-building in our client countries is a critical challenge that we all must embrace.

1 Public institutions are broadly defined here to include any institutions that shape the way public functions are carried out. As will be seen throughout the discussion, the private sector and civil society can have an important role in helping to provide some public services and monitor public sector performance. In the World Bank's 1992 report *Governance and Development,* governance was defined as "the manner in which power is exercised in the management of a country's economic and social resources." The 1994 report *Governance: The World Bank's Experience* stated "Good governance is epitomized by predictable, open, and enlightened policymaking (that is, transparent processes); a bureaucracy imbued with a professional ethos; an executive arm of government accountable for its actions; and a strong civil society participating in public affairs; and all behaving under the rule of law."

2 A concern with the functioning of public institutions spans all pillars of the CDF. Those that most centrally relate to the functioning of core public sector institutions are the first and second: governance and legal and judicial reform.

3 For a recent summary of the Bank's anticorruption activities over the past three years, see World Bank, *Helping Countries Combat Corruption: Progress at the World Bank since 1997,* June 2000.

4 For a more thorough analysis of issues and listing of references and activities in various areas of public sector reform, as well as extensive data, toolkits, and links with partners, visit our websites at *www.worldbank.org/publicsector, and http://worldbank.org/wbi/governance.*

PART ONE

Reforming Public Institutions and Strengthening Governance: Main Strategy

[T]he causes of financial crises and poverty are one and the same . . . [I]f [countries] do not have good governance, if they do not confront the issue of corruption, if they do not have a complete legal system which protects human rights, property rights and contracts . . . their development is fundamentally flawed and will not last.

—James D. Wolfensohn, President,
The World Bank Group,
Address to the Board of Governors
(September 28, 1999)

Overwhelmingly, the poor want to be heard; and they want governments and other institutions to do more, and to do it well.

Voices of the Poor (Global Synthesis)

Dysfunctional and ineffective public institutions—broadly defined here to include all institutions that shape the way public functions are carried out[1]—and weak governance are increasingly seen to be at the heart of the economic development challenge. Misguided resource allocation,

excessive government intervention, and arbitrariness and corruption have deterred private sector investment and slowed growth and poverty-reduction efforts in numerous settings. The recent financial crises in Asia have exposed problems of governance and public sector performance in that region. The latest work on aid-effectiveness points out the risks of lending to countries with bad policies and poorly performing public sectors. Just as it became evident in the 1980s that potentially good projects often fail in poor policy environments, so it became evident in the 1990s that policy reforms are less likely to succeed when public institutions and governance are weak. Furthermore, much of the Bank's poverty work—including the new *WDR2000/2001* on poverty—points to the high cost of malperforming government and inadequate service delivery to the poor (Box 1 and Annex 5). Building effective and accountable public institutions is arguably *the* core challenge for sustainable poverty reduction.

Responding to this accumulation of evidence, the World Bank has increasingly focused its attention in recent years on reform of public sector institutions.

BOX 1

Accountable Public Institutions are Key to Poverty Reduction

Poverty reduction is the goal of development work, including work to strengthen public institutions and governance. Public sector reform supports the goal of poverty reduction through a variety of distinct channels, as described in depth in *World Development Report 2000/2001: Attacking Poverty*. The World Bank is increasingly integrating concerns about governance and public sector effectiveness in its poverty-oriented work, including its work with clients to support the preparation of the first set of Poverty Reduction Strategy Papers (PRSPs) and related toolkits (see Annex 2).

The most direct channel through which governance affects poverty is via its impact on service delivery. Poverty reduction depends on improvements in the quality and accessibility to poor people of basic education, health, potable water and other social and infrastructure services. Achieving this generally calls for government action-financing, active facilitation, and in many instances the direct delivery of services. Yet in all too many countries, public actors in the social and infrastructure sectors have neither the incentives nor the resources to play this role. Reforming the institutional "rules of the game" thus becomes key to improving the availability of services for the poor.

A less immediate impact comes via the now well-documented contribution of good governance to growth (see Annex 5) and the expansion of income-earning opportunities, and via related changes in the ways in which scarce public resources are allocated and policies are formulated. In countries where institutions are weak,

policymaking and resource allocation typically proceed in nontransparent ways, with decisions generally skewed in favor of those who are well connected to centers of power. All too often, the result is that services valued by elites (for example, tertiary rather than primary education) receive disproportionate funding, and policies are adopted (for example, the granting of monopoly privileges) that benefit a few at the expense of society more broadly. Institutional reforms in both policymaking and budgeting foster openness and explicit debate among competing alternatives, thereby making it more difficult to conceal decisions that are systematically biased against the poor.

Perhaps the most profound impact of institutional reform on poverty comes via the potential for increases in citizen participation. There are a variety of ways in which strengthening "voice" in general—and the voice of the poor in particular—can improve public performance. At the micro-level, they include fostering participation of parents in the governance of schools or working with communities to provide access to water. At the macro-level, they include well-designed modes of decentralization and, more broadly, various forms of representative decisionmaking and political oversight. As this strategy emphasizes, institutional reform is not simply a matter of changing the ways in which public hierarchies are arranged. Its focus is on the broad array of "rules of the game" that shape the incentives and actions of public actors—including the "voice" mechanisms that promote the rule of law and the accountability of government to its citizens.

The Bank has acknowledged the harmful economic consequences of corruption—a fundamental symptom of public sector malfunction—and is working with partners and clients to address it in both country settings and international forums. Institutional development and capacity building have been identified as major goals under the Strategic Compact. The Bank's activities in core areas of public sector functioning—such as public expenditure analysis and management, tax administration, civil service reform, regulation, decentralization, and judicial reform—grew rapidly from 1997 to 1999 (see Figures 1 and 2). Much of its work in public service delivery (whether in the social sectors or in infrastructure) has focused on institutional concerns, including private provision or decentralization in addition to capacity building. Indeed, virtually all Bank projects approved in recent years try in some way to reform the institutions of the public sector. About one-quarter of the Bank's lending in fiscal 1997-99, equivalent to about $5 billion to $7 billion per year, was allocated to institution-building as broadly defined, with about one-tenth being spent on direct technical assistance (see Annex 1).

The *World Development Report 1997: The State in a Changing World (WDR97)*, provides an in-depth look at the forces that shape public sector performance. It is an outward-oriented document intended to inform policymakers, donors, and academics working on development issues. The goal of this strategy paper is to complement and build on *WDR97* by taking stock of the Bank's recent work on governance, public sector institutional reform, and capacity building (particularly at the core of government) and addressing how the Bank can best further the goals laid out in *WDR97*. While the strategy is intended primarily as a guide for our own work, the lessons and approaches discussed in this strategy are also relevant for many external parties.

The strategy paper is timely not only because of its centrality to development, but also because of the mixed track record the Bank has had in this line of

FIGURE 1
Governance-Related Lending Has Grown Rapidly

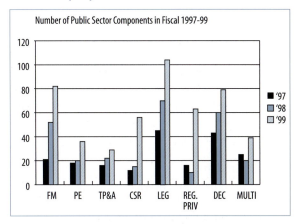

FM: Public Expenditure and Financial Management
PE: Public Enterprise Reform
TP&A: Tax Policy and Administration
CSR: Civil Service Reform
LEG: Legal and Judicial Reform
REG.PRIV: Regulation of the Private Sector
DEC: Decentralization
MULTI: Multisector (more than one of the above)

FIGURE 2
Governance-Related Nonlending Activity Has Also Expanded

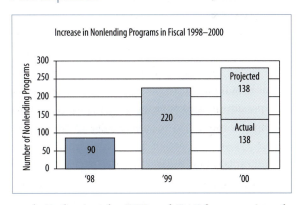

work. Evaluations by OED and QAG have consistently indicated weak performance in the Bank's portfolio of public sector management projects and in the institution-building components of projects in other sectors, although recent OED and QAG data indicate a marked improvement over the past three years. Bank and other donors efforts at technical assistance have been criticized for over a decade, and questions have been raised more recently about the quality and impact of analytic work, in particular Public Expenditure Reviews. The ongoing process of renewal within the Bank, including the formation and development of the PREM Network, the piloting of the CDF (see Box 2), and the renewed focus on poverty reduction through the PRSP process, provides an excellent opportunity to retool our skills and redefine the ways in which these skills are deployed in our operational work.

The conditions for governance reform in the developing world are better now than they have been in decades. *We have a real chance to make a difference.* The challenge of this strategy is to define a direction for change that increases the Bank's effectiveness within the scope of our mandate and comparative advantage. Part I of this strategy paper, prepared by the Public Sector Board (PREM Network) with extensive consultation and assistance from internal and external partners,[2] addresses this challenge as follows:

- **Theme.** Section 1 defines the topic and why it matters for development.

- **Experience.** Section II reviews our efforts to reform the public sector and improve governance over the past 15 years.

- **Looking Forward.** Sections III through VI build on experience and lay out a forward-looking strategy to foster client ownership and commitment, expand our knowledge, design more effective assistance programs, and enlarge our capacity to help build institutions.

- **Plan of Action.** Finally, Section VII summarizes our plan of action and specifies objectives and performance indicators to gauge Bank outputs and country outcomes.

Part II includes strategies and examples of innovative activities undertaken over the past year by each of the Bank's six regional vice-presidencies and by the Development Research Group and the World Bank Institute.

This strategy also serves as an update on the Bank's governance work, building on the 1991 report, "Governance and Development," and the 1994 update, "Governance: The World Bank's Experience." Governance—defined in the 1994 governance report as "the way in which power is exercised in managing economic and social resources for development"—is a broad topic. Core issues of governance, such as the structure and functioning of state institutions, "voice" and participation of civil society in public decision-making, transparency and accountability, public sector capacity building, and rule of law are all central concerns of this strategy paper, and the annexes review our large number of recent activities in these areas. However, in order to maintain its focus, this particular paper does not fully address some specific topics that fall under a broad vision of governance, including post-conflict issues, detailed Bank policy with regard to military expenditure, and gender equality. Given the expansion in the Bank's work in many of these areas in the 1990s, full treatment in one concise document is not feasible. These topics will be treated in greater depth in focused studies or policy notes, such as the gender strategy paper currently under preparation.

BOX 2

Public Sector Reform and the Comprehensive Development Framework

The emphasis on institutional reform in the public sector is currently high on the Bank's agenda, with the heightened focus on anticorruption since 1997 and the 1999 introduction and ongoing piloting of the Comprehensive Development Framework (CDF). The first leg of the CDF is governance—a well-functioning and accountable core public sector—and this document discusses the Bank's contribution to this goal in great depth. The second leg of the CDF is the law and justice system. This strategy also covers this topic to a significant extent, because the justice system is a major part of the public sector and a well-functioning legal system is critical to good governance. The other legs of the CDF deal with other thematic and sectoral areas,

but progress along virtually all of them requires a well-functioning and accountable public sector. Thus, this strategy paper can be seen touching on concerns across the wide span of the CDF in a kind of "L" shape, with a central focus on the first leg, a major focus on the second, and an interconnected focus on the others as they relate to the performance of public institutions.

Not only are the topics of the CDF deeply interconnected in this strategy, but the underlying philosophy and approach of the CDF is also reflected here. This strategy is concerned with long-term institutional reform and capacity building. It sees the Bank's overarching goal of poverty reduction as requiring first and foremost a strengthening of institutions in developing countries, and it urges the Bank and all donors to work together in partnership with each other and with receptive client governments to put this at the top of their agendas. This demands changes in approach, focus, analytic and lending instruments, and staffing, as suggested below.

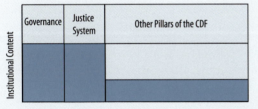

Focusing Our Agenda: Moving Institutional Development and Capacity Building to Center Stage

A person doesn't have the strength or power to change anything, but if the overall system changed, things would be better.

Voices of the Poor (Interviewee, Bosnia)

For the first few decades of its history, the Bank as well as other donors addressed development primarily as a technocratic challenge. The implicit model was that good advisers and technical experts would design good policies and projects, which good governments and an adequately resourced public sector would then implement for the benefit of society. As *WDR97* highlighted, however, at least as important as the policies and resources for development are the *institutions* within which public action is embedded— the "rules of the game" and the mechanisms through which they are monitored and enforced. Institutions can include organizational rules and routines, formal laws, and informal norms. Together they shape the incentives of public policymakers, overseers, and providers of public services (see Box 3).

Following *WDR97*, this strategy takes as its focus the reform of public institutions, as broadly defined to include all institutions that shape the way public functions are carried out.

Institutions and policies interact in complex ways.

A focus on institutions complements, but is broader than, the Bank's long-standing efforts to foster policy reform.[3] As Figure 3 (taken from *WDR97*) shows, both policies and institutions have independent impacts on development performance.

Yet while "first-generation" economic reforms have proceeded rapidly in many settings over the past 15 years, institutional reform has moved far more slowly, and weak institutions have become the main constraint to more robust and sustained growth in many settings.

Policies and institutions are closely interlinked in several ways. First, policy design should take institutional capacity carefully into account. When institutions are weak or dysfunctional, simple policies that limit administrative demands and public discretion

BOX 3

Why an Institutional Focus in Public Sector Reform?

The recent revival of "institutions" as a focal point for research and policy is not only a reflection of our need to grapple with the complexities of public action. It also is a result of the development of an extended set of analytic tools within the social sciences. The study of institutions has been enriched by a growing body of work that combines "rational choice" theory, information economics, game theory, law, and organization theory. Building upon insights made, among others, by Nobel Prize winners Buchanan, Coase, North and Vickrey and by other leading analysts, including Joe Stiglitz, this work has developed analytic tools that focus on the incentives and information that shape decisionmaking by public actors and enable us to open the black box of "the state." This institutional perspective complements recent empirical work in public economics that highlights the costs in terms of foregone investments and growth of over-regulation, corruption, and other manifestations of bad government. It also complements the work of public sector management specialists, who for years have argued for a systemic approach to public sector reform, noting the dangers of piecemeal project interventions.

A key starting point of this analysis is the recognition that public actors are often motivated not just by social goals, but by the private political and economic costs and benefits of their actions—and that these costs and benefits are shaped by institutions. If the institutions that countries use to govern themselves were perfect and ensured that the private rewards of government decisions were aligned with the social costs and benefits, the distinct incentives of public actors would not matter. But the institutions of governance are imperfect in all countries. First, those who suffer from poor policies generally lack the clout and information to impose costs on the policymakers who designed them, particularly in governments without meaningful checks and balances. Second, often multiple actors (cabinets, political parties, legislatures) provide input to policy decisionmaking, and bargaining processes may be nontransparent and favor some actors and their private interests over others. Third, even if policymakers agree on the socially optimal policy, their control over bureaucratic officials is always imperfect—and can be exceedingly weak in Bank client countries. Furthermore, institutional obstacles may obstruct feedback from beneficiaries that could improve policy implementation. By better understanding how institutions shape public action and by undertaking more empirical analysis to measure the economic costs of poorly performing public institutions, the Bank and its clients will be in a better position to help improve governance and public sector performance.

FIGURE 3
Institutional Capability Improves Economic Growth

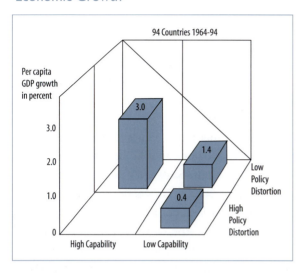

94 Countries 1964-94

Per capita GDP growth in percent

work best. Where institutions are stronger, more challenging public initiatives can be effective. Box 4 provides an illustration in the area of tax policy, and similar principles hold in many other areas of public sector activity, including infrastructure regulation,[4] the choice of service providers,[5] the design of social safety nets,[6] and the role of the judiciary,[7] indeed, the role of the state in general. Matching policies and institutions is key.

Second, policies do not emerge from a vacuum but generally are the result of bargaining among contending groups—with the interplay among them shaped by the institutional and political "rules of the game." As Box 5 illustrates in the case of public expenditures, the Bank may thus be able to help improve policy outcomes by directing attention not just to the policies themselves, but to the "rules of the game" that shape policy outcomes. Indeed, the Bank's Public Expenditure Reviews (PERs) used to be primarily analyses of expenditure policies, but in recent years they have increasingly focused on institutional issues of budgeting and financial control. A PER is now considered incomplete if it does not address the institu-

tions of public expenditure management (see Section IV below).

Third, the causation also works in reverse: policy choice can significantly influence the way institutions develop. A decision to reduce tariffs or move from highly varied to uniform tax rates can dramatically shift incentives and responsibilities within customs and tax administrations, making it harder for officials to extract bribes in return for lower taxes. This is one example of why economic reform is a key pillar of an anticorruption program.

Institutional and governance concerns touch all sectors.

The Bank has traditionally classified "public sector management" (PSM) as a sector, focused somewhat narrowly on the workings of core areas of government. Certainly our specialist skills on how to reform the core of government will continue to be important in the future. The approach proposed in this strategy, however, goes beyond a compartmentalized approach to PSM. It emphasizes the links between core public institutions (including not only the executive arm but also the legislature and the judiciary) and sectoral institutions, and ultimately between reform of the institutional system and the reduction of poverty at the grass roots.

The economic functions of the public sector can be broadly classified into three distinct categories, each with its corresponding institutional challenges:

- *Making and Implementing Economic Policy.* Good performance in designing policy requires more than economic analysis. Institutions are needed that can maintain discipline in fiscal and monetary aggregates, effectively set priorities among competing demands for resources, and mobilize revenues. Institutions for macroeconomic planning and

BOX 4

Tax Policy, Tax Administration, and Institutional Reform

It makes little sense to discuss tax policy or tax administration in isolation from one another, particularly in developing countries. On the one hand, tax policy should not be designed without looking carefully at administrative capacity. When public sector institutions are weak, tax policies need to be simple and transparent, even if this means forgoing "fine-tuning" that might seem to enhance equity or efficiency. For example, rates of sales tax or VAT should be as few and as low as possible. Multiple rates force administrators to differentiate goods and inevitably leave room for uncertainty and bargaining. High rates provide greater incentives for tax evasion and greater room for bargaining and corruption. Income taxes should also be simple, which may mean few deductions (for example, no deductions for charitable contributions, health costs, or insurance premiums), a heavy reliance on simple withholding rules, and no differentiation between rates on income and rates on capital gains, or a forgoing of tax on capital gains altogether. Significant exemption levels are useful in both sales and income taxes to keep most people out of the tax net altogether and focus limited administrative capacity on higher-income taxpayers. Presumptive methods may be needed to determine taxable turnover or income for many small and middle-size firms, using rules of thumb (for example, rules that "presume" turnover based on physical indicators) to determine tax liability rather than relying on detailed records. Although presumptive methods may be less exact (and, as a result, appear less fair) than methods based on detailed record keeping, the latter may not be feasible in many cases.

On the other hand, efforts to strengthen tax administration should not be undertaken without taking a careful look at tax policy. For example, computerizing a tax system with an excessively complex design or unreasonably high rates may well be a misuse of scarce resources—and can be futile if not counterproductive. Rather than train many administrators and auditors to enforce a complex tax, one should *first* consider how to lessen the administrative load through changes in design, and only then look for ways to improve administration.

Finally, both appropriate tax policy and efforts to strengthen tax administration may fail if the broad institutional setting reinforces counterproductive norms and incentives. In many transition economies, for example, systemic corruption, discretionary and often arbitrary imposition of tax rules, and an absence of accountability mechanisms so undermine rule of law that neither the public nor the government expects themselves or others to abide by formal tax law. The result is widespread tax evasion, large "unofficial" economies, and macroeconomic instability. In such a setting marginal changes in tax policy or tax administration are unlikely to have much impact. The only answer is likely to lie in more fundamental institutional reform.

monetary policy should generally be structured to provide autonomy and avoid pressures from spending ministries for over-optimistic forecasting. In contrast, institutions for strategic prioritization are intrinsically political and should be structured to provide participation and buy-in from interest groups, with legislative oversight where appropriate.

- *Delivering Services.* The public sector delivers or fosters private delivery of a broad range of public services—infrastructure services, social services and also the legal and regulatory services needed for an efficient private sector. This broad range of services can be delivered through a variety of institutional arrangements and with widely varying degrees of effectiveness. A central challenge is to

---

BOX 5

Reforming the "Rules of the Game" for Policymaking Through a Medium-Term Expenditure Framework

Resource allocation is about choice and, as such, is fundamentally political. The challenge is to design institutional arrangements that nudge choices in favor of the public good. In his 1998 Budget Speech, South Africa's Finance Minister dwelt on that country's decision to introduce a medium-term expenditure framework (MTEF). He emphasized the role it was expected to play in strengthening political decisionmaking, but also noted that it was intended to enhance cooperation in governance, foster more cost-effective performance, and create an environment where public service providers have greater predictability and can thus plan for the medium term.

The central coordinating role of the budget has been weakened in many countries because it has been delinked from policymaking and planning. The result has often been budgets that are unrealistic or have little relation to expressed strategic priorities. A medium-term expenditure framework is an institutional device that formally and transparently tries to link policy, planning and budgeting. If used well, it enhances the capacity of government to maintain aggregate fiscal discipline while prioritizing (and if needed, reallocating) resources to reflect changing strategic priorities. An MTEF imposes the following "rules of the game":

- An aggregate budget constraint defines what overall envelope of resources is available.

- Policy proposals must compete with each other—both as ideas and for funding over the medium term—and what is demanded must be reconciled with what is affordable.

- Proposals for policies and projects must be accompanied by cost and results information over the medium term, and

- Evaluation influences resource allocation decisions and provides information to drive improvements in the quality of service delivery.

A growing number of developing countries have introduced MTEFs, often with Bank support. The experience of OECD countries shows that institutional reforms along these lines can contribute to fiscal discipline, better allocation of resources, and improved service delivery.

---

put in place institutional arrangements for service delivery that are workable in specific country contexts and that promote the goal of poverty reduction. This goes well beyond a narrow concern with activities within relevant line ministries—that is, the allocation of sectoral funds or the configuring of ministerial organizational charts.

- *Ensuring Accountability for the Use of Public Resources and Public Regulatory Power.* Well-functioning public sectors do not operate in a vacuum. They are grounded in multiple mechanisms that insure accountability. The key to accountability is the capacity to monitor and enforce rules—within the public sector, between public and private parties, and, sometimes, among private parties. The internal regulatory mechanisms of government—accounting and audit, procurement, and personnel—have long received sustained attention as the centerpiece of reforms to promote accountability, and should continue to be a key part of the agenda. Additionally, the monitoring and enforcing functions rooted in countries' constitutional separation of powers have recently come to the forefront of development discourse. These include the mutual monitoring roles of legislatures and executives, the vertical division of power associated with decentralization, and the monitoring function of an independent judiciary and an informed citizenry.

This strategy focuses primarily on core public institutions and their sectoral linkages.

Most of the Bank's traditional categories of public sector work directly address more than one of the three broad functions noted above, as shown in Table 1. The table also summarizes our broad objectives in each area and the links with the Bank's goal of poverty reduction.

Because institutional issues span the full range of Bank work, and are thus the responsibility of all the networks, this strategy paper does not cover all of them thoroughly. Rather it focuses primarily on reforms of core public sector institutions and their interface with sectoral institutions. It touches only lightly on institutional concerns within specific sectors (including related institutional issues in the private sector; see Box 6 on corporate governance), and it does so primarily to point out generic issues that concern many sectors. Sector-specific institutional issues are addressed in greater detail in the respective sector strategy papers.

Our agenda covered in this strategy involves many parties inside and outside the Bank. The Public Sector Board (PREM network) and the sector families in other networks are increasingly working together to mainstream institutional concerns in Bank work and integrate them in country settings as much as possible. The Public Sector Board is also interacting closely with other groups in the Bank working on particular specialized topics of public sector reform in client countries, including OCS (in its work on systemic procurement and financial management reform), Controllers (financial management systems), LEG (legal/judicial reform), OED (evaluation capacity development), and WBI (anticorruption and parliamentary strengthening). We also deeply value our external partnerships with other donors and with NGOs and private actors, as discussed further in later chapters. They bring valuable and complementary perspectives, roles and skills to the work.

A broad view of capacity building must encompass institutional reform.

Institutional reform is sometimes used interchangeably with "capacity building," a term that has become increasingly common in recent years. The meaning and scope of "capacity building" can, however, be ambiguous. If narrowly defined as the provision of training and materials to build skills within organizations, capacity building is only part of the challenge of reforming public institutions. A technocratic supply-side approach does not go very far in addressing the complex political economy of public sector reform, as discussed further in Section II below. When more broadly defined to include reforms of incentives and institutions as well as strengthening skills and resources, however, the term capacity building is essentially synonymous with the concept of institutional development.

TABLE I Institutional Topics: Their Fit with Broad Functions of Government and with Poverty Objectives

Institutional Topic	Fit with Broad Functions of			Links with Poverty Objectives
	Policymaking	Service Delivery	Accountability	
Public Expenditure Management	x	x	x	Redireciton of government spending for better development outcomes; improvement in service delivery; empowerment of the poor in overseeing government actions and expenditures
Tax Policy and Administration	x		x	Increased public resources for development purposes; promotion of economic opportunities through growth
Administrative and Civil Service Reform		x	x	Improved service delivery; empowerment through reduction in corruption
Decentralization	x	x	x	Increased resources for development purposes; improved service delivery; empowerment of the poor to direct the use of government resources
Legal and Judical Reform		x	x	Improved security in person and property; promotion of economic opportunities through contract enforcement; delivery of dispute resolution services; empowerment of the poor to hold government accountable for its decisions
Anticorruption	x	x	x	Empowerment of the poor to hold the government accountable for its actions and use of resources; improved service delivery
Public Enterprise Reform		x	x	Increased resources available for development purposes; improved quality of service delivery through competition
Sectoral Institution-building	x	x	x	Improved service delivery

BOX 6

The Links Between Public Governance and Corporate Governance

This strategy paper does not directly address issues and strategy surrounding corporate governance, that is, the governance of companies (generally majority privately owned) by owners and other stakeholders, which is a distinct topic with a rich literature and professional base. However, it is important to note that the state of corporate governance in an economy is likely to be connected in intricate ways with the state of public governance. First, shareholders—particularly minority shareholders—of private firms will have great difficulty asserting their shareholder rights in countries with weak legal systems, and the likely result is a corporate ownership structure characterized by highly concentrated (often "insider") ownership and few minority share-

holders. Second, unaccountable and nontransparent public governance can lead to a blurring of the lines between the public and private sectors and to dysfunctional corporate governance—manifest through excessive government interference, corrupt capital market or utility regulation, or government "capture" by private interests, as in "crony capitalism." The Bank's research and operational work on corruption and public governance often encounters these linkages (as laid out, for example, in the recent report on corruption in Europe and Central Asia entitled "*Anticorruption in Transition: A Contribution to the Policy Debate*"), and we are interacting with our partners inside and outside the Bank to understand and address them where appropriate.

Building on Lessons of Experience

World Development Report 1997 was the culmination of a long process of learning inside and outside the Bank about the centrality of institutions for development rather than a radical break with the past. The need for institutional reform was on the Bank's agenda in the early 1980s, with the establishment of a public sector management division in 1981 and the World Development Report, 1983: Management in Development. The Bank's work on sector-based institutional reform and public sector management expanded in the 1980s, and governance was added to the range of Bank concerns with the 1989 From Crisis to Sustainable Growth—Sub-Saharan Africa: A Long Term Perspective Study, and the two Board papers on governance in 1991 and 1994. The issue of corruption entered explicitly in 1996, and governance and systemic legal reform are now key pillars of the CDF. Yet even with this expansion in attention and activity, a significant level of ambivalence remains about both the Bank's role and its success in this area of work.

Our performance has been uneven . . . but is improving.

Two primary findings emerge from the evaluations of the Bank's Operations Evaluation Department (OED) and its Quality Assurance Group (QAG). First, their findings strongly support the view that the quality of institutions is a key determinant of development impact. OED has repeatedly stressed that a good enabling environment—a credible government, little corruption, sound economic policies—is crucial for high quality projects and strong implementation capacity.[8] Second, despite this first finding, both OED and QAG consistently report that many Bank interventions do not adequately address institutional concerns. For example, only about one-third of projects completed in the mid-1990s are considered by OED to have had substantial institutional impact[9]—although, as Figure 4 shows, there has been significant improvement in recent years, suggesting that a gradual learning process is underway.

This mixed performance on institution-building applies to projects across virtually all sectors. In line with organizational responsibilities in the Bank, it is useful to divide the Bank's institutional interventions into two broad types:

- those that address core functions of governments (such as administrative and civil service reform, public expenditure management, tax administration, public enterprise reform, and legal and judicial reform)—typically classified in the "public sector management" (PSM) or "multisector" categories; and

- those that deal primarily with sectoral concerns (in health, education, infrastructure, environment, etc.).

Public sector management loans. The performance of the Bank's PSM portfolio has traditionally been quite weak but appears to have improved markedly in recent years (see Figure 4).[10] OED and other Bank reports in the early and mid-1990s consistently showed that projects and TA and adjustment loans that focused directly on public sector management performed worse than the average for Bank interventions.[11] In contrast, recent data from OED indicate that PSM projects evaluated in the late 1990s outperformed the Bank average, with 94 percent of PSM projects evaluated from 1998 to 2000 being rated as "satisfactory" compared to only 73 percent for the Bank as a whole. Similarly, QAG data show the percentage of PSM projects at risk in 1997 (24 percent) to have been very close to the Bank average for that year (26 percent) and the percentage of total monetary commitments at risk (42 percent) to have been significantly above the Bank average (24 percent). By mid-2000, however, the percentages of PSM projects and commitments at risk (11 and 5 percent, respectively) were significantly below the Bank average (15 and 16 percent, respectively).

Detailed evaluations of particular types of PSM interventions have supported this mixed but improving picture of project performance. A recent OED evaluation of the Bank's work up to 1997 on civil service reform (CSR) concluded that only 33 percent of the Bank's completed interventions and 38 percent of interventions ongoing at that time had achieved satisfactory outcomes[12] (although, again, the percentage of satisfactory CSR projects appears to have risen significantly since 1997). The mixed impact of the Bank's technical assistance—most of it in the area of public sector management—has been the subject of numerous studies over the past decade, the most recent being a study completed in 1998 that found a lower rate of success in PSM TALs (43 percent) than in the TAL portfolio as a whole (65 percent) in the 1990s.[13] A 1998 QAG review of four technical assistance projects in the Europe and Central Asia region rated only one of them as "satisfactory" overall and three of them as "marginally satisfactory" in quality at entry and quality of supervision. The Bank's

FIGURE 4
The Impact of Bank Lending on Institutional Development

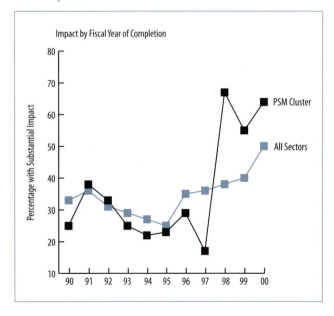

Impact by Fiscal Year of Completion

Percentage with Substantial Impact

PSM Cluster

All Sectors

interventions in the area of systemic legal and judicial reform are relatively new and have not yet been formally evaluated, but the general view of practitioners is that their success to date is also mixed. A recent internal review of the Bank's interventions in the area of tax administration also indicates a mixed record of quality.[14]

What led to these mixed results, particularly in the first half of the 1990s? Four consistent messages emerge from OED and QAG reviews, seconded by the "common wisdom" gained over the past decade by Bank operational staff.

- First, projects are not likely to be successful when they fail to take fully into account the complex political and institutional realities on the ground—and thus the *real* incentives for implementation. The Bank (not unlike other donors) has sometimes taken a rather narrow and "technocratic" supply-side view on PSM and TA in the past, interacting exclusively with government interlocutors and funding consulting services, computers, and other inputs in the absence of a deep and sustainable demand for institutional reform on the part of the borrower. In some cases, the Bank has failed to consult with key stakeholders whose support is critical or who could help mobilize pressure for change. Often a few reformers in the central ministries want reform, but they cannot mobilize the support from broader groups in society to push it through. Furthermore, in some cases the Bank has tried to provide technocratic solutions within government when changing the role and scope of government activities (for example, contracting out or decentralizing public service delivery) might have led to more fundamental institutional change.

- Second, the Bank has sometimes relied on models of "best practice" that may not be feasible in the particular country setting. Unrealistic optimism is a persistent strand of weakness running through Bank work, as reported regularly by OED and QAG. Bank staff, enthused by some new "best practice" breakthrough in one country, have sometimes rushed to recommend it in an entirely different setting, with little attention to the impact of these country differences on the prospects for success. While comparative knowledge and broad principles can help illuminate options for reform in any situation, they are no substitute for in-depth country knowledge. That "the perfect is the enemy of the good" is often true in this complex area of work. For example, the recent OED report on CSR concludes that, "the Bank has relied on small groups of interlocutors within core ministries to design and implement one-size-fits-all CSR blueprints in diverse country settings."

- Third, in addition to the shortfalls of a narrow technocratic or one-size-fits-all approach, public sector management interventions have been hampered in the past by shortcomings in traditional lending instruments, which have made it difficult to address systemic problems in the public sector over the medium-term time horizon needed for institutional change (see Section V).

- Fourth, some OED reports have also pointed to problems within the Bank, including deficient staffing and weak incentives for timely and cost-efficient delivery of Bank products. A 1998 OED study of Public Expenditure Reviews, for example, surveyed 35 PERs conducted prior to 1998 and found that many had weak analysis or limited ownership and impact in client countries.[15] The report acknowledged that PERs had improved during the past few years but recommended that further efforts be taken to increase quality, timeliness, ownership, links with the IMF and other partners, and impact. QAG's 1999 review of ESW also highlighted weaknesses with PERs, finding only 56 percent of PERs to have satisfactory quality (based on the sample of 11 that were reviewed).

While more needs to be done to improve our performance, these lessons of experience are being heeded by practitioners in the Bank (as evidenced by the recent improvements in portfolio performance). In the area of judicial reform, for example, a 1992 project in Venezuela was criticized by the NGO community for not involving a wide range of stakeholders in the design of the project; drawing in part from that experience, more recent projects in Venezuela and Guatemala have been careful to include extensive consultations with the private sector, civil society, and other donors in the design phase. With regard to PERs, extensive efforts are being made to link PERs more closely to country strategies, to increase country participation and ownership of the PER process and outcomes, to focus PER analysis more centrally on institutions for budgeting, implementation, and accountability, and to build stronger partnerships with the IMF and other donors. As described below, the strategy laid out in this paper envisions a central role for PERs and related analytic work (Section IV), and for new, more participatory and longer-term lending approaches (Section V).

Sector-based institution-building. This strategy paper does not go into detail in evaluating institution-building efforts in particular sectors. That task should be a primary concern of strategy papers for the individual sectors. However, similar lessons are likely to apply across a variety of sectors, particularly those involved in the delivery of services to the public.

First, in the past the Bank often took too narrow a view of institutional reform, focusing heavily on capacity building in traditional public organizations and under-emphasizing the need for competition and "voice" and participation. Quoting from a recent OED/PREM/HD study of projects in health, nutrition, and population, there are "a great variety of institutional options available to Bank operational staff and their clients on service delivery projects. The adoption of these better practice options would have been Pareto improvements, which the Bank failed to secure by relying largely on public monopoly arrangements in infrastructure, social, and rural services."[16]

Second, the importance of understanding and taking into account the complex realities on the ground—and the danger of relying primarily on "best practice" detached from the specifics of the situation—applies to sectoral interventions as much as to interventions in core government institutions. The Bank's sector lending may have an advantage in this respect, to the extent the Bank has had longer and more in-depth association—often over several projects—with sector institutions in particular countries. However, the report cited above found that "overall, the Bank has a poor track record in building country knowledge of institutional endowments that affect service delivery. Specifically, service delivery support across sectors has rarely incorporated assessments and models of state, political, and social institutions into project design."

As with PSM projects, the Bank's sector projects are taking these lessons of experience to heart. Since the late 1980s, Bank support for service delivery in infrastructure, rural and social sectors has begun to move away from an exclusive reliance on public monopolies—because of their operational inefficiency, poor incentives for performance, and inability to meet growing sectoral demand—and has increasingly recommended the participation of both the private sector and private citizens in service delivery. The Bank has focused on "voice" and competition in addition to—or sometimes in lieu of—internal government reforms. Private participation in infrastructure is becoming standard practice, and the Bank is shifting its support increasingly toward policy, regulation, and risk mitigation. More health, nutrition, and population (HNP) projects since 1990 have worked to employ NGOs and civil society in a participatory role in service delivery. The Bank is actively encouraging private participation in the education sector in Latin America, and water supply and sanitation projects such as those in Uzbekistan, Paraguay, and Pakistan have been noted as models of participatory development.

It is important to maintain realistic expectations.

Reforming core institutions of government and addressing governance and anticorruption concerns are extremely difficult challenges, in part because of social and political dimensions. Given the nature of the task, many attempts at reform will fail to meet their full objectives. Some may fail entirely despite the Bank's best efforts, and others may be judged as failures even though our interventions resulted in substantial gains relative to the earlier status quo. In the area of anticorruption, for example, Bank interventions are unlikely ever to eliminate corruption, and even making a significant dent in the problem may be difficult in certain countries no matter how well the Bank performs. Defining a standard for success is particularly tricky in such a situation. Rather than aim for the same percentage and standard of success in all types of projects the Bank undertakes, success should be measured in part against the difficulty of the challenges addressed, and if possible against what would have been in place without the intervention. Furthermore, a mere yes-no (successful/unsuccessful) indicator will not properly capture the outcome. Not all successes have equal benefits, and the benefits of successful interventions may be particularly high in core areas of public sector reform. A lower success rate may be offset by higher benefits in the cases that do succeed.[17]

The need for institutional reform challenges our conventional ways of doing business . . .

The first step in doing better is to recognize the mismatch between the requirements of successful institutional reform and traditional ways of going about the aid business. Effective governments work in integrated, not fragmented, ways. Public decisionmaking is an ongoing process of making choices among competing ends. As Box 5 noted, good governance rests upon "rules of the game" that make overall budget constraints explicit to political and bureaucratic decisionmakers, facilitate the flow of information on alternatives, and provide effective forums (cabinets, for example) for choosing among competing goals and interests.

. . .in projects. Recognizing the advantages of integrated decisionmaking by governments poses a fundamental challenge to a core product of the aid business—projects. Almost by definition, projects target some specific facet of public action for detailed attention, rather than the broader institutional environment. In so doing, projects can preempt domestic budget decisionmaking by earmarking resources (including technical assistance) for preferred donor objectives. As Box 7 illustrates, the proliferation of donor-driven projects in some low-income countries has undermined domestic institutional arrangements for budgeting more broadly. Moreover, to achieve their specific objectives, projects often support specialized implementation units, with higher pay scales than the civil service as a whole. These institutional enclaves deplete government of scarce human and financial resources.

At the same time, in countries where the core institutions of government are very weak, an enclave, project-driven approach may be the only way to get anything done at all and perhaps begin a cumulative process of change. Clearly there is a need to reconcile investment and institution-building objectives, both short-term and long-term. So far, the Bank and other donors have not done so systematically and effectively.

. . .and in topics addressed. WDR97, the previous two Bank reports on governance, and the Bank's anticorruption policy all highlight the fact that successful governments have not only workable, integrated rules,

but also properly functioning monitoring and enforcement mechanisms. These include both the internal regulatory mechanisms of government and the monitoring and enforcement functions rooted in countries' constitutional separation of powers (the legislature and the judiciary) and in the participation of its citizenry. Addressing these concerns has taken the Bank beyond the realm of comfortably compartmentalized technocratic support—into sensitive terrain such as judicial independence and government transparency and accountability.

We will achieve much more if we work closely with our development partners.

The Bank is only one of many organizations involved in resource transfer and capacity building in developing countries. Other major players include UNDP and other agencies of the UN system, bilateral donors, the regional development banks, the European Union, OECD, the WTO, professional organizations, and the NGO community. The private sector also has a major

---

BOX 7

How Foreign Aid Affects Public Management in Poor Countries: PIUs, Salary Supplements, and Other Distortionary Practices

Although foreign aid budgets have fallen in most industrial countries, many poor countries continue to receive aid inflows in excess of 10 percent of GDP. Unfortunately, the ways in which this aid is provided can severely undermine public management in recipient countries and unwittingly block rather than promote progress in public sector reform and institution-building. Examples of the unintended consequences of aid abound. Donors' payments of salary supplements to local project staff can draw skilled manpower away from core government functions. The establishment of project implementation units (PIUs) within or outside ministries and agencies can subordinate the coherence of the machinery of government to the narrower goal of project implementation and the achievement of short-term gains that might not be sustainable. The availability of grants and concessional loans can weaken budget discipline and encourage line

ministries to focus more on preparing a menu of initiatives to "market" to donors than on making difficult choices among competing priorities within their sectors. Donors' insistence that their aid be "additional" can further distort the process of considering tradeoffs. And the multiple procurement and disbursement procedures of donors can add additional administrative burdens and inhibit the development of coherent domestic systems. In sum, when foreign aid becomes the most reliable source of budget funding, governments lose their capacity to reprioritize and reallocate, staff incentives are distorted, and accountability is externalized. Recipients and donors share responsibility for these problems, and both need to change their ways. Recipient countries need to increase their capacity to manage aid. And donors need to reconsider the instruments and modalities for delivering aid, as discussed in greater detail below.

---

role to play in private resource transfer and capacity building. Each of these players brings somewhat different skills and advantages to the development arena, and we can achieve more collectively if we work toward common goals and strategies, respect and build on our respective comparative advantages, and avoid the disruptive effects of disjointed enclave activities as noted above.

The Public Sector Board has recently undertaken extensive discussions with our external partners in various locations (including, among others, Abidjan, Copenhagen, Harare, London, Maastricht, Manila, New York, Paris, Stockholm, Warsaw, and Washington) to share strategies, explore our various roles, and build opportunities to work together. We have deepened our relationship with UNDP, expanded the work of our MDBs' Governance and Anticorruption Working Group, forged new working relationships with OECD (including the Anti-bribery Working Group and the Public Management Service (PUMA), joined a new governance working group organized by the Conference Board with representatives of major multinational private firms, continued our interactions with Transparency International and other NGOs (including through the EAP and ECA Regions' advisory groups on anticorruption), expanded our dialogue with the professional associations (including those covering accountants, government auditors, and police: IFAD, INTOSAI, and INTERPOL) and had extensive discussions and workshops with major bilateral partners. Our strategy is embedded in a broader view, widely shared by our partners, of how the development community as a whole should move together to address the challenges of governance reform, anticorruption, and institutional strengthening. As discussed more extensively below, we are well-placed to take the lead in some areas while deferring to others' strengths in other areas. In some areas (depending in part on the country concerned) numerous donors can make important contributions, and our goal is to work cooperatively through coordinated analytic work, policy advice, resource transfer, and monitoring and evaluation. Given the enormous amount of work to be done and the tight resource constraints faced by virtually all development agencies, we all have great interest in working together.

Our strategy is fourfold.

The themes and lessons of experience outlined above point to the primary challenges for the Bank if it is to be more effective in reforming public institutions.

- First, we need to continue to move beyond a narrow, technocratic, supply-side approach and work with clients and other partners to explore a broad range of mechanisms that promote demand for accountable, responsive, and effective public sectors.

- Second, we need to start with what exists on the ground in our client countries and work with our clients to understand institutional and political realities and their implications for reform.

- Third, we need to focus more of our lending on long-term, systemic institution-building and to fully recognize the institutional implications of all our interventions and the relationships among them.

- Finally, we need to put in place the skills and incentives to enable and encourage staff to focus on the institutional dimensions of reform in their work, to enhance the quality of their work, and to interact with partners effectively.

The next four sections of this paper describe how these challenges can be addressed.

Broadening Our Approach: Empowering Our Clients and Fostering Accountability

The policy of the party is that the people know, the people discuss, the people do, but here people only implement the last part, which is the people do.

Voices of the Poor (Ha Tinh, Vietnam)

The starting point for institutional reform in the public sector must necessarily be some point of reference as to the characteristics of effective government. While a wide variety of institutional arrangements within the public sector are workable, well-functioning governments are generally thought to have certain important characteristics in common. They are responsive to the citizenry and reasonably efficient in the delivery of public services. Their decisionmaking processes and the decisions they result in are in general transparent and predictable. Oversight mechanisms (checks and balances) exist to guard against arbitrariness and to ensure accountability in the use of public resources, but these oversight mechanisms do not eliminate the flexibility and delegation that are needed to respond quickly to changing circumstances. In sum, they are accountable and results-oriented.

Most governments in the developing world are a long way from this model, although a growing number are devoting great efforts toward reform. Nontransparency, a lack of accountability, excessive intervention, a lack of delegation, and poor results on the ground are commonplace and contribute to arbitrariness, corruption, and poverty. The fundamental and very difficult question is how to move from this current situation toward a better-functioning one, and what the World Bank can do within its mandate to help clients progress toward this goal.

Public sector reform requires not only internal bureaucratic change—but also "voice" and competition.

WDR97 provides a starting point for translating theory into practice. It distinguishes among three mechanisms that can help provide incentives for public actors to pursue social ends, hold them accountable for results, and restrain arbitrary action. Looking across the spectrum of countries, and as Figure 5 (taken from

WDR97) illustrates, a broad set of arrangements are evident. These include:

- *Rules and Restraints Within the Public Sector.* These include the constitutional separation of powers, divisions of responsibility among levels of government, budgeting rules across public organizations, formal rules and oversight arrangements within public organizations, and organizational culture.

- *Mechanisms That Promote Citizen "Voice" and Participation:* These include various forms of representative decisionmaking and political oversight; direct involvement by users, nongovernmental organizations and other groups of citizens in the design, implementation, and monitoring of public policies; and the transparent production and dissemination of information.

- *Mechanisms That Promote Competition:* These include political competition (for example, between regions or parties); market competition among public agencies, or between public and private providers of information, goods and services;

FIGURE 5
Mechanisms to Enhance State Capability: Three Drivers of Public Sector Reform

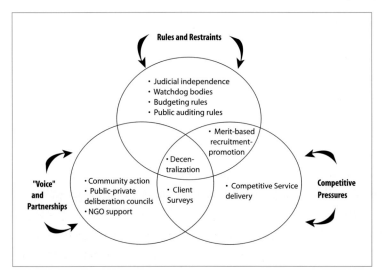

and internal competition within public bureaucracies. In some cases they might mean complete privatization of certain market-based activities. Because introducing market competition and private participation often involves a fundamental rethinking of the role of the state, public sector reform and private sector development are intimately interconnected.

It should be noted that decentralization of public sector activity—an accelerating trend in many countries and the focus of extensive work in the Bank—lies at the intersection of the three circles in Figure 5. It entails a change in the legal and regulatory framework for government activity, and it often holds the promise of increasing both "voice" and participation (by moving the administration of public services closer to the citizenry) and competitive pressures (including competition among levels of government and between subnational entities). But while decentralization holds many promises, it also entails risks that must be addressed, including the risk of "capture" by local elites or lack of capacity within local government (see Box 8).

It is not being suggested here that countries must have all of the checks and balances shown in Figure 5 in place to have effective governments. Indeed, countries differ greatly in the relative emphasis they give to different mechanisms—and we still have much to learn about how different systems of accountability work in diverse country settings. But what *is* being suggested is that countries need some critical mass of checks and balances to ensure accountability and state effectiveness.

It is also not being suggested that active involvement to build all of these types of institutions falls within the Bank's mandate. The question of the Bank's mandate was considered in designing its anticorruption policy in

BOX 8

Decentralization: A Key Element of the Public Sector Strategy

Central governments around the world are decentralizing fiscal, political, and administrative responsibilities to lower-level governments and to the private sector. Political pressure probably drives most decentralization efforts. Whatever the roots of change, decentralization can have significant repercussions for public sector performance, including resource mobilization and allocation, macroeconomic stability, service delivery, and equity.

Designing decentralization policy within a particular country context is a complex task. There is no right or wrong degree of decentralization or standard "best practice" that can be applied across countries, although most developing countries tend to relatively centralized public sectors and could benefit significantly from greater decentralization if well-designed and implemented. The best design will vary depending on circumstances, and this complexity has sometimes been overlooked by the Bank and other donors in the haste to offer policy advice. Fragmentation of policy advice has also sometimes been a problem. Decentralization is a cross-cutting issue that affects most topics in which we engage our clients—from macroeconomic stability to service delivery. Although country teams are increasingly trying to bring a comprehensive, coordinated perspective, the traditional Bank approach has handled public finance and sectoral issues separately and has sometimes focused disproportionately on the fiscal aspects of decentralization without considering the political and administrative aspects that are critical to success.

Our overall public sector strategy outlines three mechanisms to enhance state capability: "voice" and partnerships, competitive pressures, and rules and restraints. Each one of these corresponds to a critical aspect of decentralization design and is a key consideration in our operational approach:

Voice. Local residents need greater "voice" in decisions that affect their lives. The political rationale for decentralization is the desire to move decisionmaking closer to people to foster greater democracy. The economic rationale is based on gains in allocative efficiency— that is, the view that greater local involvement in expenditure and taxing decisions will lead to services that better reflect local needs and preferences. To achieve political or economic objectives, appropriate mechanisms need to be in place to ensure the accountability of local governments to citizens. For example, a recent World Bank program in Campo Elias, Venezuela used an innovative approach involving citizen surveys and "participatory budgeting" in an effort to build an institutional framework that could help lower corruption and raise the efficiency of service delivery. Similarly, the Honduras Social Investment Fund, like many social action programs throughout the world, supported the development of local communities and helped provide a collective voice for individuals to express their views to government.

Competitive Pressures. The concepts of "choice" and "exit" are key to effective decentralization. Decentralizing service delivery away from central government monopolies should open the door for alternative service providers, including local governments, the private sector and NGOs. The pressure of competition provides incentives for government to be responsive to demand, which often leads to higher quality services. A growing number of our sector operations are stressing alternative options for service delivery in the context of decentralization. For example, the Colombia Secondary Education Project has supported the distribution of school vouchers to give low-income students the choice of attending private schools.

Rules and Restraints. Effective decentralization requires an active role for *central* governments, because rules and restraints are absolutely necessary to distribute responsibilities across levels of government and to encourage fiscal discipline, enable effective service delivery and promote poverty-reduction objectives. A particularly complex set of rules revolves around the design of an internally consistent system of intergovernmental fiscal relations, which is a central topic of our operational policy dialogue in many countries. These rules assign functional responsibilities to the most suitable level of government (depending on

the nature of the service and national objectives), assign revenue sources and transfers adequate to meet those functions (no "unfunded mandates") and design transfers to enable both local flexibility and accomplishment of central objectives. These rules, perhaps above all else, must be transparent and predictable to enable subnational governments to plan and execute their functions in a responsible way. Other critical rules set clear parameters within which subnational borrowing can occur, including a legal framework for local bankruptcy, regular auditing and financial reporting requirements. Still others govern political processes that link citizens to their government and determine pay and employment conditions for civil servants. Taken together, rules and incentives provided by a central decentralization framework are essential for creating fiscal discipline and enabling effective service delivery. The Bank supports the development of comprehensive decentralization frameworks through ongoing policy dialogue, analytic work, training, and innovative projects such as the recent Mexico Decentralization Adjustment Loan and the Thailand Public Sector Reform Loan.

1997, and the tests and limits set in that policy apply here as well. If a country requests assistance from the Bank (such as when it requests help in combating corruption, as discussed in Box 9), it is proper for the Bank to respond if the activity will contribute to economic development and if the Bank has the requisite skills and resources to help. And if weak governance and ineffective state institutions are hampering economic development prospects in a country, the Bank should take this into account as it considers

the content of its assistance strategy, the size of its lending program, the design of projects, and the program of economic and sector work for that country.

We are exploring new ways to empower and enable clients.

Institutional reform and capacity building in the public sector will succeed only when it is "owned" within

BOX 9

An Integrated Approach to Helping Countries Combat Corruption

The Bank's anticorruption activities have grown steadily since 1997, and we have assisted at least 50 countries, including, among others, Albania, Georgia, Latvia, and Slovakia in ECA; Benin, Nigeria, Tanzania, and Uganda in Africa; Argentina, Bolivia and Ecuador in LCR; Indonesia, Philippines and Thailand in East Asia; the Indian state of Uttar Pradesh in South Asia, and Morocco in MNA—with anticorruption and governance reforms of significant depth. The Bank's mainstreaming agenda now requires all CASs to diagnose the state of governance and the risks that corruption poses to Bank projects. In response to country demands and mainstreaming imperatives, the Bank is developing an integrated approach to analysis and intervention that can be tailored to the specifics of each individual country situation. Progress in implementing the Bank's anticorruption strategy over the past three years is summarized in a new publication, *Helping Countries Combat Corruption: Progress at the World Bank since 1997* (June 2000).

Because the Bank views corruption as a symptom of underlying weakness in public sector institutions, its approach spans all three types of accountability mechanisms noted in the text. With regard to internal rules and restraints, the Bank's approach builds on its long expertise in economic policy reform and its growing experience with public expenditure management, decentralization, civil service regulation, tax policy and administration, public sector accounting and auditing, and other public sector institutions that affect the incentives of public officials. It works with client countries to identify weaknesses in these institu-

tions and ways to address them that are workable in the country's social and political milieu—employing explicit analysis of political economy issues when appropriate.

But it is increasingly clear that reforming internal rules is not likely to be effective by itself in combating deep systemic corruption. It is also important to ask which responsibilities the state can shed altogether (such as excessive regulations), and which ones it can share with the private sector (such as many types of service delivery)—in other words, where competition can be introduced. Furthermore, it is critical to look at the "voice" through which citizens provide feedback to governments. The Bank is becoming increasingly involved in helping strengthen "voice" mechanisms through workshops involving civil society, journalists' training, and partnerships with NGOs such as Transparency International. One recent innovative initiative is WBI's "core course" on controlling corruption, which brings together senior government officials, civil society representatives, and journalists to develop (or modify existing) national anticorruption strategies. The Bank is also developing new diagnostic tools (including surveys of citizens, firms, and policymakers) to provide an in-depth understanding of a country's corruption patterns and to help in catalyzing action and setting priorities for specific interventions. These innovative activities, when undertaken as part of integrated anticorruption programs requested by client countries, can be very important catalysts that complement the more traditional focus of Bank activity on economic and institutional reform.

the country and driven by a country's leaders, with participation and input from the legislature, the private sector, and civil society. The Bank's role is to support our clients—both committed leaders and their citizenry—and provide assistance and advice to help them succeed. When local conditions are amenable to change, Bank support can be invaluable:

• Increasing *transparency* can help to reveal problems and set priorities, and Bank-financed analytic work can help in this regard. Corruption surveys in Albania, Latvia, and Georgia, public officials' surveys in Armenia, Bangladesh, and Bolivia, and the expenditure tracking survey in Uganda are recent examples (see Box 9 and Section IV). Innovative uses of the internet and other forms of information technology to disseminate information on public spending and procurement, judicial decisions, regulatory activities, and data on service delivery can also help to improve accountability and performance, and we are undertaking a new initiative in fiscal 2001 to collect information and disseminate experience with *E-government* (see Box 10).

• Mechanisms to promote *citizen feedback* are fundamental to accountability and efficient service delivery, and Bank-supported consultations and citizen surveys can contribute. Our strong efforts to promote *citizen consultation* in strategy preparation for public service delivery in Guinea (Box 18), project preparation for judicial reform in Guatemala, and budget formulation in Campo Elias, Venezuela (Box 8), and the growing stress on *community action* and participation in decisionmaking across all sectors are recent examples.

• Well-designed *technical assistance* and other *capacity building* efforts can also be very helpful, as long as governments are in the driver's seat. One of many examples is the Bank's recent loan to Guatemala (which won a 1999 Award for Excellence) to support development of a cus-

tomized financial management system. Another is the innovative Partnership for Capacity Building in Africa, initiated by the African Governors of the World Bank and facilitated by Bank staff and Africa's other development partners, which has endeavored to proceed in a substantially more participatory way (see Box 11).

• Building on the *fiduciary* concerns in our own lending to provide broader advice and assistance to build in-country capacity for *financial management, procurement,* and *monitoring and evaluation* (including OED's initiatives in the area of evaluation capacity development) can spur systemic reforms and a much-needed focus on results on the ground in our client governments.

But selectivity is also key . . . and difficult.

Government is not monolithic but is itself a collection of interests. Institutional change can significantly alter the incentives facing politicians, bureaucrats and other powerful groups. Reforms to spur development may not be desired by one or more of these groups, and they may be in a position to block change. At the extreme are countries locked into a dysfunctional political equilibrium, where powerful interests block any actions with the potential to promote development. The experiences of countries as diverse as Argentina, Poland, and Uganda suggest that it can take a major system-wide crisis—and a resulting transfer of power to reform-oriented leaders—to "unlock" dysfunctional equilibria of this kind. Prior to crisis, the prospects for reform to succeed are very low in such situations. At a less extreme position are those countries where some scope for reform exists, but where there is still significant opposition. In these circumstances parties committed to reform need to find and take advantage of existing windows of opportunity, in ways that progressively build constituencies committed to development. Often the resulting agendas of the reformers may look "second-best" or "roundabout" in their aims from a narrowly economic perspective, but they can result in useful improvements because they take political reality into account.

It is important for the Bank to understand the political economy of a country, to recognize where efforts at reforms might have a chance and where they do not, and to allocate resources accordingly. In countries with strong domestic leadership and substantial capacity, the Bank's main contribution to public sector reform may well be through technical assistance for further capacity building in public sector management. Ghana, Latvia, and Thailand are three of numerous cases outlined in Part II. In other settings

---

BOX 10

Realizing the Potential of E-Government

E-government is the use of information and communications technologies (ICT) to enhance the efficiency, transparency, and accountability of government. These tools, particularly the Internet, are increasingly used in developing and developed countries alike to provide public services that for years were delivered only in person or by mail (if at all). These innovative technologies can:

- meet citizens' demands more efficiently, saving time and money for both service providers and their clients,

- cut through red tape and associated opportunities for corruption, discrimination and harassment, and

- enhance access to public information and services, leading to greater transparency and equity.

According to a recent survey carried out by Andersen Consulting, E-government is expanding rapidly in many countries (with the U.S. and Singapore being among the leaders), although even in those settings only a small part of the internet's potential has been tapped to date. Developing country governments are fast adopting these new technologies and adapting them to their particular needs and constraints. One area that has witnessed remarkable changes in recent years is government procurement. The Chilean and Mexican governments, for example, have implemented new Internet-based systems for public procurement. In Chile (*www.compraschile.cl*), for example, all companies that wish to be considered for a public contract register themselves according to their business activity (for example, construction, IT consulting, office furniture, etc.). When a public agency needs to purchase goods or services, it files a request in the new electronic system. An e-mail message soliciting bids is then sent automatically to all companies registered in the relevant business area. And once a decision is made, all information concerning the companies, their bids, and the results of the decisionmaking process are posted electronically. E-government solutions like this can generate cost savings for government and reduce opportunities for corruption, leading to increased public confidence in government.

BOX 11

The Partnership for Capacity Building in Africa (PACT)

PACT is an African initiative aimed at strengthening human and institutional capacities in sub-Saharan Africa. It arose from the resolve of the African Governors of the World Bank to address what they agreed has been a major cause of Africa's development difficulties—a lack of capacity to plan, implement, and monitor the development process properly. It enjoys strong ownership among Africa's political leadership and segments of the private sector and civil society, and is the product of an extensive consultative process among the African Governors, African political leaders, donors and other development partners.

PACT has four underlying principles. First, African ownership and leadership form an essential cornerstone of the initiative. Second, PACT recognizes the centrality of capacity in the development process in Africa and the responsibility that African countries must take in creating a conducive policy and operational environment for capacity building. Third, the initiative recognizes the importance of partnership toward a common goal and approach—partnership within African countries themselves (among government, civil society, and the private sector), and with national, multinational and bilateral donors, international business and trade interests and nongovernmental organizations. Fourth, PACT calls for practical and realistic phasing of all actions.

Implementation will thus need to proceed in ways that respect the principle of country-level ownership and commitment, and at the same time assure that resources are focused on initiatives where the institutional environment is sufficiently supportive to offer a reasonable prospect of success. PACT will address this challenge by defining a series of distinct categories of technical and financial support: country program support, provided annually and accessible by countries that meet eligibility thresholds as to the quality of institutional environments; project support for country-based initiatives to build key public sector capacity and to strengthen the interface between government, civil society, and the private sector; and project support for regional and sub-regional initiatives and other proposals initiated independently by civil society and training institutions.

In July, 1999 the World Bank Board of Executive Directors voted to provide initial funding of $30 million for the initiative, with the possibility of up to $150 million overall depending on PACT's performance and impact, the amount of matching funding from other donors, and the availability of Bank net income. A further $23 million was approved in July, 2000. To capitalize on capacity building initiatives currently underway, arrangements for implementation of PACT will be led by the already existing Harare-based African Capacity Building Foundation (ACBF), established in 1991 as a collaborative effort between the World Bank, the African Development Bank, and the United Nations Development Programme (UNDP).

BOX 12

Linking Governance Concerns and Country Assistance Strategies

The 1997 Bank anticorruption policy, *Helping Countries Combat Corruption: The Role of the World Bank*, establishes an explicit link between the Bank's lending activity and the extent of corruption and willingness of a country to deal with it. It does not provide any guidelines on how to implement that link in practice, however. This issue is coming increasingly to the fore, and the Bank is now formulating strategies to link anticorruption goals and lending more closely. Recent discussions on a fiduciary framework for adjustment lending, for example, suggest several broad principles to guide our approach:

CAS Diagnosis and Prescription. The CAS should be the central focal point for addressing the country's overall anticorruption strategy. Every CAS should diagnose the state of governance and lay out in broad terms the condition of financial management and other accountability institutions in the country concerned. Where corruption is a serious problem, the CAS should include a monitorable program to address governance and corruption concerns that has been agreed with the government (and designed to the extent possible through a participatory process), with clear benchmarks and performance indicators.

Fiduciary Safeguards. Safeguards should be in place in all loans to fulfill the Bank's fiduciary requirement that its resources be used for development purposes. Safeguards for investment loans include procurement and disbursement rules as well as innovations in project design. Safeguards are also now being adapted for adjustment loans. While adjustment lending provides general external financing and counterpart funds for the budget that are not tied to specific expenditures, safeguards can help insure that the funds enter the consolidated government budget and that the budget is accompanied by an adequate financial management system, audited regularly, and monitored for development impact.

Impact on Bank Programs. Risks posed by poor governance and ineffective financial management to both development outcomes and the Bank's fiduciary requirements should be taken into account in the design of Bank strategies. High levels of risk may lead to changes in lending amounts, the balance and sequencing of lending and nonlending services, the choice of lending instrument, or project design. The Bank is currently exploring the standards needed for different forms of lending and is developing methodologies to measure both the levels of risk and borrower progress in addressing it.

Content and Conditionality of the Lending Program. For countries with particularly high levels of corruption, the Bank's assistance program should be directed at least in part on helping to improve systems of financial management and strengthen public sector accountability. Not only is this critical for development, but good financial management of *all* public spending represents the best assurance that Bank funds are used appropriately. In some cases, adjustment lending could be directed toward this goal; in other cases technical or project assistance may be the more appropriate vehicle. The key here is to focus more of the Bank's lending on achieving systemic improvements—in economic policies, public sector management, legal and judicial reforms, citizen participation, etc.—that improve gover-

nance and accountability. Because improvements in financial management and control take time, programs of institutional reform—whether supported through adjustment lending, technical assistance, or project lending—should in most cases be stretched over a longer period of time (3 to 5 years or more) than self-standing adjustment loans have traditionally been.

more of a "demand-side" approach may be appropriate, focusing on activities that help build transparency and momentum and consensus for change. Selectivity in approach is also critical for fiduciary reasons. While

general principles are being developed and can help (see Box 12), this inevitably requires balanced and informed judgment on a case-by-case basis.

Analytic Work: Grounding Individual Project and Broader Country Strategies in Institutional Reality

When we approach the block agriculture office for paddy seed, the official would force us to buy other seeds like Dhanicha, for which we do not have money, and neither do we cultivate those seeds.

Voices of the Poor (India).

As outlined in Section I, the challenge of reforming public institutions is relevant for the full variety of activities in which the Bank is engaged, from economic policymaking to service delivery to the range of check and balance mechanisms that ensure accountability for the use of public resources. Certainly, action within each activity calls for specialized skills that are appropriately the responsibility of the relevant technical networks. But applying those skills in individual country settings must start with a thorough and broad understanding of the realities as they exist on the ground. Against the backdrop of these realities, the reform challenge is to identify specific actions that support change and continued momentum for development, even if the actions themselves may seem quite imperfect from the perspective of some ideal notion of "best practice." We must work

with our clients to find reforms that fit local conditions while also reflecting broad fundamental principles of efficiency, equity, and poverty-orientation. While broad end goals may be similar, "best practice" in achieving them is not uniform across countries; rather "good fit" that builds on basic principles is in essence "best practice."

An emphasis on "good fit" in the reform process has two implications for Bank work. First, it means that in the preparation of Bank projects and adjustment loans, we need to help our clients undertake whatever analytic work is necessary on the ground to identify reform options that are feasible, can be readily implemented, and have a positive long-term effect on institution-building. Institutional analysis to understand realities on the ground—including, for example, the capacity of local institutions and the extent of political support for reform—should be a routine part of the design of Bank projects (as illustrated for a recent Bank project in Box 13). To help address this need, a draft Operational Policy (OP) has been prepared on institutional assessment in Bank projects. As part of this strategy for reforming public sector institutions, we propose to work with the sector families across the Bank to pilot the draft OP in 3 to 5 projects in fiscal 2001, with the goal of refining and finalizing it by the end of fiscal 2001.

A second implication of the emphasis on "good fit" is that we need to be more attuned to how the range of public institutions fit together and reinforce (or undermine) each other in any particular setting. Sector institutions (such as public health providers, transportation ministries and schools) and institutions at the core of government (such as parliaments, cabinets and finance ministries) do not operate separately but rather interrelate in complex ways. This strategy proposes that we move upstream where possible and try to understand linkages in institutional systems and integrate this knowledge into country assistance strategy formulation.

Country Assistance Strategies (CASs) play a central role in allocating resources for country programs and are thus a key focal point for ensuring that the Bank's programs within individual countries—both the choice of operations and their design—reflect a deep understanding of existing institutions and a well-considered approach to reforming them. A growing number of country strategies (such as those for Albania, Armenia, Azerbaijan, Bangladesh, Bolivia, Bulgaria, Cambodia, Kenya, Mexico, Mozambique, Papua New Guinea, Philippines, and Thailand) are already designed around a core goal of improving public sector performance and governance. Given the Bank's current direction and the findings of the aid-effectiveness literature, most CASs can be expected to address this goal in the future. Pursuant to the fiscal 1999 Anticorruption Action Plan, all CASs must at a minimum diagnose the state of governance and the risks that corruption poses to Bank projects in the country concerned. As corruption is a symptom of public sector dysfunction, an effective strategy to address corruption will inevitably involve reform in public institutions.

Careful diagnostic work can help us focus our assistance.

More systematic diagnosis of the institutional, political and organizational dimensions of development in both projects and country strategies will better position us, our client countries, and our partner development agencies to answer a variety of questions that are key to the success or failure of Bank work across the range of activities, including the following:

- *Is there a "window of opportunity" for reform?* All too often Bank resources have been used to promote reforms in countries that are locked into dysfunctional political equilibria. Sometimes it may be more effective to postpone reform efforts until a genuine "window of opportunity" is evident—and to focus Bank resources on countries with a more favorable environment. As an intermediate step when windows of opportunity appear small, it may be possible to focus Bank efforts on certain activities (such as WBI workshops or private sector surveys) that help educate key stakeholders, build constituencies for reform in the future, and keep the Bank engaged in policy dialogue without a major commitment of resources.

- *What approach to reform "fits" best with prevailing institutional constraints?* What is feasible in a particular country may be only second (or third or fourth) best compared with some global optimum, but may nonetheless help to advance that country's development. While there are clearly lessons that are important in all settings—such as the importance of focusing on *accountability, transparency,* and *outcomes* and of building the capacity for in-country monitoring and evaluation—even these must be approached with a full understanding of nuances on the ground in each setting (as noted in Box 14).

BOX 13

The Importance of Institutional Analysis: The Latvian Revenue Modernization Project

Computerization can become an end rather than a means in tax administration reform projects, if the institution-building necessary for sustainable reform is inadequately addressed. The State Revenue Service Modernization Project in Latvia could have gone the same way, as the Latvian government was initially looking primarily for assistance with information technology. However, with help from the World Bank, the government integrated an "institutional development" component in project design. The resulting balance of institutional development and information technology earned the project a "Highly Satisfactory" and a "Best Practice" ranking from the Quality Assurance Group's (QAG) Quality At Entry Assessment for "sustainable institutional reform." Two of the most important factors mentioned by QAG were:

Project concept, objectives and approach. The Government of Latvia took the initiative, requesting help only after considerable prior work and a Cabinet discussion of the issues. The Government had clear objectives for both tax reform and capacity building to qualify for EU entry, and it showed commitment by providing almost 90 percent of the project cost. Preparatory work addressed important institutional issues such as "vulnerability to corruption" and "institutional gaps." The project utilized relevant lessons of

experience in project design and implementation, such as introducing performance indicators as benchmarks for revenue agency staff and managers, and complementing the IT-dominated operational components with components aimed at the organization and management aspects of revenue administration. An alternative project design was considered and dropped because it did not fit the desired criteria.

Institutional capacity analysis. The central importance of institutional development for sustainability was recognized and explained, and a comprehensive analysis of the executing agency's capacity and incentives to carry out its mission was included. This analysis identified gaps and solutions and served as the base for project design.

Stakeholder analysis. A limitation of the project design process, according to the QAG report, is its apparently limited assessment and incorporation of stakeholder views. It was considered too difficult to arrange the direct participation of taxpayers in the project, although there were brief surveys of businesses, households, public officials, and taxpayers to assess their perceptions of the State Revenue Service. Consultations were also carried out with major accounting firms and a few large taxpayers, but it is not clear to what extent their views were reflected in project design.

- *Where should one start in trying to build institutional capacity?* The long-term goal is to strengthen institutions—not just to operate within the constraints of what is currently workable. But where to start and what sequence to move in is not always obvious.

- *Is an enclaving approach likely to help or hurt over the long run?* Where the institutional starting point is very weak, or where the political window of opportunity for reform is narrow, a common approach is to begin by creating institutional "enclaves". Project implementation units are one example, but there are many others. When judicial systems are weak, for example, the temptation is to bypass the judiciary and set up special courts or out-of-court mechanisms for problem resolution (such as debt workouts or bankruptcy, for example). Or when government procurement or financial controls are unreliable, donors establish special rules to govern their projects. Such enclaves can create highly visible islands of success on which to build and can help loosen constraints to sustained development (for example, in taxation, mining, or agribusiness). Yet the potentially harmful long-term effects described earlier of an "enclaving" approach, especially if multiplied over many donors, must also be taken into account (see Box 7). Furthermore, bypassing mainstream structures takes away the "demand" that can put pressure on them to improve. The costs and benefits of enclaving, in both the short and the longer run, should be carefully weighed in every relevant case, and enclaves should in general be avoided.

Adapting "New Public Management" to Developing Country Settings

Governments in many OECD countries have undergone extensive "reinvention" in the 1990s toward models of "New Public Management" (NPM). The basic idea of NPM, pioneered most notably in New Zealand, is that governments should seek to improve quality by giving managers broad discretion in running their programs and holding them accountable for results. The first part of this bargain is designed to "let managers manage"; the second part, to make managers manage. Letting managers manage means shifting decisions on the use of resources (staff, money, space, supplies, etc.) from central controllers and headquarters staff to line managers. Making managers manage means specifying in advance the performance expected of them, comparing results against targets, and auditing both financial and substantive performance.

Understandably, many developing and transitional countries have explored NPM models as opportunities to accelerate their development and improve public sector performance. While many aspects of NPM are valuable in any setting, moving too fast may be risky and open the door to corruption and abuse if basic public institutions are not sufficiently developed. These include the rule of law, an independent judiciary, sturdy property rights, a formal civil service system based on merit and rules, proper and efficient use of public funds, and robust internal controls. It took generations for most developed countries to embed these capabilities; the process can be accelerated but cannot be bypassed altogether.

In rule-based public management, managers internalize the norms for spending funds and carrying out operations as authorized by law. Controls are effective, not only because they are enforced by outside controllers, but also because those who spend the money, appoint civil servants, and purchase goods and services accept the administrative rules as fair and legitimate. When the norms and practices are internalized, governments can safely improve managerial performance and the quality of public services by eliminating many procedural rules and empowering managers to use public resources in carrying out authorized programs according to their best judgment.

Where the rules are not internalized, however, and public management is highly informal—where, for example, managers routinely ignore civil service and procurement rules and actual spending deviates significantly from the approved budget, broadening managerial discretion may encourage "anything goes" behavior. It would be prudent, therefore, for countries attracted by the promise of NPM to take a two-pronged strategy: to try to build basic institutions as quickly as possible—including, importantly, institutions for monitoring and evaluation—while preparing the way for broader managerial flexibility.

A move to NPM may make sense under certain circumstances even when institutions are weak. For some time Mongolia sought to undertake government reforms along general New Zealand lines (albeit with some important qualifications), in part to provide a politically acceptable means to cut the share of government spending in GDP, shed excess public employment, and reverse inappropriate styles of public administration carried over from communist days. The Mongolian reformers knew that the result would be far from perfect—in part because the country lacks many of the fundamentals noted above—but they believed it would be an improvement over what they had. Because the country is small and homogenous, levels of education and skills in the civil service are quite high, and corruption is not thought to be endemic, Mongolia could well benefit from immediate improvements through NPM-style reforms without some of the risks noted above.

Waiting to adopt full-scale NPM does *not* mean that governments should wait to adopt performance management. A focus on *monitoring and evaluation* of results and on *transparent reporting* of those results is *always* called for, even if not accompanied by full-fledged managerial flexibility. A major thrust of Bank work should be to help countries improve their ability to produce, disseminate, and evaluate data on the quality and cost of public services, as has been pioneered in Australia and other advanced government reformers.

"Upstream" diagnostic work—Public Expenditure Reviews and Institutional and Governance Reviews—can help.

The diagnostic work described above requires tools that enable practitioners to understand country-specific starting points and match options for public action to these starting points. While important knowledge gaps remain, the immediate priority is not more fundamental research but rather a systematic effort to codify, adapt, and make accessible to practitioners the insights that already exist—albeit often in fragmented and haphazard forms—on the political and institutional dimensions of development. PREM and WBI are currently working to develop several types of country-focused diagnostic tools for public sector reform, including:

- tools that evaluate the quality of a country's institutions (including those at the "core" of government) and help measure the severity and pattern of institutional dysfunction, and

- tools that assess a country's readiness for specific reform initiatives and likely political and institutional obstacles to implementation.

We propose to move to two core types of economic and sector work—Public Expenditure Reviews and Institutional and Governance Reviews—to provide a full range of public sector analysis to underpin the Bank's lending and assistance programs. Where possible we propose to work with our clients to undertake this analytic work—to foster ownership, transfer skills, and heighten the accuracy and relevance of the analysis.

Public Expenditure Reviews. PERs have been in use in the Bank since the 1980s, and the Bank now undertakes about 30 to 40 annually, primarily in the Africa Region. As noted in Section II above, recent reviews of PERs by OED and QAG point to problems of variable quality and the need for change in several

directions—toward greater institutional content, client ownership, quality of analysis, timeliness, and focus on impact and results. In addition, the IMF and other donors have expressed concerns about the availability of timely budget information needed as input to their programs. The Public Sector Board and the Public Expenditure Thematic Group have developed new draft guidelines for PERs, which are currently being discussed with our sector and IMF colleagues, that will bring better clarity to their scope and better quality to their content, taking the needs of partners into careful account.

With regard to content, PERs will continue to provide information on budget allocations as needed but will also focus increasingly on institutions for budget decisionmaking and implementation. As noted earlier, the purpose and scope of PERs has broadened in recent years from an economic analysis of public spending allocations to a broader analysis of both spending patterns and the institutions for public expenditure management. For example, a recent China PER focused on institutional reforms in budget management and won a wide hearing, while the Macedonia Public Expenditure and Institutional and Governance Review will analyze the sustainability of the fiscal program and its institutional drivers. The fiscal 1999 West Bank and Gaza Public Expenditure Review, Jordan Public Sector Review, and PERs in the Pacific Islands and Cambodia also have an institutional focus. While maintaining these constant core themes, each PER may also look at specific expenditure topics of particular importance to the country, and they will necessarily vary somewhat in scope, size, and timing, depending on country demand. In some cases (such as Ethiopia), PERs may be undertaken annually but may have a rotating focus that covers individual topics only once every few years.

With regard to quality, the Public Sector Board is working with the Regions (particularly AFR) to develop stronger criteria for task team leadership and membership, more thorough monitoring programs, and stricter peer review procedures to complement the guidelines on scope and content. Half-day public expenditure clinics are now offered by the Public Expenditure Thematic Group to teams about to embark on PER field missions.

With regard to country ownership, some PERs are now undertaken by clients themselves with Bank assistance, with both client and Bank staff participating in any pre-mission training provided. In the recent case of Argentina, the country carried out the PER on its own, and the Bank provided a clinic for country staff. In some cases there may be tradeoffs between objectives of quality, timeliness, and ownership. For this reason

PERs (particularly those focusing more heavily on assessments of spending programs) must not be the only elements in the public expenditure program through which the Bank engages with clients; other forms of technical assistance, training, and analysis may also be appropriate as complements to PERs.

A focus on results—moving beyond budget allocations to what those allocations actually buy—must also increase as part of the improvement program for PERs. A recent PER for Uganda included an innovative "tracking" survey to determine how much of the funding budgeted for schools and clinics actually reached them.[18] It identified significant gaps between amounts budgeted and amounts spent, and this has resulted in a strengthened effort at citizen monitoring of budget dis-

---

BOX 15

Gender and Governance: Gender Budgets

One outgrowth of the growing appreciation of the links between good governance and poverty reduction has been the increasing recognition of the importance of making public institutions more accountable to women's interests. Strengthening women's representation and participation in economic and political life can contribute significantly to poverty alleviation and to more effective and accountable governance. One tangible result has been the formulation of "gender budgets" in a wide range of countries in different regions. Such analyses of national budgets to determine their impact by gender have been undertaken, among other places, in Australia, Bangladesh, Barbados, Canada, Fiji, South Africa, Sri Lanka, Tanzania, and Uganda.

Gender budgets—or women's budgets—are

not separate budgets for women, but analyses of public spending from a gender perspective. Typically they assess (a) spending specifically targeted to gender issues, (b) spending related to equal employment opportunities in the civil service, and (c) the differential impact of mainstream expenditures by gender. The experience to date has shown the potential of such analyses not only to further gender equality, but to improve transparency and good governance. Gender budgets have contributed to reprioritization of public spending and to other policy changes in areas such as child care, family tax credits, and domestic violence. In addition, they have proven useful in exposing general budget and policy weaknesses, in furthering economic literacy, and in fostering political participation.

bursements in that country. Similar surveys are planned in Albania and Macedonia, and over time they are expected to become standard instruments for monitoring expenditure outputs and outcomes on the ground. Another initiative that several countries have undertaken is an effort to analyze the incidence and impact of public spending from a gender perspective through "gender budgets" (see Box 15).

Institutional and Governance Reviews. To complement PERs and facilitate institutional analysis in other areas of public sector reform, we worked with our clients in fiscal 2000 to pilot variants of a new family of analytic instruments, called *Institutional and Governance Reviews* (IGRs), in four countries: Armenia, Bangladesh, Bolivia, and Indonesia (see Box 16). At least five more are being undertaken in fiscal 2001. These IGRs (whose variants may also be called simply Institutional Reviews or Governance Reviews) attempt a broad assessment of the quality of accountability, policymaking or service delivery institutions in a country, and propose a comprehensive strategy for institutional change (see Annex 2 for further description). Two particular characteristics tend to distinguish the family of IGRs from PERs and other analytic work done in the Bank to date: First, they focus heavily on actual performance, starting from a problem (such as inadequate health service delivery in the Armenia case) and working backward to establish a chain of causation that links sector problems to upstream weaknesses in public expenditure management, policymaking, judicial oversight, intergovernmental relations, or other systemic functions of the public sector. Second, they attempt to enrich our understanding of actual incentives on the ground and may include analysis of the political economy of the situation, and they draw on local knowledge and expertise to provide such knowledge to the extent possible.

Our medium-term strategy is to solidify the institutional focus of both the IGRs and the PERs, with the latter being concerned more centrally with public expenditure issues and the former with other core functions of government and their connections with the quality of public service delivery (Annex 2). Such analyses can help support CAS preparation (particularly as we move toward the approach laid out in the CDF) and the design of lending programs (see Section V below). The individual toolkits that underlie them should also be useful in further downstream analytic work and the design of individual projects in specific areas of institutional reform. These institutional analyses complement the analytic instruments (Social and Structural Reviews) being developed for wider country analysis; one of the key areas of concern in the Social and Structural Reviews (SSRs) is public sector effectiveness, and the tools being developed for IGRs and PERs can be straightforwardly used in the SSRs.[19] The tools also complement the Country Procurement Assessment Reports (CPARs) and the Country Financial Accountability Assessments (CFAAs) being undertaken by OCS and Controllers as part of the Bank's fiduciary mandate to improve procurement and disbursement mechanisms both system-wide and for Bank projects. These various analytic tools all deal with accountability institutions in our client countries, and we are taking steps at the regional level to integrate them more closely. Finally, all of these tools need to feed into Poverty Reduction Strategy Papers (PRSPs), and we are piloting a toolkit for governance and poverty analysis to help clients bring these various strands together with an explicit poverty focus.

New options are also needed for knowledge transfer and capacity building.

The Bank has also sought to promote public sector reform through transferring knowledge and building capacity in client countries. This is critical if clients are to take on the ownership role envisioned in the CDF.

BOX 16

Pilot Institutional and Governance Reviews: Armenia and Bolivia

Two of the pilot Institutional and Governance Reviews (IGRs) completed in fiscal 2000 are those for *Armenia* and *Bolivia*. Having gone through "first-generation" reforms that focused on economic stabilization, privatization, and trade and price liberalization, both countries now face the new challenge of "second-generation" reforms that focus on institutional development to promote better service delivery, policy quality and responsiveness, and accountability. In this context, the IGRs were designed to provide analyses of public sector performance and its institutional causes and to help craft reform strategies tailored to each country's institutional realities.

The Armenia IGR focused on four areas: public expenditure management, civil service reform, policymaking institutions and regulations within the public sector, and service delivery, with the health sector as an example. This information and analysis serves as input to the CAS, helping it to address institutional concerns. While the IGR drew on already published and available data, it also commissioned background papers from local academicians and journalists and undertook surveys of public officials and households. The survey of public officials focused on practices related to public administration, budget management and accountability. The survey of households focused on their use and satisfaction with key public services. This broad data collection enabled the IGR to consider cross-cutting issues, such as the relationship between agency characteristics and poor service delivery, the impact on policymaking of fragile budget institutions and a poorly supported cabinet system, and the efficacy of horizontal and vertical accountability mechanisms.

In *Bolivia* the IGR was designed to provide analytic input useful for refining the design and formulating an implementation strategy for the Government's public sector reform agenda (supported by a Bank-funded Institutional Reform Project). The reform agenda aims at introducing merit-based civil service and performance-oriented public management, agency by agency, with the intention of spreading the reform through the entire public sector over a 10-year period. Based on case studies, secondary literature, a survey of public officials, and in-depth interviews with former and current government officials, the IGR identified several key political and institutional factors (such as particular constraints presented by the country's coalition politics) that influence public administration, reviewed past institutional reform efforts in the country (including successful efforts to build autonomous regulatory agencies), and offered operational recommendations (including sequencing for gradual introduction of advanced public management techniques such as results-oriented budgeting). The recommendations emphasized the importance of political feasibility given the country's own political and institutional realities, and proposed several measures that are both realistic and critical for improving public management in Bolivia.

Several other IGRs are being piloted in different regions. The methodology developed for institutional diagnosis in Armenia and Bolivia, with a strong emphasis on political economy analysis and the selective use of public officials surveys and other diagnostic tools, will be applicable to other countries facing similar challenges to institutional development.

Traditionally, the main instruments for this knowledge transfer have been economic and sector work (ESW), research, training, and policy dialogue with client governments. ESW and research have worked well to raise the level of country-Bank discussion by providing transparent, empirical documentation on public sector issues and offering new ways of thinking about difficult problems. ESW, research, and training have also been effective in transmitting global and cross-regional lessons and in distilling accumulated wisdom in a systematic way.

For several reasons, however, the Bank's knowledge transfer has not always been fully effective in fostering public sector reform. In research and ESW, institutional analysis has sometimes been an add-on to more traditional policy analysis. Knowledge disseminated through WBI training has sometimes been poorly coordinated with country program priorities. Knowledge has not always been available when most needed because of delays in research and ESW. Furthermore, these instruments have not always been linked to sustained and continuous dialogue with the government. Rather, the ESW may have been done to fill a need for a one-shot operation or single policy issue. By contrast, the process of reforming public sector institutions takes time, often requiring a social and political consensus that must be nurtured and developed incrementally with short but punctual interventions on the part of the Bank.

The new forms of IGRs and PERs outlined earlier provide one means to work more actively with our clients to focus knowledge generation and transfer on operationally relevant institutional concerns in the public sector.[20] The programs of the World Bank Institute are another important means of knowledge transfer and stakeholder involvement, and the formation of the networks and closer integration of staff and client learning will help link such programs more closely with operational concerns, as is already being done in the area of anticorruption (see WBI strategy, Part II). DRG has a rich research agenda (see DRG strategy, Part II), and the network boards (which include active membership from DRG) will need to continue to foster close coordination between this agenda and operational needs. DEC's and WBI's expanding efforts to support the development of local research institutes in client countries are also valuable initiatives to transfer knowledge and build capacity.

In addition, some countries may from time to time want technical advice on specific topics but be unable to pay for it, and the Bank should have a way to provide the advice without tying it to a project. A model is the SIGMA program in Central and Eastern Europe, which has proven popular among policymakers and reformers. Sponsored by the European Union and administered by OECD, SIGMA provides financing for a network of professionals (ranging from senior government officials to academics and practitioners) in the area of public sector reform that can be activated at the request of beneficiary countries. A technical secretariat helps prioritize the requests and can offer initial technical assistance. Although the same services could perhaps be provided by the Bank through an IDF grant, the advantage of SIGMA has been its flexibility and the continuity of advice and institutional memory that it can provide. The Commonwealth Secretariat provides similar technical assistance to countries belonging to the British Commonwealth, and donors such as DFID also provide large amounts of assistance. The Bank should work with these organizations to tap into or build more of these types of flexible nonlending services.

Lending Instruments: Focusing On Long-Term Institution-Building

Among the urban poor in Indonesia, 'neither any government services/programs nor a single NGO was among the institutions rated by urban groups as important, effective, trusted, or open to community influence.'

Voices of the Poor

To have a bigger impact on poverty, the Bank must make a quantum leap in its ability to address critical systemic concerns. Does the Bank have an appropriate mix of lending approaches to this end? In this section, we identify the advantages and limitations of the Bank's traditional approaches and discuss several promising new approaches. The design of Bank lending programs is changing continuously. While we have much to learn and risks are inevitably high, we are optimistic that we are heading in the right direction for significantly enhanced impact.

The Bank's traditional approaches remain useful in certain circumstances.

The Bank's traditional lending instruments include quick-disbursing policy loans, technical assistance loans, and investment project loans. Each has played an important role in promoting institutional change, although each also has inherent limitations.

Quick-disbursing adjustment loans, usually Structural Adjustment Loans (SALs) or Structural Adjustment Credits (SACs), are used to encourage policy shifts that are needed to set new "rules of the game" for public sector institutional behavior and governance. Frequently, they reinforce government actions that are on the critical path to reform but, for political economy reasons, are too difficult to undertake without external urging and assistance. Through the leverage they provide, adjustment loans have been effective at focusing country political leadership on important policy issues, at bringing a strategic framework to otherwise disparate reform measures, and at triggering crucial initial steps in a reform process. For example, a structural adjustment credit and supporting TA in Albania is tackling two key sources of corruption: patronage in judicial appointments and the civil service. A structural adjustment credit in Georgia is supporting the creation of a legal and institutional framework for procurement. And a planned SAC in Vietnam will have a substantial focus on state enterprises and financial sector reform.

Quick-disbursing loans are ideally suited to discrete policy actions, such as the reduction of trade barriers. In contrast, institutional programs that require ongoing attention and support can fit awkwardly within a short-term adjustment framework. The timeframe of an individual adjustment operation often forces us to focus on those tasks that can be accomplished in the very short span of the loan (see Box 17). Sometimes "the tail wags the dog": SALs typically form part of comprehensive macroeconomic programs, so a disbursement may in practice be deferred only for major violations. Formal SAL conditionality tends to be narrow and specific, thus often too limited in scope to foster sustained institutional reforms.

Technical Assistance (TA) loans provide an alternative and complement to adjustment lending. In principle, technical assistance can provide needed help in performing tasks that are beyond the capacity of local governments and can help train country personnel to carry on with activities after the loan is completed. And its timeframe affords a more extended window in which to realize institutional objectives. The Economic Law Project in China has influenced the crafting of legislation to enable the market-driven sector to flourish in a modern system of business regulation. The TA for fiscal policy in China is contributing to the development of a more modern budget system and new regulation for fiscal management and macroeconomic planning. Technical assistance loans have also promoted an institutional agenda in Korea, Thailand and Indonesia.

As it is currently practiced, however, the impact of freestanding TA is often limited, lacking the influential weight of SAL resources and the policy leverage to bring off difficult reform measures. TA loans for institutional reforms in different areas or sectors of government often end as uncoordinated activities without a strategic or programmatic impact. Even when used in tandem with SALs, ongoing technical assistance often sputters when the SAL has been disbursed and high-level attention has waned. In resource-poor environments, TA sometimes amounts to "substitution" assistance, where tasks are performed by experts with little transfer of capacity or even involvement of host country clients. Increasingly, technical assistance lending is considered too expensive by those countries where other donors provide assistance through grant aid.

Traditional investment lending and, increasingly, *sector investment programs (SIPs)* can also be instruments for institutional strengthening, and indeed a substantial percentage of investment loans have contributed to sustainable institutional development. As noted in Section II above, however, a significant share of Bank projects have not had a sustained institution-building impact, either because they have tilted resources toward hard investments or because they have lacked the design characteristics needed to address institutional issues effectively. Furthermore, where projects have positive institutional impacts, they may be limited to individual sectors without systemic impact on other sectors or the core of government. SIPs offer a promising approach to integrating institutional programs in particular sectors and provide a more demand-driven vehicle for institutional reform. They also create incentives for greater results-orientation, because they force governments and donors alike to focus on sectoral outputs and outcomes rather than individual donor inputs. However, they do not address the need for cross-sectoral integration or coordination with reforms of central government institutions.

The Bank has relied for several years on *Institutional Development Facility (IDF) grants* for initiating upstream, non-project work on public sector reforms. These grants use indigenous capacity as much as possible and have proven useful in stimulating early work on institutional topics. The separation of IDFs from subsequent lending can impede the continuity of institutional work, however, and raises concerns about scaling up from these small initiatives to larger programs with greater impact.

And new approaches to longer-term institution-building look promising …

While better diagnostic and sector work will be helpful, our operational interventions pose the most

---

Civil Service Reform and Structural Adjustment Lending

Much of the Bank's early work on civil service reform (CSR) originated in the context of structural adjustment programs. As a feature of adjustment lending, CSR was often construed to denote government downsizing. In concert with IMF programs, radical adjustment of macroeconomic policies came increasingly to include conditionality focused on wage bill containment and government employment reduction to meet specified, short-term fiscal targets. Between 1987 and 1996, adjustment loans accounted for over half of all CSR-related operations. Over two-thirds of all adjustment lending for CSR was carried out in the Africa Region.

The pairing of CSR and structural adjustment lending has been useful in providing focus and leverage for reforms that have been perceived by governments to be politically difficult to undertake on their own. But this advantage has been offset by various disadvantages associated with adjustment-led CSR. The short time horizon, narrow prism, and supply-driven nature of adjustment has led CSRs to emphasize one-off employment cuts rather than longer-term sustainable rightsizing and performance improvements. As a result, when the adjustment crisis abates, reforms tend to unravel: employment and wage bills have sometimes tended to re-expand, subject to the myriad pressures that caused them to grow in the first place.

Overall, one-off adjustment lending has driven CSR toward excessive focus on issues of fiscal balance. While sound wage bill management and appropriate staffing levels are fundamental to good civil service performance, they alone cannot ensure improved administrative quality. Rather, programs need to emphasize building merit-based systems of recruitment, promotion and evaluation, and improving client-orientation in service delivery. Quick-disbursing structural adjustment lending, even when accompanied by technical assistance, rarely affords enough time to support these institutionally focused reforms, which require sustained effort and country ownership.

---

important test of whether the Bank can do better in promoting public sector reform. Several new approaches look like promising adaptations of existing instruments in situations where government commitment is strong.

Adaptable Program Loans (APLs) or Credits (APCs) can provide a flexible approach to institutional reforms in individual sectors or at the core of government, lengthening the timeframe for reform and promoting a more programmatic rather than project-oriented approach to reform.[21] APL/Cs have recently been chosen as an instrument for promoting public sector institutional reform in Bolivia, Ghana, Tanzania, and Zambia.

In Bolivia, for example, the government, project team, donors, and Bank management agreed that an Adaptable Program Credit (APC) was preferable to a traditional Technical Assistance Credit to support Bolivia's public sector reforms, because of the need to address systemic reforms (including a fundamental reform of human resource management and compensation) and to ensure flexible long-term commitment by both the borrower and the Bank. The APC is phased in three operations over 10 years. Phase I, the Institutional Reform Project, supports reforms in human resource management, national integrity, budgeting by results, and performance evaluation, to be implemented in several pilot agencies through a program of organizational restructuring and change management. Specific trigger indicators will be used to assess achievements at the end of each phase and to decide on the financing for subsequent phases that extend the reforms to additional entities. Project design is being informed by a Public Expenditure Review and an Institutional and Governance Review, and the operation has attracted considerable donor co-financing. The operation is a keystone of the Bolivia CDF pilot.

Learning and Innovation Loans (LILs) offer a new instrument that allows for more experimentation and piloting of promising but unproven reform approach-

BOX 18

Bringing Government Closer to the Guinean People

For the quarter century following independence in 1958, Guinea was governed by a top-down, centralized, bureaucratic "command and control" state. The result was economic stagnation, deterioration of basic infrastructure, and reduced availability and quality of social services, especially in rural areas (where over 70 percent of the population lived). In 1984, a new government committed itself to a new institutional framework with much greater emphasis on decentralization: the new legal framework for decentralization established 33 urban and 303 rural communes (CRDs). Yet despite these changes in the formal rules, participation by rural citizens—and the provision of services to rural areas—remained low.

In the mid-1990s the newly appointed Prime Minister and reform-minded government, working closely with the World Bank, initiated an intensive process of civic consultation to identify what could be done to more effectively show results at the rural 'front-line' of development. As a follow-up to this consultative process, the Bank prepared two complementary Adaptable Program Loans to support the government's effort to implement a new approach: a Village Community Support Program, which works directly with local communities, and a Capacity Building for Service Delivery Program, which works to strengthen the ability of the public sector to support communities. Taken together, these programs will help foster the following governance, fiscal and administrative reforms:

Politically, the representativeness of the elected CRD councils is being enhanced by broadening their membership to include representatives from a wide range of social, cultural, ethnic and economic groupings. Furthermore, Prefecture Development Councils (PDCs) are being established, with membership elected by and accountable to CRDs, and authority to advise on programs and budget trade-offs across CRDs. Increasingly, regional administrations will become accountable to these PDCs, and not just to the hierarchies of central government.

Fiscally, a $10 million demand-driven Local Investment Fund has already been established to support, with matching grants directly to CRDs, basic social and infrastructure projects identified by communities. Additionally, a pilot initiative is underway which will enable some CRDs to keep head taxes (which have until now been paid into the central fiscal authorities within their locality—with revenues shared according to a fixed formula between prefectures, subprefectures and districts. Furthermore, as an initial step in increasing direct access of rural communities to the national fiscal authorities, these head tax resources will be matched by direct transfers of budget and donor funded resources from the center.

Administratively, a major initiative is being introduced to realign subnational administrations to reflect the growing shift in accountability to rural communities. This initiative includes: a revision of the detailed administrative framework governing roles and responsibilities of different levels of government under decentralization; the establishment of decentralized delivery and management systems—and capacity building more broadly— at the prefecture and CRD levels; improving participatory mechanisms (such as school parent-teachers associations, health center management committees, and farmers' groups) at the point of service delivery; and the introduction of a performance-incentive system which will reward high performing CRDs and teams of public officials at the prefecture and central level on the basis of results as measured by the quantity and quality of service delivered to the local population.

The aim is that at the end of a 10 to 15 year process of reform there will be an overall increase of 80 percent in access to and in the quality of all services to the rural population. Underlying such gains are major prospective fiscal reforms: whereas currently close to three-fourths of funds budgeted for sectoral line ministries are spent on administrative activities upstream, the Guinean program aims to ensure that at least 70 percent of all operating funds allocated to the sectors reach the service delivery level.

es. Given the uncertainties of applying lessons from developed to developing countries, LILs provide an excellent opportunity to "get it right" at a pilot level before investing on a wider basis. The first LIL, the 1997 Venezuela Supreme Court Modernization Project, supports judicial reform. In Georgia, the Georgia Ministry of Transport Project is a LIL aimed at reorienting the Ministry from an old Soviet-style entity to an agency charged with policymaking and regulation of private transporters. In China, a LIL is being used to promote pension and enterprise reforms.

APLs and LILs are both investment loans. A series of *Programmatic SALs or SACs (PSALs or PSACs)* offers an alternative vehicle for supporting coherent public sector reform. PSAL/Cs are a series of typically two or three one- or two-tranche adjustment operations that together support a medium-term government program of policy reforms and institution-building. Their design relies on a solid foundation of completed or parallel analytic and advisory work, especially in the areas of public expenditure management and public sector governance and reform. Key features of PSAL/Cs are as follows:[22]

- The medium-term reform program supported by a PSAL/C series is laid out at the outset in the government's Letter of Development Policy for the first PSAL/C. It is reflected in a multi-year matrix of policy and institutional reforms with monitorable indicators and progress benchmarks for each loan.

- The corresponding multi-year framework of Bank support is also articulated at the outset. Typically it includes a notional (non-binding) multi-year envelope, with individual PSAL/Cs phased annually in line with the borrowing government's budget cycle.

- The conditionalities of the first PSAL/C in the series are agreed up-front. Each subsequent PSAL/C builds on the previous ones; its conditionalities are formulated and agreed when it is negotiated, drawing on the progress benchmarks

laid out at the outset as a part of the medium-term framework.

Each individual loan in the PSAL/C series depends on satisfactory progress with reforms against agreed benchmarks, based on a review by staff, and on a continued satisfactory macroeconomic framework.

Programmatic SALs were recently approved for Thailand and Latvia. A subnational loan with programmatic features was approved for the state of Uttar Pradesh in India. Loans with similar programmatic features are also under consideration for Benin, Jordan, and Uganda. This approach allows objectives to be laid out over a longer time horizon, but allows "multiple paths to get there," accommodating the fact that reforms of various agencies and institutions are likely to proceed at different paces. For example, the Public Sector Reform Loan I (PSRLI) for Thailand, approved by the Board in October 1999, is designed as the first of three annual loans that together constitute the PSAL program. This first loan disburses in a single tranche to support the initial steps of reform in five areas of the government's reform program: public expenditure management, human resources management, revenue management, decentralization, and accountability and transparency. Subsequent loans, PSRLII and PSRLIII, will depend (in addition to a continued financing need) on the continuing strong commitment of government to reform and on the satisfactory progress of reform measured against a detailed set of specific monitoring indicators. Reform progress will be measured against semi-annual benchmarks the government has set for itself.

Programmatic lending approaches also carry risks.[23] The country's institutional context is critical to the success of programmatic lending operations. Weak financial management and institutional capacity can undermine performance, yet these are precisely areas that programmatic lending seeks to help build. In addition, the broader scope of such lending—typically involving several sectors or regions and counterpart agencies—increases the risk of diminished focus and implementation problems. Design and country commitment are critical, and clear accountability arrangements and monitoring mechanisms must be built into such programs. In view of these generic risks, the CAS will need to focus on the suitability of the use of programmatic instruments in a particular country or sectoral context.

In sum, the various types of Bank lending instruments available to client countries all offer advantages in certain circumstances, and a major challenge of a CAS is to find a "good fit," that is, to tailor the mix of instruments to country conditions. The programmatic approach embodied in institutionally oriented APLs and PSAL/Cs provides a longer-term perspective that is likely to prove useful as the Bank moves to strengthen its institutional development and capacity building focus. As the Bank gains experience with programmatic lending, it can further identify good practices and delineate important aspects of design and implementation.

The fundamental challenge (drawing on the themes of Sections III, IV, and V above)—is to use both our lending and nonlending instruments in ways that not only reform internal rules and restraints, but that also bring competition to bear when feasible, and that enhance the voice and participation of the citizenry, drawing on the range of fundamental drivers for public sector reform discussed in Section III above. An innovative assistance program for Guinea (Box 18) and a push in the Africa Region more generally for programs of community empowerment provide examples of recent innovations in our thinking and our approach.

Achieving Our Goals: Staffing, Organization, Incentives, and Partnerships

nitiatives to mainstream the reform of public institutions and to expand the use of more appropriate lending instruments will succeed only if we have in place staff who are capable of taking advantage of these new opportunities—and have the incentive to do so. And Bank staff will need to make a special effort not to over-reach, but rather to step back in favor of our development partners for those aspects of institutional reform which they are better positioned than we are to take on.

We need to continue to strengthen our staffing.

Implementing the ambitious agenda for public sector reform laid out above calls for three distinct types of staff skills:

- The first is the traditional task-manager skill, which the Bank has been able to develop internally.

- The second skill is the ability to understand the forces that shape institutions at a deep conceptual level.

People with this second skill have a broad understanding of the way formal and informal incentive systems and political conditions drive behavior within organizations, especially public agencies in developing countries. This skill does not derive primarily from academic training, although some academic fields (including economics, political science, public policy, public administration, or anthropology) can provide a solid foundation. It is usually developed through in-country experience and can be strengthened through in-house training. The Bank's move to decentralize its operations can help in this regard because it is better able to incorporate local staff with in-depth knowledge of institutions and culture in client countries.

Because institutional reform is inherently complex and interdisciplinary, a good institutional specialist will be open to knowledge of different disciplines and will seek to integrate differing perspectives in his or her work. The Bank's staff represent a mix of disciplines, but this mix needs to be integrated more effectively. Developing institutional reform skills and training materials will require a core of specialists in institutional assessment and political-economy and governance analysis. There are a small but growing number of these in the Bank at present.

• The third set of skills comprises specialist, functionally specific expertise in particular areas of institutional reform.

Traditionally the Bank has lacked a sufficient number of specialized staff with extensive knowledge and practical in-country reform experience in most if not all of the following specialized areas: public financial management (tax policy, tax administration, expenditure policy, budget process, information systems, accounting, auditing); administrative and civil service reform (policymaking, service delivery, agency structure, and civil service regulation, pay and employment); legal and judicial reform; subnational government reform; and regulatory and public enterprise reform. Some of these skills can be hired on the market on a short-term consulting basis, and there has also been a need for some increase in in-house expertise in these specialties in the past three years. Of course, as is illustrat-

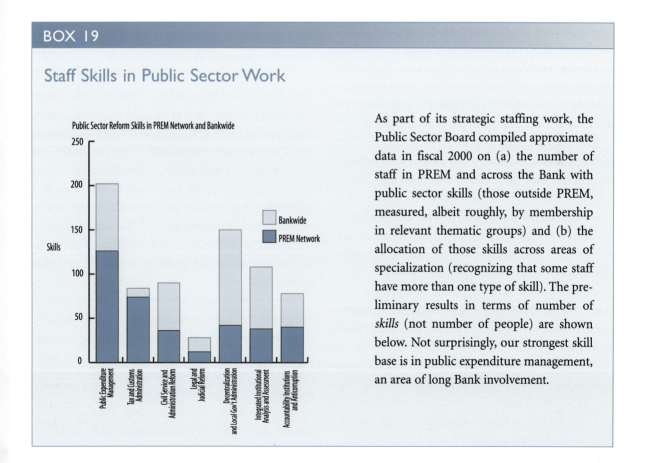

BOX 19

Staff Skills in Public Sector Work

Public Sector Reform Skills in PREM Network and Bankwide

As part of its strategic staffing work, the Public Sector Board compiled approximate data in fiscal 2000 on (a) the number of staff in PREM and across the Bank with public sector skills (those outside PREM, measured, albeit roughly, by membership in relevant thematic groups) and (b) the allocation of those skills across areas of specialization (recognizing that some staff have more than one type of skill). The preliminary results in terms of number of *skills* (not number of people) are shown below. Not surprisingly, our strongest skill base is in public expenditure management, an area of long Bank involvement.

ed by some of the best practitioners already in the Bank, functional specialists will be most effective when they also have a broad understanding of the interplay between their specialty and the broader array of formal and informal incentives that shape behavior within the public sector.

Addressing remaining deficits in the second and third skill categories requires actions on several fronts. First, we need to continue (to the extent budgets allow) to externally recruit people with relevant academic training and public sector experience. Second, we need to strengthen the capabilities of existing staff (including general economists and sector specialists) to address questions of public sector institutional reform. This requires training and experience aimed at increasing staff capabilities to analyze the incentives of public officials and the institutional arrangements that shape these incentives. In organizing this training, we should make a special effort to include as trainers officials from developing countries who have led successful reforms of public institutions. Third, we need to revisit the incentives and organizational arrangements that encourage task management at the expense of specialization.

The Bank's matrix structure implies that we may need special arrangements to recruit new staff. Regional budgets rest with the Country Directors, and there is inevitably a lag between their expression of "demand" for work from the sector units and the ability of those sector units to expand their staff if demand exceeds current supply. Country Directors are sometimes understandably hesitant to commit funding to tasks without commitment from pre-identified, well-proven staff. This situation can create impediments to expanding our staff skills in new and somewhat untested areas of high priority.

The Public Sector anchor can help to some extent by bringing new staff into the Bank for an early "tryout" phase; if the staff prove to fit well in operations, they can move to a Region after a period of time. To date, the anchor has had the funding to bring in 2 to 3 new staff per year, and the regional units have also been able to augment their staff, albeit incrementally and with some lag. The Public Sector Board has recently agreed to pilot a new recruitment initiative, through which the Sector Board will collectively work to identify and hire 3 to 5 new fixed-term recruits in fiscal 2001. The recruits' salaries will be partially funded by a central human resources budget during their first year on the job and will be located in specific VPUs while maintaining a group identity for purposes of orientation, training, and support. The initiative is designed to foster a more worldwide search for talent, a greater focus on diversity objectives, and a better ability to provide support and training to new hires, without these new hires being obliged to support their positions fully with operational activities from the first day on the job.

We need to continue to fine-tune our organizational structure.

The Bank's matrix structure, although not without problems, is a major step in the right direction. Country directors are more apt than under previous organizational arrangements to demand "value for money" and thus not contract for analytic and lending products with little immediate impact (a critique of OED's study of past PERs). Furthermore, the existence of the network and associated thematic groups[24] has clearly enhanced the incentives and ability of staff working on public sector reform across the Bank to cooperate and share knowledge.

Important efforts were made in fiscal 2000 to strengthen the matrix structure across the Bank, particularly to increase the authority and flexibility of sector managers with regard to the specific use of budget resources allocated in work program agreements. The experience of the past three years points to the benefits of having sector board members who are clearly accountable in their Regions or central units for delivering effective programs of support across the range of relevant topics to country directors or other clients, and who have the authority and resources to hire and manage the staff needed to do the job. The network family should then be jointly accountable to the whole of the Bank to set strategy and priorities, recruit and train staff, and oversee quality. The cohesiveness and sense of shared vision of the Public Sector Board and the overall quality of management and staff in relevant public sector units have grown considerably over the past three years (recognizing that individual Board members have somewhat differing roles in their respective VPUs because of differing organizational structures among Regions). We will continue to build on these improvements, to strengthen the sense of shared vision, and to support each Region in implementing this strategy on the ground.

We need to continue to reassess the incentives facing Bank staff.

Even with strengthened staffing, the tension and ambiguity between the role of the World Bank as a lending institution and its role as a development institution may nonetheless constrain our ability to address the challenge of reforming public institutions. Institution-building is difficult and time-consuming. It requires detailed country-specific information, and its success can be difficult to measure. Furthermore, difficult institutional components of projects are often the first to be dropped in a pinch. And in times of tight budgets, the ability of Bank staff and country counterparts to undertake the analytic work needed to gain country knowledge and undertake effective institutional work may be constrained.

An important way to keep governance and institution-building on the forefront of the Bank's agenda is to continually emphasize these goals in reviews and evaluations of CASs and country lending programs.

The emphasis on the quality of institutional work has definitely increased in recent years as an outgrowth of the Wapenhans report and the subsequent creation of QAG and reorientation of OED.[25] The emphasis on governance has also grown dramatically, and all CASs are now required to diagnose the state of governance and the risks that corruption poses to Bank projects in the country concerned. While substantial progress has been made, still more emphasis on evaluation and development impact is needed if the Bank is to have a deep and serious commitment to public sector reform in its client countries. The Public Sector Board will continue to work actively with OED and QAG to enhance the Bank's ability to measure success in institutional development, and it will continue to work closely with country teams to help strengthen the coverage of governance issues in CASs. Over the medium term, the networks will work to upgrade the quality of institutional and governance work through staffing, professional development, and knowledge management.

With better measurement and deeper focus on quality should come greater selectivity—that is, the willingness to reduce activity when conditions are not conducive to reform. Such selectivity is already part of the Bank's anticorruption strategy, but it needs to be continually reinforced in individual country situations.

We need to deepen our partnerships...

As noted in Section II, we will achieve more as a development community if we work closely and collaboratively with our partners—both within developing countries and among donor organizations. This is not only because they each have a particular comparative advantage, but also because if they fail to work together they risk undoing each other's contribution—and

TABLE 2 Examples of Bank Partners in Institution-Building

Thematic Area	International Organizations and Associations	International Financial Institutions	Bilateral Donors and UN Agencies	Other
Anticorruption and Governance	Council of Europe, Financial Action Task Force on Money Laundering, Global Coalition for Africa, Interpol, OECD, Organization of American States	Asian Development Bank (ADB), African Development Bank (AfDB), European Bank for Reconstruction and Development (EBRD), Inter-American Development Bank (IADB), IMF	Canadian International Development Agency (CIDA), Department for International Development (DFID), Development Assistance Committee (OECD DAC), UNDP, Swedish International Development Agency (SIDA), Danish International Development Agency (DANIDA), USAID, NORAD/Min. of For. Affairs (Norway), Min. of For. Affairs (Netherlands)	Transparency International (TI), International Chamber of Commerce, Institutional Chamber of Commerce, Institutional Reform and the Informal Sector (IRIS at U. Maryland), Centro Latinoamericano de Administracion para el Desarrollo (CLAD), Carter Center, Asia Foundation
Civil Service Reform	Commonwealth Secretariat, Commonwealth Association for Public Management (CAPAM), Public Management Committee and Public Management Service (OECD PUMA), Support for Improvement in Governance and Management in Central and Eastern Europe (OECD SIGMA)	ADB, AfDB, IADB, IMF	UNDP	Civil Service College (UK), International Institute for Administrative Sciences, International Personnel Management, Tinker Foundation
Decentralization	OECD (Fiscal Affairs)	IADB	UNDP; many bilaterals, including the United States, Canada, Switzerland, Denmark, Italy, Netherlands, Belgium	IRIS (at U. Maryland), Georgia State University, One World, University of Toronto, Wharton School, British Know How, Open Society Institute Eurasia Foundation, Escola de Administracao Fazendaria (Brazil), Instituti de Estudios Superiores en Administracion (Venezuela)
Legal/Judicial Reform	European Network on Justice, International Development Law Institute, Inter-American Institute for Human Rights (Costa Rica)	ADB, AfDB, EBRD, IADB	Caisse Centrale de Co-operation Economique (CCCE), CIDA, DANIDA, DFID, Deutsche Gessellschaft fur Technische Zusammenarbeit (GTZ), Japan International Cooperation Agency, SIDA, UNDP, USAID	Asia Foundation, Ford Foundation, Lawyers Committee for Human Rights, National Center for State Courts, U.S. Department of Justice, Singapore Supreme Court, Federal Judicial Center (U.S.), Danish Center for Human Rights
Tax Policy and Administration	Inter-American Center of Tax Administrations (CIAT), OECD (Fiscal Affairs)	IADB, IMF	United Nations Conference on Trade and Development (UNCTAD)	Arthur Andersen, Barents Group, Crown Agents, CRC-Sogema, Data Torque Ltd., Group Systems Corporation, Intertek Testing Services, KPMG, TransSenda International, WM-Data, Western Australian State Revenue Department

TABLE 2 Examples of Bank Partners in Institution-Building, *continued*

Thematic Area	International Organizations and Associations	International Financial Institutions	Bilateral Donors and UN Agencies	Other
Public Expenditure Analysis and Management	Commonwealth Secretariat, CAPAM, International Federation of Accountants, INTOSAI, OECD PUMA and SIGMA	ADB, IMF	CIDA, DFID, Ministry of Foreign Affairs (France)	Center for Budget Policies and Priorities, Institute for Democracy in South Africa
Parliaments	International Parliamentary Union, Commonwealth Parliamentary Association		UNDP, CIDA, DFID, Min. of For. Affairs (Norway), Min. of Foreign Affairs (Netherlands)	Canadian Parliamentary Centre, National Democratic Institute, Institute for Democracy and Electoral Assistance (Sweden)
Media	Commonwealth Press Union, Commonwealth Broadcasting Association, Commonwealth Journalists Association, International Federation of Journalists, OECD, OAS (Trust of the Americas)		CIDA, Ireland, Ministry of Foreign Affairs , (France) Ministry of Foreign Affairs (Norway)	TI, Centre Quest-Africain des Media et du Developpment (WANAD), Association of Journalists (Tanzania), Uganda Management Institute, Radio Nederland, Groupe de Recherche et d'Echanges Technologiques

perhaps causing more harm than good. Several types of partnerships are worth highlighting:

...with clients. The most important partner is of course the client, and the Bank's primary responsibility is to serve its clients. Although the proximate client is the government in the borrowing country, the ultimate client is the public interest, that is, the citizenry of a country. "Serving the client" is often but not always synonymous with serving the interests of the government, and the Bank needs to be sensitive to the broad public interest and the ultimate objective of poverty reduction in all cases. As noted in Section III, a country's leaders must be in the driver's seat for institutional reform and capacity building efforts to succeed. When feasible, the Bank (and other donors) should support the client government as the government designs and implements strategies for development, and this situation is envisioned in the CDF process. In the worst case scenario, when the Bank and the government do not share a common view of the country's needs, the Bank may need to devote its resources elsewhere. One key to effective partnership is selectivity.

... across the Bank. Because virtually all of the Bank's operational activities involve institutional development and capacity building, internal Bank units must be willing and able to work together to share ideas, experiences, and staff resources as needed. In addition to the sector families, key groups in the Bank include the Public Sector Group in PREM (reforms at the core of government), WBI (external and internal knowledge transfer and capacity building), OCS and Controllers (procurement and financial management), LEG (legal and judicial reform), DRG (knowledge creation), and OED (evaluation capacity development). The various perspectives and disciplines all bring important contributions to the table, and we must continue to seek interaction and mutual support and avoid creating "cylinders."

...with other donors. Different donors bring different skills and comparative advantages to recipient countries. Because of their size and leverage, the Bank and regional multilateral banks may be best suited to undertake high-level policy dialogue and broad interventions to reform institutions. In the case of civil

service reform, for example, the Bank's comparative advantage is likely to lie in stimulating major reforms (such as downsizing, contracting out or privatizing service delivery where appropriate, changing the rules for civil service hiring and promotion, or institutionalizing citizen feedback mechanisms) rather than in specific capacity building activities (such as civil service training). In contrast, the comparative advantage of some bilateral donors and the private sector is often seen to lie more in longer-term organizational strengthening, because of the technical skill-bases they can tap into in their countries and their ability to commit to sustained involvement and careful monitoring. Furthermore, many donors bring more expertise in certain areas than the Bank. In some cases the Bank simply has not built expertise, while in others (particularly certain areas of political governance) the Bank does not have a mandate like some of its partners. Public sector reform requires work at all levels, and donors must keep trying to find better ways to recognize and coordinate the unique and complementary contributions of each other. Examples of some of the Bank's partners are listed in Table 2 by thematic area. This is not an exhaustive list but is included here primarily to give an idea of the range of organizations we work with on an active basis.

The Bank's partnership with the IMF is particularly critical in the area of public sector reform. The Bank and Fund are both active in fiscal policy and administration, albeit with somewhat different emphases.[26] The Bank has more in-depth involvement in many other aspects of institutional reform, such as civil service reform, judicial reform, decentralization, and reform of sectoral institutions, although many Fund programs have important impacts in these areas. Both organizations have a growing focus on governance and anticorruption, and we benefit greatly from our collaboration and mutual contributions, both in our country work (as, for example, in our governance conditionality in Indonesia and Kenya) and in our broader work

on strategy and research. The Bank is very supportive of the Fund's work on the Code of Fiscal Transparency and is working with clients to facilitate its dissemination and application. We are also working closely with the Fund on monitoring of expenditures under the HIPC initiative. Continued coordination of approaches is needed (as discussed further in Annex 3) and will be sought as part of this strategy.[27]

The Bank's partnership with UNDP is also a critical one, particularly as both organizations have recently expressed heightened commitment to helping client countries improve governance and build institutional capacity. UNDP's grant-making ability, its close client relationships built through long-term in-country residence, and its expanded mandate (reaching, for example, to issues of political governance) all make UNDP's role both important and in many cases complementary to that of the Bank. Our goal is to work closely both at the country level and at the international level to collaborate in the design of work programs and the sharing of learning and experience, in order to make the most of scarce resources and avoid unnecessary duplication of effort. Countries where there is already substantial collaboration between UNDP and the Bank include, among others, Bolivia, Ghana, Indonesia, and Vietnam—and we intend to highlight these and other good examples in order to stimulate further work in that direction. The Public Sector Board is in close touch with our UNDP counterparts, and we are undertaking a series of meetings over the current year toward this end.

Bilateral donors are also important partners of the Bank in the area of public sector reform. Many bilateral donors focus extensively on issues of governance. Like UNDP, bilateral donors often work in areas of political governance (such as election monitoring and political party development) that the Bank is not involved in. They are able to draw on experience and expertise in their own countries that can deepen their contributions to development. We are working

BOX 20

Promoting Partnerships Through Governance Trust Funds

Trust Funds form an important area of Bank partnerships and provide significant resources to develop innovative approaches to address governance issues worldwide.

The Danish Governance Trust Fund (DGTF) was established by agreement between the World Bank and the Government of Denmark in December 1997, with a planned disbursement of approximately $4.5 million over three years. The objective of the Trust Fund is to support innovative proposals in the field of governance that will add to our knowledge, help build consensus for reform, and test new ideas in the field. The Trust Fund is managed by the Public Sector Board in close cooperation with Danish authorities. This arrangement enhances collaboration while ensuring close alignment between the use of funds and overall Bank priorities and strategies for governance and public sector reform.

The Danish Trust Fund has allocated $3.4 million to date in support of 57 projects, some managed within the Bank and some by external partners (including NGOs). For example, it has funded new modes of governance assessment for local governments in Bolivia, an experiment to develop a "special governance (corruption-free) zone" in Indonesia, efforts to prevent bribes in bidding for a major infrastructure privatization in Papua New Guinea, surveys to track public spending in Albania and Macedonia, and investigations of citizens' experience with judiciaries in Latvia and Paraguay.

The **Bank-Netherlands Partnership Program (BNPP)**, which focuses on cross-country initiatives, has contributed $2.6 million to fund nine projects on governance and public sector reform over the past two years. These include, for example, a series of surveys of public officials in a dozen developing countries to understand the incentives they face, an in-depth look at the impact of IDA lending on institutional development in three countries (Bolivia, Laos, and Senegal), and a study of the impact of decentralization on governance in the Philippines, Sri Lanka, and Uganda. Like the projects funded by the DGTF, these projects are grounded in the Bank's overall strategy for public sector reform and directly support our work and that of our development partners on the ground.

The focus of the overall BNPP is on several broad themes, only one of which is governance. Beginning in 2000, the Bank's Sector Boards are being brought more centrally into the process of decisionmaking on allocations under the BNPP (as with the DGTF), according to theme.

The experience to date shows that Trust Funds can be important means to encourage innovation and experimentation in critical areas, such as governance, in our client countries. The Bank's plan is to build on the initial experience and use of these Trust Funds, also as a means to enhance partnerships both in strategy-setting and at the operational level. During our recent strategy discussions, numerous other bilateral partners expressed an interest in closer collaboration, and in widening the Trust Fund mechanism to encourage broader and deeper collaboration and to help prioritize among the various projects and programs in need of financing.

increasingly with bilaterals on particular analytic work and cofinancing of public sector projects in numerous countries. For example, we are working closely with DFID on governance analysis in Kenya and budget management in Ghana, we have joint anticorruption work with USAID in Slovakia, and we are collaborating with various bilaterals on initiatives ranging from judicial reform in Guatemala to public expenditure analysis in Vietnam. We are very grateful to the Danish Foreign Ministry and DANIDA for sponsoring the Danish Trust Fund on Governance, which over the past 2 years has funded a wide variety of innovative governance programs carried out by task leaders both inside and outside the Bank. The Dutch, through their Bank-Netherlands Partnership Program (BNPP), are also generous sponsors of innovative governance initiatives (see Box 20).

We have expanded our relationships with the four other large multilateral development banks (ADB, AfDB, IDB, and EBRD) through the creation of a formal Working Group on Governance and Anticorruption. The Working Group has held annual meetings for the past three years and maintains year-round contacts to share ideas and information. We cofinance many public sector projects jointly with our MDB partners and are currently exploring opportunities for joint in-depth analytic work (in line with the recommendations in this strategy).

We are also active partners with OECD on numerous *global initiatives*. We have participated regularly in the OECD Working Group on Bribery in International Business Transactions, and we strongly support the OECD Convention (which went into effect in February 1999 and has been ratified by most OECD countries) to outlaw the bribery of foreign public officials and end the tax deductibility of foreign bribes. Two other OECD initiatives related to governance include the technical assistance work of SIGMA (see Section IV) and the governance work of DAC. Among other activities, DAC is coordinating a joint effort by numerous donors (with in-depth participation by the Bank) to develop and put together rigorous and credible indicators of governance.

... and with NGOs. WDR97, the Bank's anticorruption agenda, and this strategy paper all recognize the important role that civil society plays in public sector reform. NGOs can be important partners to the Bank, both on the "input" side—in communicating with civil society given that the Bank deals primarily with governments, and on the "output" side—in delivering services when public sectors cannot effectively do so. NGOs are also sometimes important educators and monitors of the Bank itself: like other public sector organizations, the Bank needs feedback from external "voice" mechanisms to strengthen its own accountability. The Bank values its expanding relationships with various NGOs (such as Transparency International) that focus on issues of governance, public sector reform, or human rights, and we hope to continue to build these relationships in the future. The challenge is to find ways to work in tandem without compromising each party's independent voice.

Conclusions and Summary: Our Plan of Action

Our strategy to help strengthen public institutions and governance has four broad objectives.

Building on the lessons from our experience and the themes of *WDR97*, our strategy is predicated on the four broad objectives described in Sections III through VI above:

- *Approach*: to continue to broaden the range of reform mechanisms we support, maintaining our efforts to strengthen internal rules and restraints within government while expanding our complementary emphases on competition and "voice" and participation—and to focus our efforts where a country's overall commitment is strong and in ways that put a country's citizens in the driver's seat,

- *Analytic Work*: to work with clients and other partners to strengthen our tools for institutional analysis and for knowledge transfer to underpin both projects and country programs,

- *Lending Approaches*: to advance long-term institutionally oriented programmatic approaches where appropriate, and

- *Internal Capacity and Partnerships*: to strengthen our internal capacity to assist countries in public sector reform through continued improvements in staff skills, organization, incentives, and relations with partners.

And these can be translated into objectives and monitorable indicators of country performance by thematic area.

Table 3 summarizes our long-term goals for performance improvements in client countries *by thematic area* for the main cross-cutting topics in our public sector work program. It also lays out specific objectives for Bank work on these topics to further those in-country performance goals, as well as monitorable indicators we can use to assess progress in reaching those goals.

TABLE 3 Monitorable Progress Indicators for Country Outcomes

Strategic Governance Objectives	Actions Needed in the Bank
More efficient use of public resources for development through improved **public expenditure analysis and management**	• Greater integration of public expenditure management and related institutional concerns into PE analysis (including PERs) and lending • Closer link between public expenditure work and country strategy and lending • Careful attention to quality, timeliness, and relevance of PERs • Better coordination between individual analyses of expenditure topics (including analyses in individual sectors) to develop an integrated systemic picture
Increased public resources and reduced market distortions through improved **revenue policy and administration**	• Greater attention to institutional environments, incentives, and anticorruption strategies in our revenue policy and administration work
More efficient use of public resources and more effective government action through improvements in the **civil service**	• Greater attention to and upstream analysis of institutional environments, incentives, and anticorruption strategies in our civil service reform work • Greater attention to sectoral linkages and the impact of civil service policies on service delivery • Broaden use of longer-term programmatic lending approaches for civil service reform
More accountable, efficient and effective government through **decentralization** *of decisionmaking and service delivery*	• Integration of institutional concerns (including governance at the national and sub national levels) into analysis of government structure, the distribution of public functions among different levels of government, intergovernmental fiscal and administrative relations, and the costs and benefits of decentralization
Growth, security, and accountability through better access to timely, affordable and just **dispute resolution services**	• Greater attention to and upstream analysis of institutional environments, incentives, and anticorruption strategies in our legal and judicial reform work • Deepening of our knowledge base and our partnerships with foundations and other donors working on legal/judicial reform
Improved accountability through **other institutions**	• Greater cognizance and support of the role and functioning of Parliamentary over sight bodies, Ombudsman offices, Public Audit Institutions, etc. • Greater support for organizations that collect, evaluate, and publicize data on public sector performance

Desired Outcomes in Client Countries	Possible Indicators of Performance
• Better integration of planning, policymaking, and budgeting through medium-term expenditure frameworks • Pro-development public spending allocations • Improved accountability for public spending policy and implementation through closer links between budgets and actual spending	• Extent of policy volatility • Delays in audit • Variance by functional appropriations • Budget comprehensiveness • Extent of audit of military expenditures • Difference between projected and actual annual expenditures • Fiscal deficit relative to target agreed with IMF
• Improved revenue performance in client countries—including lower budget deficits, more equitable and efficient revenue policy design, and lower corruption in revenue systems • More open avenues for citizen feedback (for example through regular taxpayer surveys)	• Revenue adequacy (budget deficit) • Revenue stability • Revenue predictability • Extent of perceived corruption in tax administration
• Civil service employment and aggregate wage bill levels roughly in line with international norms (recognizing that these norms vary widely and that local capacity and values will influence what is considered optimal) • Transparent and largely non-discretionary civil service pay, at levels appropriate to national labor market conditions • Transparent and merit-based civil service recruitment and promotion • Effective sanctions for poor performance or corruption	• Public sector wage bill as percent of GDP • Pay structure • Extent of political appointments in civil service • Percentage of civil servants recruited through competitive procedures • Average turnover rate of civil servants recruited through competitive procedures
• A more appropriate match between responsibilities, resources, and capacities in subnational governments • More effective and efficient delivery of public services • Significant levels of citizen "voice" and participation at the subnational level	• Number of central government "bail outs" of local governments in the last 5 years • Citizen perceptions of corruption in service delivery • Performance and price in various areas of public service delivery compared to international and regional norms
• Transparent and predictable judicial decisionmaking • Effective judicial oversight of the legality of public sector activities • Reasonably timely and low-cost judicial process • Low levels of corruption in the judiciary • Existence of alternative providers of legal services where appropriate	• Case backlog • System user and staff satisfaction • Population with access to courts • Population with access to legal information • Percent of private land formally titled • Existence of extra-judicial bodies with coercive powers
• More frequent and reliable independent monitoring of public sector performance by various watchdog institutions inside and outside government	• Regularity and timeliness of public audit reports • Availability to the public of public audit reports • Number of complaints received and investigated by ombudsman's office • Staffing and funding levels for budget and public accounts committees of Parliament

Strategic Governance Objectives	Actions Needed in the Bank
*Improved service delivery and more efficient resource use through privatization and restructuring of **public enterprises***	• Continued focus on reaching an appropriate role for the public sector and on privatization of public enterprises or contracting out of public service delivery where feasible
*Improved service delivery through **sectoral institutional building***	• Continued focus on enhancing the accountability and efficiency of sector service delivery and regulatory institutions through internal reforms, the expansion of competitive service delivery where appropriate, or greater "voice" and participation by citizens or consumers.

We will prioritize our activities in order to staff effectively under current resource constraints. We aim for the Bank to be considered one of the leading authorities worldwide in several core areas where we have a track record or a comparative advantage, including (a) public economics (economic analysis of the role and functioning of the public sector), (b) decentralization and intergovernmental fiscal relations, (c) core system-wide administrative and civil service reform, (d public expenditure analysis and management (including financial management and procurement), and (e) sectoral institution-building, particularly in social sectors and infrastructure (including regulation of private service delivery). We aim for the Bank to be considered an expert, along with other partner organizations, in several other areas, including (a) revenue policy and administration, (b) legal and judicial reform, and (c) other accountability institutions (such as ombudsmen and parliamentary oversight bodies). For reasons of either limited mandate or limited expertise, we do not envision the Bank becoming involved in some other areas of public sector reform, such as (a) police reform, (b) criminal justice systems (including prosecutorial and prison reform), (c) general parliamentary process-

es, or (d) political governance (including election processes or the structure and financing of political parties). Many of our partners, including UNDP, bilateral donors, and NGOs, have clearer mandates or a likely comparative advantage in these areas of work.

It is difficult to forecast specific levels of lending for public sector reform.

Country assistance programs are formulated through a process of country dialogue between the Bank's country director (and his or her team) and country authorities. Because of the demand-led nature of this assistance, it is not possible to specify up front the exact size or composition of our assistance program for public sector reform. The regional strategies in Part II discuss specific challenges and lay out the strategic directions for the lending program in each of the Bank's six Regions. We anticipate that virtually all of the Bank's projects will continue to have institution-building objectives and in many cases specific capacity building or institution-building components (totaling some $4 billion to $7 billion of institution-building assistance

Desired Outcomes in Client Countries	Possible Indicators of Performance
• A role for the state in line with economic rationale and existing institutional capacity • Progress in reaching that role through privatization of commercially oriented activities and contracting out of other public functions where feasible	• Public spending as share of GDP • Concentration ratios in industry
• Accountable institutions that result in high-quality, efficient, and equitable delivery of public services in the social sectors, agriculture, infrastructure, etc. • Easy entry of alternative service providers and contracting out public functions where feasible and quality-enhancing (with government regulatory oversight as needed)	• Various indicators of outcomes in sectors (health, education, infrastructure, etc.)

per year, divided approximately evenly between investment and adjustment lending), and that the number and aggregate amount of stand-alone public sector management and multi-sector projects will continue in the $2 billion to $4 billion range annually. Because public sector reform pervades almost everything the Bank does, the key to increasing our effectiveness lies more in improving the quality and impact of what we do rather than in transferring more resources per se. We prefer to focus this strategy not on aggregate lending amounts but on proactive ways to work with our colleagues across the Bank to improve the quality of this work.

But the proactive elements of the strategy are clear.

Table 4 summarizes the "proactive" elements of this strategy—that is, the additional work to be undertaken to help inform and influence Bank activities (including CASs, ESW, and lending) to achieve both the broad and the thematic strategic objectives laid out above. It includes indicators we will monitor to gauge implementation of the strategy.

Mainstreaming in Bank projects and in CASs and PRSPs. Major tools for mainstreaming institutional concerns are the OP on institutional analysis in projects and toolkits for integrating governance concerns into CASs and PRSPs. The OP was prepared in fiscal 2000 in draft form and is being piloted in fiscal 2001 in projects, with an aim to finalize the OP in fiscal 2001. The CAS is the main instrument for mainstreaming institutional concerns in the design of broader country programs. All CASs are now required (since January 1999) to diagnose the state of governance and the risks that corruption poses to Bank projects. A growing number of CASs go beyond this to focus their proposed programs centrally on building public sector institutions and improving public sector effectiveness. PRSPs are also important means for our clients to mainstream governance and poverty concerns, and the Public Sector Board is working actively to develop and pilot toolkits that can be useful in this regard. These trends are likely to continue with the further development of the CDF and the further mainstreaming of the anticorruption agenda. PREM's Public Sector Board

TABLE 4 Proactive Initiatives in Support of Strategic Objectives

Issue or Past Problem Area to Address	Strategic Objectives	Responsible parties[28]
Insufficient focus on institution-building in Bank activities	• To place long-term institution-building center-stage in our work, recognizing that is the key to sustainable development and poverty reduction	• PSB • PSB, OCS, and others
Imbalance in our approach toward a narrow technocratic emphasis	• To continue to broaden the range of reform mechanisms we support (increasing our emphasis on competition and "voice" and participation)	• Regions • PSB, WBI, Regions
Inadequate ownership of the reform agenda by clients	• To help enhance client ownership and ensure that a country's leaders are in the driver's seat • To ensure selectivity in our engagement	• PSB, Regions • AFR Region • OCS, PSB
Inadequate knowledge of institutional realities (including political dynamics) on the ground	• To strengthen our tools for institutional analysis and assessment to underpin both projects and country programs	• PREM regional units, PSB • PREM regional units • PSB, WBI, with input from other sectors • PRMPS, WBI
Lending approaches that are not fully conducive to institution-building	• To move progressively toward longer-term institutionally oriented programmatic lending where appropriate	• PREM regional units
Shortage of qualified in-house expertise	• To ensure adequacy and quality in Bank staffing for public sector work	• OVPs • PSB • PSB • PSB, WBI

Activities to Achieve Objectives	Goals by End of Fiscal 2003
• Preparation of Public Sector Strategy and dissemination across Networks and with partners outside the Bank • Preparation and piloting of draft OP on institutional assessment in Bank projects • Establishment of process of regular CAS and PRSP advice and review (both upstream and downstream) • Development and successful implementation of Anticorruption Action Plans annually	• Widely held consensus on donor approaches to public sector reform • Regular application of OP on institutional assessment in at least 25 percent of Bank projects • Adequate diagnosis of governance situation in 90 percent of Bank's CASs. Upstream advice and downstream review of all major CASs and PRSPs by public sector network, and positive evaluation by CAS teams of timeliness and utility of advice • Full implementation of annual Anticorruption Action Plans
• Enhancement of work on decentralization and community-driven development • Development and testing of survey instruments to measure the extent and causes of corruption or track public expenditures and service delivery, and thereby to increase citizen feedback	• Implementation of community action programs in at least 10 low-income client countries. • Implementation of citizen, firm or public official surveys in at least 15 client countries • Implementation of public expenditure tracking surveys in at least 5 countries
• Further progress on CDF piloting and mainstreaming of anticorruption and governance agenda • Implementation of PACT (Partnership for Capacity Building in Africa) • Preparation of fiduciary framework for adjustment lending	• Integration of governance concerns in all CASs and country programs • Successful implementation of PACT • Finalization of fiduciary framework for adjustment lending
• Initiation and substantial progress on pilot IGRs • Progressive strengthening of institutional components of PERs • Completion of set of toolkits for institutional diagnosis in IGRs, PERs, PRSPs, SSRs, and anticorruption surveys • Development of institutional analysis website for easy access to toolkits and relevant data	• Regular use of IGRs/PERs and the individual component toolkits and surveys as analytic instruments that are found to be integral and useful to Bank operational work
• Design of new approaches, including long-term APLs (ex: Bolivia, Ghana, Tanzania) and PSALs (Latvia, Thailand, Uttar Pradesh, Uganda) focused on public sector reform	• Broader use of programmatic approaches in Bank lending with strong client ownership, where appropriate. Governance-oriented APLs or PSAL/Cs in at least 10 client countries
• Designation of units with clear accountability for leading governance work and anticorruption initiative, each Region • Determination of staffing needs for those units and development of strategic staffing plan for the public sector group • Development and implementation of external recruitment plan to identify expertise in areas with unmet need • Design and delivery of a professional development plan for existing staff (including training courses, informal seminars, mentoring program, PREM Fellows program, and professional development grants)	• Appropriate staff resources to meet the needs of clients and country directors • Widespread recognition of the Bank as among the world's expert organizations in at least 3 areas of public sector reform • Well-functioning and integrated system of institutional recruitment for public sector specialists • Well-regarded and integrated system of professional training and staff development for public sector specialists

Issue or Past Problem Area to Address	Strategic Objectives	Responsible parties
Incomplete quality-control mechanisms in public sector portfolio and ESW	• To assure high quality in the Bank's work on public sector institutional reform	• PRMPS • PSB • PSB • PSB • PSB, DECRG
Inadequate mechanisms for sharing and preserving knowledge	• To build and share a knowledge base among practitioners inside and outside the Bank	• PSB • PRMPS • PSB

will continue to monitor CAS and PRSP processes and provide assistance to country teams on governance issues as needed.

Analytic instruments. The networks will continue to work with country teams and other interested groups in the Bank—and with governments and other groups in our client countries—to develop diagnostic tools for institutional analysis. Four pilot Institutional and Governance Reviews were completed in fiscal 2000, and five more are underway in fiscal 2001. These IGRs and the toolkits that are being developed to guide them are providing valuable links to the PRSP process (with intensive efforts in Benin, Cameroon, and Uganda, among other countries). In addition to these IGR pilots, anticorruption surveys were carried out in several ECA countries in fiscal 1998 (see Part II, ECA strategy), and WBI is working with regional PREM

units on additional surveys in other countries, including Benin, Cambodia, Ecuador, Ghana, Nigeria, Russia, and Thailand (see Part II, WBI strategy).

The other major tool for upstream diagnostic work is the PER, expected to be undertaken in at least 20 countries in each of the three years fiscal 2000-02. The Public Expenditure Thematic Group will continue to work with operational staff to integrate institutional analysis more thoroughly into PERs and to finalize and implement new PER guidelines that further define and, where desirable, standardize their content.

We aim for a well-defined set of products and toolkits (with many flexible variants in practice) that country teams can use as needed to undertake analytic work on institutional settings as input to a CAS or PRSP. We also expect that the individual toolkits will be useful in framing individual pieces of economic and

Activities to Achieve Objectives	Goals by End of Fiscal 2003
• Preparation of portfolio database to monitor public sector loans • Adoption of active program to identify and collectively review at-risk and flagship projects in the pipeline • Active participation of Public Sector Group members in QAG reviews • Formation of peer reviewer list by thematic group (with the goal of having at least one reviewer from the list for each major Bank project) • Preparation of new PER guidelines and upgrading of PER monitoring and peer review process	• In conjunction with OED and QAG, development and consistent use of monitorable indicators for measuring institutional impact of Bank's services • Rating of satisfactory or better on institutional components in 90 percent of QAG reviews for public sector loans • Clear consensus among Bank's clients and partners on the purposes and contents of PERs of various types • QAG rating of satisfactory or better quality for 80 percent of PERs
• Building of 6-8 active thematic groups dealing with various areas of public sector institutional reform • Launching of 7 or more websites on public sector reform • Publication of series of PREM Notes on various topics of governance and public sector reform • Exploration of new knowledge sharing approaches with partners	• Full integration of virtually all Bank public sector staff around the world into the Bank's knowledge management activities, and regular use of KM systems and resources in their everyday work • Large set of succinct and readable PREM Notes for wide dissemination of lessons of experience • Quicker access to a wide range of external expertise as needed by the Bank or its clients

sector work or projects undertaken downstream of the CAS.

Knowledge management. The Public Sector Group will have seven sites on the Bank's Knowledge Management System (KMS) on various topics of public sector reform. These include KMS sites on anticorruption, administrative and civil service reform, public expenditure analysis and management, tax policy and administration, public enterprise reform, decentralization (in collaboration with the other three networks), and reform of legal institutions (in collaboration with LEG). Five of the seven have already been made available on the external web, and all will be available to external audiences by mid-fiscal 2001. A strong effort will be made to disseminate country cases (including outcomes of the IGRs) through the Knowledge Management System.

Lending instruments. It is proposed that the Bank gain experience and broaden the use of programmatic lending approaches for public sector reform (PSALs and APLs) with at least 5 to 10 operations in fiscal 2000-02. As noted in the earlier discussion, innovative PSALs focusing on public sector institutional reform have been approved for Thailand, Latvia, and Uttar Pradesh, India, and governance-oriented adjustment loans are also under preparation in numerous other settings. Long-term APLs are focusing on public sector reform in a variety of countries, including Bolivia, Ghana, Tanzania, and Zambia. The development of these lending approaches is expected to be closely aligned with progress on the CDF, because both share very similar goals.

Staffing and organization. The Bank's expertise in public sector reform has expanded significantly since

BOX 21

An Emerging Quality Assurance Plan for the Public Sector Board

As a result of the Bank's recent review of matrix management, sector boards throughout the Bank have been asked to take on an enhanced quality assurance role. Summarized below are elements of the quality enhancement plan adopted by the Public Sector Board:

Delineation of portfolio content and monitoring responsibilities

- Sort out portfolio and align project classification to network responsibilities to the extent possible.

- In cases of overlap of responsibilities, establish mechanisms for collaboration on quality assurance with other networks and with the Economic Policy Board (within PREM).

Upstream quality assurance (public sector lending and ESW products)

- Continue upstream work of the network on strategy, knowledge management, instruments, staffing, and professional development, which are the key fundamentals to quality in the medium- and long-run.

- Establish an Operations Support Group (OSG) to share experiences among operational task managers in the design and implementation of major public sector reform initiatives.

- Identify quarterly, for each region, the pipeline of public sector lending and ESW products under preparation in the next 6 to 12 months that fit into two categories: (1) major flagship initiatives and (2) loans with high levels of risk.

Discuss lists at Sector Board meeting and agree on next steps for each activity (whether more extensive discussion by OSG or Board, Quality Enhancement Review, etc.).

- Provide feedback as requested by regional sector managers on anticipated task leadership and team membership for public sector lending and ESW activities.

- Provide the option of a menu of organized "just-in-time" clinics and other training opportunities for project teams (including, as appropriate, country counterparts) embarking on public sector reform projects and ESW.

- Draft a new set of guidelines for the content and process of PERs (distinguishing more clearly between two objectives: capacity building and assessment). Work with QAG to review assessment guidelines for PERs in light of these new content and process guidelines.

- Take steps to increase the quality and impact of the peer review process:(a) Prepare guidelines on the selection of peer reviewers and the responsibilities of peer reviewers. (b) Provide a list of qualified peer reviewers from which at least one of the peer reviewers for major products should be selected. (c) Create a system for sharing and tracking peer review comments on all public sector projects and ESW tasks, and explore the possibility of setting up a special website for sharing such comments along with other project information.

Downstream quality assurance (for projects identified by QAG to be at risk or projects with weak supervision)

- Carry out, in collaboration with QAG, a semi-annual portfolio review (with Sector Board discussion) to assess the extent and nature of quality issues.

- Review and discuss with QAG the indicators used to monitor the portfolio.

- Review list of problem projects (including names of task managers and peer reviewers) on a quarterly basis. Agree on next steps for each project on the list.

the creation of PREM in 1997, both through new hiring and through expanded training.[29] There is still strong demand in most regions, in part attributable to the rapid expansion in the Bank's anticorruption activities. Overall numbers, however, are expected to expand slightly if at all in the coming one to three years, given budget constraints and possibilities for internal redeployment, and anticipated retirements and redundancies. Another three to five qualified staff are expected be hired in fiscal 2001 through the sector board's pilot recruitment initiative, resulting in the total number of core public sector specialists (not including institutional specialists in particular sectors) of approximately 160.

Quality assurance and evaluation. The recent review of matrix functioning by senior management is resulting in an expanded role for the networks in quality assurance. Enhancing the quality of projects, policy-based loans, and analytic work (particularly PERs) is high priority for the Public Sector Board in fiscal 2001. The first step has been to develop a clear picture of the relevant portfolio; this has proven more difficult than originally envisioned, because many projects originally labeled as "public sector management" are managed by staff outside the PREM network. The PS Board is currently working closely with other sector boards to delineate their portfolios and their respective

responsibilities for quality assurance for those projects.

Several steps are being taken to enhance quality where accountabilities are already clear, and an emerging quality plan for public sector activities is outlined in Box 21. The Board has begun a process of early identification and collective review of high-risk and flagship loans in the pipeline, with the primary goal being the provision of upfront support and assistance to task teams. It has begun to undertake Quality Enhancement Reviews of high-risk projects and ESW (cofinanced with QAG and the Region) upon request from the Regions. It has formalized a list of peer reviewers by thematic group to participate in the review of major Bank products, and it is working to enhance the reporting requirements and follow-up for peer reviews. It has established an Operations Support Group of task managers for major public sector reform initiatives to encourage further peer monitoring. Its ongoing work on staffing, staff training (including "just- in-time clinics" for teams undertaking PERs) and promotions, knowledge management, and thematic group development are all oriented toward long-term quality enhancement. It works closely with OED and QAG as they undertake their important roles in quality monitoring. OED is planning to undertake an evaluation of the Bank's anticorruption program in fiscal 2000-01. As noted in Section II above, the quality of the public sector portfolio has already improved significantly over the past three years, and we hope these organizational and quality control activities will lead to continued improvements in the future.

Partnerships. Many partners in the international community are centrally concerned with governance and capacity building, and we will continue to strengthen our relations with the IMF, UNDP, other MDBs, bilateral donors (including OECD DAC), and NGOs—with a central goal being strong collaboration in implementing the capacity building mandate laid out in President Wolfensohn's 1999 Annual Meetings speech. We will continue to help coordinate the MDBs' Working Group on Governance and Anticorruption and to disseminate this strategy and share approaches to governance and public sector reform with bilateral donors.

One of the many areas where such partnerships can be enhanced is in the design of new, more flexible ways to finance technical advice on public sector reform. The Public Sector Board has already begun to expand its partnerships with the OECD (including SIGMA) and the Commonwealth Secretariat, and we will seek ways to draw on their abilities to provide quick and flexible technical assistance from expert practitioners on demand. We will also continue to monitor the existing public sector and technical assistance portfolios and work with other donors (including the DAC Working Group on Technical Cooperation) to improve the design and delivery of these programs.

Partnership is also needed in research and knowledge generation, with analysts and researchers both inside and outside the Bank. Although research on institutions and their contribution to development has increased in recent years, we still face many uncertainties and knowledge gaps. In some cases it is unclear which institutional setups are optimal from an economic perspective. In others the desired institutional change is clear but how to get there is not. For example, we may have a good idea of what actions ideally need to be taken—for example, in the civil service or the judiciary—to build better accountability institutions, but we may still be uncertain about how to sequence and time our interventions and our support to help build coalitions for change. We must continue to keep our minds open to new ideas, keep searching for answers, and keep learning from experience.

Risks. This strategy addresses issues that are difficult both technically and politically, and there are inherently many risks as the Bank moves forward. First, there are risks of inconsistency in the application of Bank standards as the Bank moves to become more selective in linking governance and CASs more closely (Section III). Second, there are risks that the Bank's analytic work will not be demand-driven, linked sufficiently to operational needs, sufficiently high quality, or carried out in a manner that builds local capacity and strengthens partnerships (Section IV). Third, there are risks of corruption and financial mismanagement in Bank programmatic lending (as noted in the discussion in Section V). Finally, there is a risk that staff skills and incentives will not be adequate to carry out the strategy (Section VI). We are cognizant of these risks and are collaborating in efforts already underway or under discussion that will help to address them (for example through possible CAS and ESW reform, adapting fiduciary and safeguard policies to programmatic approaches, and re-balancing the management matrix). We also know from experience that failure to move forward is fraught with even more risk.

Closing. The Bank will make the above goals and actions the centerpiece of its strategy for public sector reform over the coming months and years and will work with others to try to make them reality. We realize that reforming public sector institutions is exceedingly difficult and complex and will not be achieved quickly or completely, but we believe that well-functioning governments are so fundamental to sustainable development that the Bank must embrace the challenge.

NOTES

1 As will be seen throughout the discussion, the private sector and civil society can have an important role in helping to provide some public services and monitor public sector performance. For purposes of this strategy paper, private entities that perform public functions are included in the broad category of public institutions.

2 An earlier version of the present two-part strategy was discussed by a subcommittee of the Board's Committee on Development Effectiveness (CODE) in December 1999 and by the full CODE in January 2000. Following the CODE discussion, extensive consultations were held with external partners (including UNDP, various bilateral donors, the regional development banks, NGOs and the private sector), and the current draft attempts to take these many views into account. The Bank's Board of Executive Directors reviewed the entire strategy in July 2000, and the current version reflects the comments received from Directors at that meeting and in follow-up discussions.

3 From the perspective of the policymaker, institutions are the set of incentives and constraints within which policy decisions are made and implemented; policies are the decisions themselves. For example, from the policymaker's viewpoint budgeting procedures are institutions, while budget allocations are policies. The processes of interaction among various macroeconomic policymaking groups are institutions, while the specific contents of the rules that result from these institutions (such as exchange and interest rates) are policies; rules specifying who can own property are institutions, while the contents of specific zoning regulations are policies.

4 For example, "price-cap" regulation of private providers of utility services may work best in OECD countries but be inappropriate in countries where there are few checks and balances on regulatory discretion.

5 In countries with very weak institutions, channeling public funds to NGOs or citizens' groups may be the only workable way of getting at least some social services delivered – even though tighter controls over resource use might be preferred if institutions were stronger.

6 For example, although a graduated benefit tailored to prior earnings may be the optimal design for unemployment insurance, a flat benefit for all may be the only administratively feasible design in countries with weak public institutions.

7 One goal of judicial reform in countries with poorly functioning judiciaries might well be to limit their responsibilities to the most critical functions for the economy, removing those functions (such as in-depth screening of enterprise incorporation documents, probate of wills, or complex notarial duties) that are less critical or that can be handled by private parties.

8 OED, 1998 Annual Review of Development Effectiveness.

9 OED, 1997 Annual Review of Development Effectiveness.

10 Recent improvements in performance are likely to have resulted from a combination of factors, including a more accountable organizational structure; improved oversight, management, and quality control; and clearer strategic vision focused more centrally on capacity building. This strategy, already well into implementation, is intended to encourage further changes in these directions in the future.

11 OED, "1997 Annual Review of Development Effectiveness," p. 23.

12 OED, "Civil Service Reform: A Review of World Bank Assistance," March 1999.

13 World Bank, "Perspectives on Technical Assistance Loans," February 1998.

14 L. Barbone, A. Das-Gupta, L. De Wulf, and A. Hansson, "Reforming Tax Systems: The World Bank Record in the 1990s," unpublished manuscript 1999.

15 OED, "The Impact of Public Expenditure Reviews: An Evaluation," 1998.

16 Navin Girishankar, "Reforming Institutions for Service

Delivery: A Framework for Development Assistance with an Application to the Health, Nutrition, and Population Portfolio," Policy Research Working Paper 2039, January 1999.

17 An example of the problems with simple yes-no ratings is the record of the Ford Foundation in sending young Indonesians abroad for graduate school training in the 1950s and 1960s. Dozens were sent, and out of these about a half-dozen went on to be economic ministers for up to 30 years. On a pure numerical basis, the program might be judged a failure, because perhaps only one-tenth of the "interventions" contributed directly toward building government capacity; but if the magnitude of the overall benefits and costs are weighed, the program was surely a success.

18 Emmanuel Ablo and Ritva Reinikka, "Do Budgets Really Matter? Evidence From Public Spending On Education And Health In Uganda," World Bank Working Paper, 1998.

19 The chapter on public sector reform in the recent review on India (and accompanying documents) provides a good example of how public sector institutional analysis can be integrated into an SSR.

20 More generally, reforming ESW to link it more closely and more efficiently to country and Bank needs while recognizing budget limitations has been the focus of a recent Bank-wide study entitled "Fixing ESW: Where Are We?" July 2000.

21 For further discussion, see *Adaptable Lending: Review of Experience After Two Years* (R2000-31), March 10, 2000.

22 *Guidelines for Programmatic Adjustment Loans/Credits*, Operational Memorandum to staff, February 11, 2000; *Financial Crisis and Structural Reform: The Bank's Role and Instruments* (SecM98-743), September 17, 1998; and *Programmatic and Emergency Adjustment Lending: World Bank Guidelines* (R98-249), October 22, 1998.

23 Operations Policy and Strategy, *Lending Retrospectives, Volumes and Instruments: Issues Paper*, Nov. 1999.

24 The Public Sector Board sponsors six thematic groups: Administrative and Civil Service Reform; Anticorruption; Decentralization; Legal Institutions of a Market Economy; Public Expenditure Analysis and Management; and Tax Policy and Administration. We

will soon launch a thematic group on E-Government. These thematic groups together have approximately 500 internal members who together design and manage training and other professional development activities, develop intranet-based knowledge services, and provide a ready means to seek informal advice and share information. Many of the groups meet regularly, and all sponsor workshops, conferences, and brown-bag lunches. IMF staff and outside experts are included in several of the groups.

25 "Effective Implementation: Key to Development Impact: Report of the World Bank's Portfolio Management Task Force," October 2, 1992.

26 In the expenditure area, the Bank has greater responsibility for policy work, while both organizations work on public expenditure management. In the tax area, the Fund has a major program of technical assistance (on demand) in tax policy and administration, while the Bank's involvement (particularly on the administrative side) extends to major lending initiatives.

27 In FY99 the Bank and Fund completed their third review and set of regional consultations on work programs in public sector reform, as mandated in 1995 by the heads of the two organizations. The third exercise moved beyond public expenditure work (the focus of the first two) to cover a much fuller range of work in public sector reform – including taxation, civil service reform and anticorruption (see Annex 3).

28 OVP – Operational Vice Presidents; PREM – Poverty Reduction and Economic Management Network (including regional units); PSB – Public Sector Board; PRMPS – Public Sector Anchor; WBI – World Bank Institute; DRG – Development Research Group (in DEC); OCS – Operational Core Services Network

29 Training courses for staff organized in 2000 include: Decentralization; Public Expenditure Analysis and Management; Budget Reform; Public Expenditure Review Clinics (on demand); Understanding Civil Service Reform; Practical Tools and Techniques for Governance Assessment; Workshop series on Alternative Dispute Resolution, Judicial Reform, Case Management and Court Performance Standards; Building Property Systems; and An Anticorruption Strategy for Revenue Administration.

Regional, DRG, and WBI Strategies

Africa Region (AFR)

Chastened by the mixed results of an ambitious program initiated in the 1980s to strengthen public sector management, staff within the Africa Region (not just those whose explicit mandate is public sector reform) recognize that the primary obstacle to progress is not simply a shortfall in financial resources and the production of technically sound advice, but more deep-seated failures in governance. Participatory processes and capacity building comprise part—but only part—of the requisite response by the Africa Region (AFR) to the challenge of improving governance. In some countries such initiatives need to be consolidated through painstaking work to rebuild the formal state institutional infrastructure. In other countries, the grip of dysfunction may be so strong that there is little immediate scope either for building sustainable capacity or for achieving genuine ownership on the part of government of a program of reform. A key immediate challenge for AFR work to reform public institutions is to define an agenda that is more selective and more strategic than it has been in the past.

Salient characteristics of the Africa Region

Africa's institutional development problems are deep-rooted, and understanding their causes is key for the elaboration of a viable strategy. The first part of the story is familiar to many. At the end of colonial rule, the euphoria of independence disguised the reality that (beyond a consensus in favor of independence) support for many African regimes was drawn from a narrow base, often with quite weak roots in the society at large. At the same time, the starting point for many African governments was a precarious combination of overextended mandates, weak revenue bases, and low capacity. Mandates were increased further in response to ideological and social pressures. During the crisis of the 1970s and 1980s, restoring macroeconomic balance became an imperative enforced through a myriad of adjustment operations and IMF programs.

Perhaps less familiar are the ways in which the adjustment process, while resolving some emerging imbalances, compounded some pre-existing weaknesses of fragile government institutions:

- Many countries responded to the need for budget stringency, not by reducing their scope of activities and number of employees, but by reducing public service pay—especially at the higher levels of the public sector—leading to an exodus of many of the most skilled people from the public sector, and a consequent crisis of capacity within the civil service.

- The high levels of aid dependence that accompanied reform, with aid often earmarked for preferred initiatives of donors and with project employees earning above their counterparts in the core public sector have helped entrench a perverse system of incentives, undermining the ability of governments to effect rational and strategic choices in public spending.

- This institutional weakening compounded what was for many governments an already fragile basis of legitimacy and accountability. In some countries it has led to a patrimonial system in which rent-seeking absorbs much of the energy of African elites at the expense of development efforts. This contributed to further alienating the citizenry, to the related inability to raise taxes and to the absence of a culture of accountability and service delivery in the public sector.

These weaknesses have proven difficult to reverse. In many cases there was little drive for reform of the public sector from the top of governments: the danger of a low-level equilibrium exists, in which the incentives to remove poor service are nowhere to be found for any of the actors involved.

Experience to date in the Africa Region

As the above brief diagnosis of the root causes of the institutional crisis of the public sector suggests, in settings where institutional dysfunction has taken root, technocratic, supply-driven approaches to public sector management will not yield sustainable results. Today this lesson is broadly accepted within the Bank's Africa Region. But the learning process has been a long and continuing one.

The 1980s: from investment to policy and management. As in the rest of the World Bank, in the late 1970s and early 1980s, AFR moved from an exclusive preoccupation with investment-oriented development projects to an agenda that incorporated a growing emphasis on policy reform and adjustment lending. Already by the mid-1980s it had become apparent in the Region that more was needed to achieve sustainable development than simply grafting policy reforms on top of a menu of investment projects. Consequently, beginning in the mid-1980s, AFR invested heavily in initiatives to reform public sector management, perhaps more heavily than any other regional grouping within the Bank. Between 1987 and 1997, 70 of 102 civil service reform projects (and included in a recent OED review)[1] were in sub-Saharan Africa.

The Region's experience with public sector management (PSM) has been uneven: just 29 percent of the completed interventions, and 45 percent of those still ongoing, were rated "satisfactory" in the OED review (the corresponding Bank-wide figures are 33 percent and 38 percent). In retrospect, the reasons why so many technically based reform projects were doomed to fail are clear. Launching computerization programs, functional audits, or other technical inputs within a context where they enjoy little support from political leadership, and where they are radically at variance with informal "rules of the game" do not yield sustainable results. Even in those cases where leaders wanted reform, they and the donors consistently underestimated the magnitude of the challenges involved at the political, managerial and technical levels.

This very mixed track record created a certain wariness among AFR staff as to the potential impact on the ground of opportunistic public sector management reforms, initiated without careful attention as to whether institutional and political realities provided a favorable starting point. Increasingly, attention turned toward approaches that focused more on deep-rooted sources of institutional failure, as exemplified in the 1989 study *From Crisis to Sustainable Growth—Sub-Saharan Africa: A Long-term Perspective (LTPS)*.

The 1990s: Participation and capacity building. Over the course of the 1990s, the public sector management agenda was complemented by initiatives that focused less on the details of management systems and more on the challenges of fostering local ownership and participation and building local capacity. Indeed, as the results of the first round of public management projects began to become apparent, resources shifted increasingly to the latter areas—to the point that by 1998 public sector management had become something of an "orphan," with just a handful of staff, located precariously at the edges of the Region's Social Development and Capacity Building Units.

The LTPS gave a major impetus to work on capacity building within AFR, leading to the establishment (at the initiative of the World Bank) of the autonomous Africa Capacity Building Foundation in Harare in 1991. This new emphasis was given added momentum during the Bank's 1995 Annual Meetings, when the African Governors and the Bank President agreed to work together on a new program of action to support capacity building. In the three subsequent years African stakeholders, with the support of the Bank, have invested heavily to realize this vision of a new Partnership for Capacity Building (PACT). The African Governors sponsored the establishment of National Focal Points, and a series of National Capacity Assessments—with

the latter (supported by IDF grants) completed in at least twelve countries. Within AFR, determined efforts were made to "mainstream" capacity building across the spectrum of Bank work.

In May 1999, the Board of the Bank discussed a Memorandum of the President that outlines specific ways in which the Bank can support the forward momentum of this African initiative. This Memorandum recommended that the PACT be implemented by the Africa Capacity Building Foundation (ACBF), an organization based in Africa. Twelve of the twenty-two country-level members of the ACBF's Board of Governors are African (others include bilateral donors, the African Development Bank, the UNDP, and the World Bank)—underlining the principle that PACT should be an African-owned initiative. The ACBF's Board of Governors completed its preparatory arrangements to take on the PACT in January, 2000. Implementation of PACT is proceeding rapidly.

The way in which PACT has developed is just one example of a new emphasis on fostering participation across the range of AFR work. This new emphasis has come as a breath of fresh air to governments and citizens in the region, who increasingly had voiced their frustrations with the perceived arrogance, ignorance and failure to listen of 'old-style' approaches to development work. Increasingly, the full range of Bank work—from CASs to investment projects to initiatives to foster institutional reform—was evaluated on the basis of the quality of local ownership and participation.

At the operational level, Zambia's Public Service Capacity Building Project illustrates how this participatory process has worked. The Zambian government set up a technical committee, with representation from a wide range of public and private stakeholders, to take responsibility for project preparation. This committee, with only modest specialist support, identified the critical issues, prepared an objective tree for the project, converted it into a logical framework, and drafted the project concept and appraisal documents. At the strategic level, the process of preparing the Bank's CAS for

Guinea began with a commitment by the Head of State and the Prime Minister, and consisted of country-wide grassroots consultations conducted by cross-sectoral teams of trained local facilitators. A national forum helped validate the results, build a consensus on the development priorities identified by the communities, and articulate a country-owned and community-driven development strategy.

The challenges ahead

The increasing emphasis on both participatory processes and capacity building exemplifies the striking openness across all sectoral staff within AFR to new approaches to development work centered on improving governance. Yet, as noted above, while participatory processes and capacity building are a good start, they fall short of a sufficient recipe for successful institutional reforms in two distinct ways. In some countries, initial successes in partnering and building capacity will need to be consolidated through painstaking work to rebuild the formal state institutional infrastructure. In other countries the grip of dysfunction may be so strong that there is little immediate scope either for building sustainable capacity or for achieving genuine ownership on the part of government of a program of reform. Either way, the immediate challenge for AFR work to reform public institutions is to define an agenda that is more selective and strategic.

The approach: fostering selectivity and strategic prioritization. The priorities for institutional reform vary across countries depending upon the strength of a country's administrative apparatus, the political goals of the government in power, and more broadly, the character of state-society relations. In some countries, reform-oriented governments enjoy the support of broad segments of society to effect far-reaching reforms of a functioning, if cumbersome, administrative apparatus. In others, the major political players who dominate the state apparatus are fundamentally unwilling to change their behavior and to move toward more accountable governance. Sometimes, (as in Mozambique at the end of civil war, or Ethiopia after the collapse of the Derg regime) reform-oriented leaders may confront situations where the state apparatus has decayed, been destroyed, or remained underdeveloped to such a degree that the immediate agenda is to address some of the most basic elements of state structure.

Many of the earlier failures of PSM initiatives were the result of a failure to recognize this diversity in political and institutional starting points, and to tailor the reform program accordingly. Yet donors, including the Bank, persisted in providing technical assistance for improved management in contexts where the preconditions were not present. Our immediate challenge is thus to move away from a "one-size-fits-all" approach, and to broaden the menu to incorporate other options in addition to classic PSM (or for that matter, undifferentiated approaches to participation or capacity building). Four distinct, but potentially complementary, sets of approaches to institutional reform can be identified:

- Reforming the structure of the state,

- Strengthening public sector management,

- Working from the demand-side, and

- Empowering communities for service delivery.

The first two approaches focus on the "supply-side" in that they focus directly on the organizational and institutional arrangements of states, on the presumption that there indeed exists a strong constituency for reform. By contrast, the second two "demand-side" approaches aim at engaging civil society more broadly in the quest for public sector reform.

As is highlighted in the main strategy, what the relative emphasis should be among these approaches will depend on country-specific institutional and political realities on the ground. A focus on listening and participation should characterize our work in all settings. In countries where the first two approaches dominate, the immediate challenge of participatory work will be to build sustained and close working relationships with our counterparts within government, as well as to strengthen mechanisms which encourage further transparency and accountability. In countries where the latter two approaches are given more emphasis, we will need to work with counterparts in government in ways that reach out broadly to diverse segments of civil society.

The first two sets of approaches are relevant in countries where there is a favorable political environment for reform. Even within this group of countries, situations on the ground will vary widely. In some settings the focus of reform will need to be on fundamental questions concerning the role and structure of the state. In others, the challenge will be more one of consolidating and strengthening what already exists. In all cases, our aim should be to act as facilitators who help the reform's political and bureaucratic champions articulate their vision and get through the difficult early stages to the point where there is no turning back. In practical terms, this means that we should help ensure that the strategy, leadership, resources, and skills devoted to the effort are sufficient for the task at hand. Even more importantly, it means that from the beginning, national teams must take the initiative in consulting their own constituencies, planning the reforms, and selling their ideas to their own constituencies and to the Bank. If policies and programs emerge from a national debate, the leaders are likely to be held accountable for them by their own internal constituencies.

Reforming state structure. The evolving reforms in Uganda and Ethiopia have highlighted the importance, in some contexts, of getting the role, size and profile of the state well adapted to local circumstances before embarking on more focused PSM reforms. At this level, reforms include such fundamentals as:

- Amending the constitution to redefine the role of the state, introduce new governance arrangements, change the machinery of government or alter the balance of power among the executive and the parliament,

- Introducing devolution or decentralization of services to lower levels of government and related fiscal reforms, and

- Privatizing or reforming public enterprises and public corporations; changing the regulatory environment for the para-public and private sectors.

In the case of societies struggling to manage civil conflict (for example, Republic of Congo, Democratic Republic of Congo, Liberia, and Sierra Leone) these reforms will obviously constitute a high priority, yet may only materialize over the medium-term. In instances of national reconstruction, it may prove necessary to provide interim technical support to key government functions in the form of external expertise during the transition to a more stable context. Only when the latter has been achieved will it be possible to rebuild viable organizations and develop national technical skills on a sustainable basis.

Strengthening public sector management. Some of the more successful African adjusters have already gone a long way toward completing a restructuring of the state's role, including increased scope for participation and competition. In these countries, of which Ghana is a leading example, the predominant supply-side issue will be management reforms aimed at improving the performance of the public sector.

Difficult experience has taught us that in the absence of an overarching strategy for sequencing changes, piecemeal public management reforms—the so-called stovepipe approach of vertical compartmentalization among sectors and agencies—are unlikely to be more than, at best, a short-term palliative. The seemingly disparate elements of a well-functioning public sector are in fact interdependent: the impact of contracts and other mechanisms to foster performance-based management depends in significant part on the policies these agencies are mandated to pursue, the mechanisms for monitoring agency performance, and the systems that impose budget discipline. These in turn rest on the foundation of systems that perform due diligence and hold public agencies accountable for their use of resources. And performance systems yield sustainable results to the extent that pay is adequate to attract the requisite staff and induce them to perform, records are maintained, and the political will exists to impose financial discipline, confront tradeoffs, and set and adhere to a hard budget constraint.

There is thus a difficult tension between on the one hand, the gains from integration and on the other, the benefits of an incremental, sequenced approach that does not attempt to take on more than can realistically be achieved. Many reform efforts have become hopelessly confused and blurred in attempting to manage this large agenda simultaneously. Once a realistic vision is agreed on, implementation needs to emphasize phasing and sequencing—an area where we still have much to learn—as one successfully completed block builds on the last one and presages the next.

Working from the demand-side. In cases where political and bureaucratic obstacles inhibit committed African reformers from moving forward with their agenda, a realistic assessment of past failures points to the need to take a longer-term perspective. This entails working on the demand-side by undertaking activities that may, over the medium-term, strengthen the domestic impetus for public sector reforms. The latter include:

- initiating anticorruption activities within civil society and government to raise awareness and mobilize support for reform;

- collaborating with influential groups, such as parliamentarians and the business community, to bring pressure to bear for enhanced accountability and transparency within the operations of government and at the interface between government on the one hand and civil society and the private sector on the other;

- working with foreign investors and others to strengthen the regulatory and dispute-resolution mechanisms for private investors, notably including the enabling environment for private participation in the provision of infrastructure; and

- encouraging changes in political attitudes and behavior through the provision of seminars, study tours and other catalytic activities designed to make governments aware of the positive outcomes of reform in terms of service provision, growth, equity and political stability.

Empowering communities for service delivery. The fourth approach to institutional reform—empowering communities for service delivery—is actually a hybrid that incorporates elements of the first three: in aiming to close the (geographic and accountability) distance between citizens and government, it works on the demand-side; in redefining the relationships between central and local government, it reforms the structure of the state; and in realigning fiscal and administrative processes to support devolved authority it involves major public sector management reforms.

There is growing momentum across the African continents for reform initiatives that shift resources, responsibility for service delivery, and accountability for results from central government to more decentralized levels. Ethiopia and South Africa have recently promulgated new federal-style constitutions. Uganda and Tanzania have explicitly shifted authority for service delivery to local governments, with (most clearly in the former country) accompanying budget reforms to transfer resources—and allocation decisions—to local levels. Guinea is currently in the midst of a complex process aimed at strengthening democratically accountable local governments, increasing their direct access to financial resources, and strengthening the local administrative apparatus.

Because it implies profound change at so many levels, the challenge of implementing initiatives that aim to empower communities for service delivery is unusually formidable. Yet, if it can be made to work, it has the potential to provide a new foundation of legitimacy for the relationship between citizens and states. Many staff within AFR are thus enthusiastically embracing this new agenda of community empowerment.

If AFR is to contribute constructively to ensuring that this new agenda does not end in yet another round of disappointment, two tasks must be addressed urgently. First, the agenda is fundamentally a cross-cutting one: staff with expertise in public institutions have a key role to play to help reform administrative and accountability relations; public finance staff need to help realign intergovernmental fiscal relations; and staff in the infrastructure and social sectors need to identify new ways of supporting new approaches to service delivery. All of this will require AFR staff to set aside the boundaries of functional specialties and units, and renew our commitment to work together (in-country teams) in a genuinely cross-cutting way.

The second task is to identify a menu of workable sequencing options. Rarely, if ever, will countries be in a position to address simultaneously in an integrated way all the elements needed for successful community empowerment for service delivery. Sometimes the impetus for community empowerment will come from the grassroots. In such settings, civic pressures are likely to outrun the ability of fiscal and administrative systems to respond efficiently. At other times the reform impetus may come from the center of government. Here the challenge will be to ensure that redirection of fiscal and administrative responsibility does not simply result in a transfer of patronage and corruption from

one (centralized) locus of control to another (local) one. Everywhere, the process is certain to be uneven, marked by a seemingly endless sequence of new problems. Our challenge is to work with our counterparts in-country to negotiate ways through the maze that help ensure that the process does not become trapped in dead-ends, but makes step-by-step progress along a critical path toward sustainable long-run solutions. The "Sourcebook on Community Driven Development in the Africa Region," produced by a multi-sectoral team of AFR staff, comprises an important step in bringing both coherence and cross-sectoral collaboration to this important agenda.

Activities and instruments

In coming years, staff within AFR working on the development of public institutions will experiment with a variety of new approaches to both our knowledge-related and lending activities.

Knowledge generation, facilitation, and dissemination. As described above, AFR's staff who work on institutional reform have been active in fostering approaches to our work that put our government counterparts in the driver's seat and that engage stakeholders in civil society as full partners in the design of development options. While we will continue to approach our work in this way, we also need to do more intensive analytic work "upstream" in a way that enables both our clients and us to come to grips more realistically with what the institutional and political realities on the ground imply for a workable agenda of reform—not just for public sector management, but more broadly. The pivotal role now assigned to the CAS as the basic strategic planning statement for the Bank's activities, and the experiment in Ghana with the CDF, also reflect this more holistic and integrated approach to the generic and cross-cutting problems that are central to the agenda of public sector reform. Our knowledge-related work will thus incorporate the following:

- Pilot Institutional and Governance Reviews, facilitated by staff who specialize in institutional reform, and undertaken by country teams as multi-sectoral initiatives that aim to highlight the connections between service delivery results on the ground, and underlying public sector management and related institutional and political obstacles—and that lay out operationally feasible, sequenced steps in a complex multi-faceted agenda. (These pilots will be cofinanced through country budgets and the Bank-wide Public Sector Group's knowledge management resources).

- Analytic support for the institutional, public sector management and political dimensions of Public Expenditure Reviews or, for that matter, of institutionally oriented sector work in other sectors where we can offer complementary expertise;

- Surveys to benchmark service quality (the Core Welfare Indicators Questionnaire, or CWIQ) and to analyze the nature and extent of corruption, and of other dysfunctional aspects of governance, and dissemination of the results to public officials and civil society (together with WBI); and

- Participatory CASs and other mechanisms to engage civil society in an open discourse on countries' development priorities and choices and, more broadly, to help disseminate "process principles" for fostering ownership and sustainability for all the Bank's work (together with WBI)—for example, as is now being developed for Guinea, Senegal, and Sierra Leone, the implementation of a results-based model of political accountability relying on a foundation of monitorable benchmarks and indicators.

Public sector reform operations. Three principles will guide our operational work in public sector management. First, we intend to be highly selective as to

where we would be supportive of such operations. Second, where we do move forward, we will do so in a way that is strategically coherent and avoids "stovepiping" into multiple, separate projects. Third, we will work to ensure that all donors participate on the basis of a shared vision and of an agreed strategy to achieve it. Without a renewed emphasis on partnerships at the country level, an integrated strategy cannot succeed. In terms of developing interventions, we are experimenting with a variety of new instruments and more are being developed:

- Adaptable Program Loans (APLs) have been developed for Ghana, Guinea, Tanzania, and Zambia. A loan such as the APL is conducive to the long-term, sequential operations that are often required for public sector reform. It permits a phased, step-by-step approach and incorporates carefully defined benchmarks for assessing progress and defining triggers for phases two and three. The minimum package for upgrading performance and the key prerequisites for sustained reform will be included in the first phase.

- Programmatic SALs (PSALs) in Benin and Uganda reflect an attempt to help countries get the fundamentals of budgeting and expenditures right before launching into downstream reforms. The implementation through such lending operations (or other approaches to lending) of a Medium-Term Expenditure Framework may be used to help governments distinguish the desirable from the possible and to bring a realistic focus to bear on the implementation of the reform agenda, its timing and its sequencing.

- Multi-sectoral "Capacity Building for Service Delivery" loans, such as the one in Guinea, (see description below) which aim to build from the "bottom-up" through a decentralized approach to development, ensuring that our efforts to promote better service delivery at the community level are buttressed by requisite reforms not just of budget systems but also of administrative arrangements at subnational levels, and of mechanisms that give citizens "voice" and enable their representatives to hold administrators accountable for performance.

Organization, staffing and partnerships. The multi-faceted approach to reform outlined in this regional strategy points to the need for AFR to have two core competencies adequately available in-house. Some staff should have broad experience in the area of reforming public institutions, including generic strategic skills (for example, in institutional economics, analysis and political economy) that may be applied to specific country situations. Some should also be specialists in a functional area of financial, economic or personnel management.

Note that the approach recognizes that public sector management is not a discrete sector but a series of core functions that cut across all sectors. Consequently, a sustained effort will be required to mainstream reforms across sectors and among country economists and other macroeconomic specialists. Public sector specialists will be expected to lead and participate in multi-unit teams in order to help bring about the required integration.

Guinea: Capacity Building for Service Delivery

Type of Activity: Loan (Adaptable Program Loan)
Timing: Board Approval: December 1999
Loan Amount Phase 1 (2000-2003): IDA $19 million; Phases 2&3: (2004-2012): IDA $90 million

Summary of Contents

Together with the complementary Village Community Support Program APL, this Bank program will help foster the following political, fiscal and administrative reforms:

- *Politically,* the representativeness of elected local councils will be enhanced; regional development councils, accountable to local councils are being established; increasingly, regional administrations will become accountable to these local governance structures, not just to the hierarchies of central government.

- *Fiscally,* a Local Investment Fund will support with matching grants basic social and infrastructure projects identified by communities; there will be an increase in the share of taxes raised locally which are kept within the locality; a new framework is being established for direct transfers to local authorities of budget resources from the center.

- *Administratively,* subnational administrations are being realigned to shift accountability toward rural communities.

The aim is that at the end of a 10-15 year process of reform there will be an overall increase of 80 percent in access to and in the quality of all services to the rural population.

Innovative / Risky Elements

By shifting control from the bureaucratic center to localities, the program risks a backlash from center bureaucrats and politicians seeking to maintain discretionary control over the use of resources.

The program increasingly will harness donor resources to priorities set by empowered local communities; donors may resist this more fungible framework, leaving capacity stretched local authorities saddled with a multiplicity of complex, earmarked procedures.

Partnerships

An early challenge of the operation will be to bring donors on board with an integrated approach to community-driven development.

Tanzania: Public Sector Reform Project (PSRP)

Type of Activity: Loan (Adaptable Program Loan)
Timing: Board Approval: October 1999
Loan Amount: Phase 1 (2000-2004): IDA $41 million; Phases 2&3: (2005-2011): IDA $53 million

Summary of Contents

The PSRP builds on efforts by the Tanzanians since 1993 to transform a bloated, centralized, and dysfunctional public bureaucracy into a decentralized, accountable, transparent, and efficient public service. The first phase focused on reducing public employment and decompressing the civil service salary structure. The new phase of the program focuses on role restructuring and performance improvement. Direct responsibility for service delivery will increasingly shift to local authorities and the private sector, with central ministries and agencies playing a steering role. For this phase, the Tanzanians have developed a process-oriented change management model. An important feature of the approach is a Performance Improvement Fund (PIF), supported by IDA via this PSRP. Access by each Ministry/Agency (M/A) to the PIF would be in two phases:

- M/As would be supported to develop a strategic, operational, and performance improvement plan for restructuring. Each M/A will prepare and publish a social pact: setting out standards of service that the public can expect in the short- to medium-term; clarifying the resource and service requirements to meet these service standards; and committing to review progress at least twice a year.

- Once a strategic plan has been adopted, support would be made available for the capacity building activities needed for effective implementation, including training, salary supplements within the medium-term pay framework, and contract recruitment of specialized professionals.

Innovative / Risky Elements

Instead of a top-down effort to reform systems, roles and procedures, this program provides incentives and technical resources to encourage individual M/As to "buy-into" the reform process. The risk is that too few genuinely buy-in, and the reform process remains stymied by the dead weight of preexisting practices.

Partnerships

In the area of public service reform, the Tanzanian government has a proven track record of effective donor coordination; 10 donors (including UNDP) have supported the integrated program; apart from the Bank, other donors will contribute $37 million to phase 1 of the APL.

Regionwide: Partnerships for Capacity Building (PACT)

Type of Activity: Grant/Trust Fund Activity
Timing: Approved: July 1999; Ongoing
Grant Amount $30 million/$150 million (seed money from Bank), subject to approval by the Board

Summary of Contents

PACT recognizes the centrality of capacity in the development process in Africa. Building capacity calls for leadership by African countries themselves in creating a conducive policy and operational environment for capacity building; in laying out practical and realistic phasing of capacity building actions; and in building partnerships within countries themselves (among government, civil society, and the private sector), and with national, multinational and bilateral donors, international business and trade interests, foundations, and nongovernmental organizations. Implementation of PACT will be led by the already existing Harare-based African Capacity Building Foundation (ACBF), established in 1991 as a collaborative effort between the World Bank, the African Development Bank, and the United Nations Development Programme (UNDP). Working through the ACBF, PACT will make available:

- country program support, provided annually and accessible by countries that meet eligibility thresholds as to the quality of institutional environments;

- project support for country-based initiatives to build key public sector capacity, and to strengthen the interface between government, civil society and the private sector; and

- project support for regional and subregional initiatives, as well as other proposals, initiated independently by individual agencies of civil society and training institutions.

Innovative / Risky Elements

PACT governance is built upon the principles of partnership and devolution. A first risk is that the devolution of implementing authority to the ACBF will dilute the influence of individual donors, and hence reduce the attractiveness of PACT to them. A second risk is that participatory National Focal Points, to which responsibility for developing coherent country programs is being devolved, will prove ineffective, and that PACT could find itself supporting a multiplicity of disconnected initiatives.

Partnerships

The Board of Governors for the ACBF (and hence PACT) comprise three multilaterals (the World Bank, the UNDP, and the African Development Bank); 10 donor countries; and 12 African countries.

East Asia and Pacific Region (EAP)

Before the recent economic crisis that swept through the East Asia and Pacific Region, public institutions were largely thought to be working well, credited with many of the virtues associated with the "Asian miracle." Indeed, the Bank's approach to public sector institutional reform and governance was hands-off for most of the last decade; a small public management unit was disbanded for perceived lack of country demand. This view has changed in the wake of the past few years' political and economic turmoil. Public sectors throughout the region have had difficulties responding to the crisis, which has exposed previous institutional weaknesses that had escaped notice during periods of economic growth. Moreover, the context for public management and governance has changed dramatically: in addition to the crisis, both further democratization and increasing globalization have raised the requirements for accountable, transparent and efficient government. The Bank is responding by rebuilding its public sector institutional capacity in the East Asia Poverty Reduction and Economic Management Sector Unit (EASPR) and developing a strategy to address public sector and governance issues in a highly diverse set of countries. Three groups of countries, requiring distinct assistance strategies, are discussed in this note: the East Asia 5 (Indonesia, Korea, Malaysia, Philippines and Thailand); the transition countries (China and Vietnam), and the small economies (Cambodia, Laos, Mongolia, Pacific Islands, and Papua New Guinea).

Salient characteristics of the East Asia and Pacific Region

East Asia's pre-crisis reputation for competent public management was based on its macroeconomic and sectoral performance. Budget surpluses contributed to macroeconomic stability and low debt burdens; extensive public investment in education paid lucrative dividends in rising productivity; and public programs to improve agricultural productivity and improve health status combined with rapid growth to lift 350 million people out of poverty over the last two decades.

But East Asia's public sectors were vexed by underlying structural problems. State enterprises were inefficient and over-protected. State regulation was excessive and ineffectual. Government policies thwarted competition. Civil service rules were antiquated, and internal systems of checks and balances to ensure governmental accountability and probity were often lacking. The abuse of public office for private gain was widespread, but largely ignored. Such problems did not shake investor confidence, however. The *WDR97* survey of businesses ranked East Asia Pacific as among the best performing regions on measure after measure.[2]

In July 1997, the economic crisis changed all this, thrusting the need for public sector reform onto center stage. The crisis put three new pressures on the public sector. First, it forced a sharp adjustment of public finance, demanding greater efficiency in the use of government resources. Bank recapitalization suddenly and significantly increased public sector debt levels, raising concerns that interest payments would crowd out other important expenditures, including those that targeted social welfare. This came precisely when demands for government to protect the new poor and to improve overall societal living standards were rising.

Second, the economic downturn revealed poor management and regulatory practices, notably in the financial system. Implicit guarantees to the banking system and private infrastructure projects caused contingent liabilities to mount. Investments in public education declined. And without appropriate social safety nets in place, vulnerable groups were particularly susceptible to the crisis.

Third, the crisis was associated with a sea change in the demands of the citizenry for new, more accountable governance. The economic crisis brought political change in four of the East Asia 5. As financial sector liabilities made claims on the public purse, the clamor for greater transparency and accountability rose. Corruption, a hushed secret in most countries prior to the crisis, became a rallying cry in the daily press for proponents of better government. For example, in Thailand,

The Bangkok Post in a month in 1998 (picked randomly) ran more than 30 stories on corruption or other government failings. Even in the transition countries, senior officials launched programs to curb the regime-threatening corruption that wastes public resources, frustrates the business community, and alienates the citizenry. By the end of 1998, in China, for example, the Central Commission for Discipline Inspection had sanctioned 158,000 Communist party members.[3]

In short, the crisis exposed latent problems (corruption and contingent liabilities), aggravated others (inefficient tax administration), and created new ones in public sector management (budget deficit pressures). Taken together, these problems currently threaten to impede the region from recapturing the high growth momentum of the past. They also stand in the way of realizing a broader concept of development, one that incorporates dimensions of participation and national community. Throughout the region, governments have no choice but to *improve their efficiency* in resource management, improve the *effectiveness of their service delivery* and *regulation*, and augment the *progressivity of their policies* in a way that improves their *transparency and accountability*.

Experience to date in the East Asia Region

Guided by the presumption of a sound public sector, the Bank had concentrated its pre-crisis interventions on promoting public economic policy rather than on reforming government institutions. In the *emerging market economies* of the East Asia 5, for example, the Bank worked with clients on tariff structures, introducing corporatization and competition, and promoting private ownership among utilities. It worked on improving health care and education. The Bank launched projects to improve tax administration in the Philippines.

But there were no initiatives to strengthen public administration on a broader basis. In fact, by mid-1995, the Bank had virtually ceased lending to Korea, Malaysia, and Thailand altogether. Even in the state-dominated *transition countries* of China and Vietnam, the Bank's work did not focus on core government institutions except in the context of fiscal reforms in small economies. Instead, Bank programs sought to reform state enterprises and the state-dominated banking system, and to introduce economic law, while bolstering anti-poverty programs.

Now, with the rising importance of the institutional agenda to Asian governments, the Bank faces the challenge of rebuilding its capacity to help countries implement core institutional reforms. These reforms span four areas: public financial management, administrative and civil service strengthening, regulatory and legal development, and governance and anticorruption initiatives.

Although there is a good deal of commonality in the problems governments throughout the region face, the initial conditions and pressures driving reforms in each country demand quite different strategies. Dividing the region into a tripartite typology of emerging market economies, the small market economies, and the transition economies provides a framework to discuss approaches, activities, and Bank responses.

Emerging market economies

The East Asia 5 (EA5) are generally wealthier, more endowed with managerial capacity and systems, and farther along on the path toward competitive and open societies than are the other two country subsets. Nonetheless, the crisis has doubled debt levels and driven deficits to two-decade highs in the EA5. While the crisis has stabilized in all but Indonesia, the incipient recovery is uneven and fragile.

To rekindle high and sustained growth, these countries have to rethink rules, competition and "voice" to promote government performance and accountability. Improvements centering on fiscal management and service delivery can be obtained through civil service reform, budget management, and tax policy and administration. In the smaller economies, getting proper and transparent budgeting systems in place is the highest priority. Competition for state-supplied goods and services or competition among branches of government is badly needed to improve performance, by reforming state enterprises, deregulating sectors protected by policy-induced barriers, and even contracting out for selected public services. Governments also have to develop new ways to allow the "voice" of the citizenry to place new and effective demands on government to perform well.

Approaches. These countries share broad objectives for institutional change that the Bank is supporting. These are designed to:

- Improve fiscal management to achieve macroeconomic and development objectives (spending, debt management, and contingent liabilities). These require not only achieving budget targets—a task the advanced countries have generally done well in the past—*but institutional improvements:* in the strategic management of budgets over a multi-year period to better link policy objectives with budget outcomes; in coordinating fiscal and monetary policy to ensure better consistency in implementing annual programs; and in improving internal accounting standards and practices to ensure that political authorities are aware of public liabilities.

- Improve service delivery to contribute to short-term poverty amelioration and long-term development objectives (social services, human capital formation, and infrastructure). This would involve setting out-come and output performance measures for line ministries and civil service reforms.

- Reduce corruption to establish a new legitimacy in the eyes of a wary public. Countries are taking a holistic approach that includes deregulation to reduce opportunities for corruption, enforcement of sanctions through development of special watch-dog agencies and robust judicial systems, and through strengthened civil society institutions, such as an independent press to raise public awareness of the corruption problem.

- Decentralize government to reach citizens. Coun-tries now enjoying—to varying degrees—greater pluralism and democratic participation, are taking a first step toward greater accountability by involving citizens in policy and budget decisions and, in the larger, more advanced countries, by devolving fiscal and administrative responsibilities to decentralized units of government closer to constituents. Such reforms need to be planned carefully, however, to make sure that decentralization does not increase the opportunities for corruption through weakened institutional capacity and supervision.

Experience to Date. The Region is using both lend-ing and nonlending activities to achieve these objec-tives. The Bank has used adjustment lending as its cen-tral instrument of dialogue and financing. As a consequence, our regional commitments doubled from $4.5 billion in fiscal 1997 to over $9 billion in fiscal 1999 and our disbursements increased proportionately to about $5 billion annually. Adjustment loans have supported an extensive dialogue on public sector issues, including macroeconomic policy, revenue and expenditure management, social safety net issues, and state enterprise reform.

Technical assistance (TA) loans in Korea, Thailand and Indonesia have promoted an institutional agenda.

Advice and ESW have also been conduits of policy advice, some of it focused on public sector manage-ment issues, such as tax policy, tax administration, debt management and CSR in Indonesia; macroeconomic policy, revenue and expenditure management and deregulation in the Philippines; and budget manage-ment and regulation in Malaysia and Thailand. This new post-crisis institutional agenda is only just begin-ning. The Bank's contribution has been to catalyze a discussion, convene reform-minded entities, and pro-mote the shared agenda. It has been most successful in situations like Thailand, when the spur of crisis and the vision of local policymakers combined with the techni-cal expertise of the Bank to motivate reform. Indonesia remains more problematic for macroeconomic and political reasons and because the Bank's own experi-ence with the volatile governance agenda is still travel-ing up the learning curve. In all countries, much remains to be done to promote institutional reforms that can help countries weather the current crisis and help sustain reforms well into the millennium.

The challenges ahead. The Region has been pio-neering three new instruments that could be helpful in promoting the dialogue on public sector issues. The first is the use of programmatic public sector reform loans to promote institutional changes over a sustained period. Thailand's Public Sector Reform Program is the first of these. It envisages annual adjustment loans over three years to achieve improvements specified in detailed action programs. These cover expenditure management, human resource management, and improvements in accountability, and will affect core agencies and line ministries. A similar operation is con-templated for the Philippines. The second instrument is the use of the *Social and Structural Reviews.* The first Bank-wide *Social and Structural Review* was undertak-en for Malaysia, with a major focus on the public sec-tor. The Region intends to expand these to as many as five countries in the coming two-year period. In addi-tion, the Region is innovating by placing governance issues more explicitly at the center of country programs. The Indonesia country management unit, for example, now has a senior governance advisor to lead and coordinate a governance and public sector reform strategy that fully integrates cross-sectoral concerns in a coherent country program.

East Asia has also begun piloting *new diagnostic instruments* through surveys of government effectiveness. Corruption surveys have been undertaken in Thailand and Cambodia. In the Philippines, an analytic report on corruption has been presented to government in response to an official request for Bank guidance in developing an anticorruption strategy.

Risks. The emerging market countries run a series of institutional risks, as the Bank proceeds with its new work on public sector reform and governance. In Korea, Thailand and Malaysia, there is a significant risk that economic recovery will reduce country—and Bank—motivation to continue to push for institutional reform. There is also the risk that current reform-minded governments could be replaced by less committed regimes. Indonesia still poses its own particular set of risks. While political stability is not guaranteed, recent elections completed a peaceful political transition to a largely democratic regime that has displayed considerable disposition to public sector and governance reforms. Time will provide the only meaningful test of the new government's resolve to implement serious reforms that introduce a governance system based on real rule of law—which is widely seen as the fundamental requirement for restoring public credibility. On the Bank's part, capacity to help government and civil society achieve these fundamental changes will also be severely challenged. The depth of regional expertise on these issues is limited and the Bank's reputation still needs to be strengthened on these issues. But the CMU has already demonstrated high commitment to raise the visibility and priority of the governance agenda to a central focus of the overall country program.

Small economies

In the smaller economies of the region—Cambodia, Laos, Mongolia, Papua New Guinea (PNG), and Pacific Islands—bilateral donors play a larger role in resource transfers. This means that coordinated donor efforts to improve public sector management is more central—and indeed foreign aid, left uncoordinated, risks contributing to the difficulties of public sector management instead of resolving them.

Progress in smaller countries has been mixed. Fiji is one among the Pacific Island countries that has attempted to improve the management of its expenditures with steady implementation of reforms. Other countries, such as the PNG and Laos, have made much less progress, as poor governance has set back broader reforms.

In these small market countries, prospects for reforms are offset by significant risks. PNG poses particular challenges; dysfunctional administrative and political institutions adversely affect all aspects of development, and reports of pervasive corruption and clientelism abound. The Bank has stepped up the volume and quality of its analysis of these issues. Governance was the central focus of the recent Country Economic Memorandum (CEM) on PNG and features prominently in the upcoming Structural Adjustment Loan. In others among the small countries, such as Cambodia and the Pacific Islands, PERs have been a common instrument of dialogue for performance on this new agenda in the emerging market economies. In Cambodia, the focus on governance followed directions laid out in the CAS. A governance action plan is being constructed with inputs from a Bank-supported survey of households, private businesses, and public officials that polls perceptions of government quality and probity and identifies areas for reform. The Cambodia SAC with a heavy governance focus is reinforcing work on civil service, public expenditure, and legal reform that has been underway through an ongoing TA project. In Laos, an IDF is proposed to address public sector management constraints. Laos has also been the venue for Danish Trust Fund-financed analysis of the institutional impact of IDA lending, as part of a forthcoming cross-national study carried out by the Bank.

Transition economies

The transition economies of China and Vietnam are poorer than the emerging market economies, and they face fundamentally greater institutional challenges in realigning the use of state authority in the economy. To achieve their development objectives, these governments are reducing their authority over resource allocation by widening the scope of market competition and decreasing ownership of assets under state control. In the case of China, the government has taken steps at the local level toward improving fundamental relations of political accountability and institutions of government. The Chinese government has sought to match the pace of fiscal decentralization with improvements in local institutions to manage and account for public resources. The transitions in these dimensions involve a far more complex and sustained institutional transformation than for the market economies of the EA5.

Ironically, because they are less encumbered by checks and balances inherent in open political systems and have a history of command-based planning, these countries have the potential to promote sweeping reforms, once decisions are taken. Also, both countries have greater capacity to control the pace of reform because the crisis has not plunged them into recession.

To rekindle high and sustained growth, the transition countries have to take actions in three areas. First, *rules* governing the operation of the public sector are more informal and discretionary than in other parts of the region. State enterprises and state banks must be reformed and revenue and expenditure relations examined in a context of a new quasi-federalism. Second,

opening up formerly state-dominated sectors to *competition* from the private sector can reap considerable improvements; examples include state enterprise reform, and deregulation of sectors protected by policy-induced barriers. Finally, these countries, like other poor countries with low levels of per capita income, score low on business surveys of accountability, corruption and transparency, and are only now beginning to harness political competition and press oversight to their anticorruption efforts.

Approaches. These countries require sustained attention for the next decade to improvements in public sector management as they make the transition from plan to market. Three major classes of objectives comprise the shared areas of Bank-Government strategy:

- Promoting new forms of transparency in public decisions as a first step toward reducing corruption and enhancing citizen "voice."

- Redefining the relationship of the government to the productive sectors. This implies revamping the ownership and governance of the state enterprises and banks, reshaping the architecture of government to allow competition and to regulate the noncompetitive productive sector, changing civil service rules to end cradle-to-grave protections and rigidities, and implementing complementary sector level reforms.

- Mobilizing revenues more efficiently to ensure a stronger public sector while at the same time revamping revenue and expenditure assignments across levels of government.

Experience to date. To support these objectives, the Bank in China has used project lending as well as advice and ESW as its central instrument of dialogue and financing, since the Chinese government has not requested adjustment support and has been reluctant to borrow on IBRD terms for technical assistance. Vietnam has been more receptive to investment lending, but its content remains to be determined. Both have engaged the Bank amply through its analytic services. Vietnam has also provided an arena for using traditional Bank analytic instruments in new ways. The Vietnam Public Expenditure Review is being carried out on a fully participatory basis, with country nationals actively involved in shaping analysis of public sector issues.

Project lending in roads, power, health and poverty programs have often promoted the three central objectives of public sector reform, even though they were not advertised as such. In power, for example, the Bank's multi-billion dollar program has successfully helped the government unwind from antiquated socialist pricing mechanisms and blurred government and party relations in the governance of power companies. It has helped the government gradually introduce competition to power generation, and even improve transparency of procurement. These are changes of enormous import since they have begun transforming the links between government and productive activity for a major share of the old public sector investment program.

TA loans in China have promoted an institutional agenda of public sector reforms with some success. Our Economic Law Project has had a major influence in the crafting of legislation that enables a market-driven sector to flourish in a modern system of business regulation. Our TA for fiscal policy contributed to the development of a more modern budget system and new regulations for fiscal management and macroeconomic planning.

ESW and conferences have provided a broader policy dialogue in both countries. The recently completed PER for China, for example, focused on institutional reforms in budget management and won a wide hearing after launch at a high-level policy seminar. Also, the seven reports in the *China 2020* series provided advice on institutional reforms in public sector management of state enterprises and banks, environment, pensions and other social programs affecting income distribution, the huge state-managed food distribution system, and the regulation of trade. Reports and policy notes on state enterprises have also proven to be useful. In Vietnam, the Bank has provided the government a steady stream of policy advice on state enterprise and financial sector reform, the institutions of social policy, and rural development. Vietnam has requested our assistance in CSR, but so far, the Bank's ability to respond to this request has been limited.

China's program of reform has been impressive, although, given the difficulties it confronts in the financial system and labor markets, the challenge is to maintain a pace of reform that is fast enough to maintain its high growth. China has made incontrovertible progress in delinking the state's authority from resource allocation—by providing an incentive framework conducive to competition, revamping its financial system, and beginning to tackle the state enterprise questions. It has also progressed in reforming the core institutions of the public sector, notably the system of taxation, fiscal administration and decentralization. Last year's administrative reform entailed a profound realignment of the structures of government with the needs of a market economy. No less important was the adoption of reforms to separate the military from the commercial sector.

While China's economic reform strategy is clear, the government's strategy to improve government responsiveness and the institutions of accountability at all levels of government is less clear. The government is still struggling with decentralized authorities that are not fully accountable to their citizenry, and with the corruption that comes from highly discretionary authority. Vietnam's internal reforms have been more fitful, and in contrast to China, the government has not yet succeeded in unleashing a virtuous circle of market-based reforms that produce growth and new constituencies supporting further reforms.

The challenges ahead. In China, the Region is

developing Learning and Innovations Loans (LILs) to promote pension and enterprise reforms. The objectives are to adapt potential improvements in enterprise reform methods to local circumstances, demonstrate feasibility through pilots, and make lessons from these widely known among local and central policymakers, leading to the replication of promising reform methods beyond the project itself. The project will focus, among other things, public mechanisms to help retrain laid-off state enterprise employees, and promote small business development. In Vietnam, the forthcoming SAC would have a substantial focus on state enterprises and financial sector reform. Programmatic adjustment lending may be eventually useful in supporting public sector and governance reforms in Vietnam, but these programs will have to be developed. Meanwhile, Strategic Compact funding is being used to develop an anticorruption strategy that will bring a range of civil society institutions into the public discourse.

Risks. Success in helping China and Vietnam with public sector reforms hinges critically on the Bank building on its established reputation as a cost-effective source of global knowledge. Several factors confine our role to providing modest input into policy:

- First, these issues involve huge internal political constituencies—ranging from government bureaucracies and state enterprise workers in the tens of millions—that dwarf any Bank influence.

- Second, these governments want access to our financial resources and embodied technical advice, but are not dependent on them. Governments will accept our financial resources only insofar as they see that the benefits in high quality embodied technical assistance and advice in promoting reforms outweigh the financial and preparation costs.

- Third, financial support has been confined to project assistance, and recent limitations on IDA avail-

ability as well as Chinese reluctance to accept TA on IBRD terms precludes much direct help on these issues. This underscores the importance of upgrading the Bank's advice and ESW, and of working intensively at the margin to promote high quality, intellectually driven interventions such as the TA embedded in our regular portfolio and in new instruments such as LILs.

Risks in the region

Threats to the realization of an ambitious policy dialogue in the East Asia and Pacific Region emanate from various sources, but two are particularly noteworthy. For prudential reasons, the Region will not be able to continue adjustment lending in large amounts for long. This may mean that countries, such as Korea, Thailand, and Malaysia, will become less interested in a dialogue with the Bank on these issues. This risk can only be mitigated through ensuring high-quality advice, appropriate structuring of conditions to consolidate steps forward in policy areas of mutual interest rather than dictating conditions high-handedly, and using multiple vehicles of dialogue of interest to the client. Much the same could be said for China.

A second constraint is that in some client countries, domestic politics may prevent effective policy formulation or implementation. The Bank can only deploy a reduced form of *advice and ESW* to maintain a sustained dialogue; simultaneously it can use *advice and ESW* to build bridges to private, reform-minded constituencies. Since these activities are usually not accompanied with a lending program, our internal budgeting mechanisms tend to require that managers assess the effectiveness of these investments against the probability of near-term pay-off in renewed political will to implement public sector reform.

Organization and staffing

The Region has begun to build a public sector cluster in the EASPR unit to help governments implement the institutional agenda. While this will spearhead the agenda described above, it will need to match resources and skills to the demand for specialized expertise on public sector reform and governance. Given the cross-sectoral nature of this institutional work, it will need to coordinate closely with other EAP units, which will play important roles. The PSI unit is heading up the state enterprise reform agenda in China, for example, and advises on competition policy and deregulation. The Legal Department is handling most legal and judicial reform activities and has advised on regulatory reforms in other areas. The Bank's Special Financial Operations Unit (SFO) has headed up the Region's activities in the financial sector. ESSD, HD, and FPSI staff are deeply involved in social, sectoral and subnational aspects of the larger governance agenda. A social policy and governance group has been meeting regularly in the Region to facilitate cross-sectoral institutional work.

To build an effective public sector cluster within the Region, EAP has hired a full time Lead Specialist in the Public Sector and has now recruited four additional professionals (including the Indonesia governance position) to begin to fill the skill gap in the areas of administrative and civil service reform, public financial management, and decentralization. With such constrained resources, public sector work in EAP has to be selective. Direct operational support for CSR, anticorruption activities and broader governance work has, of necessity, been limited. The cluster's efforts have been leveraged through its work in concert with the eight or so economists in PREM—in HQ and the field—and with CMU and sectoral staff who are presently spending a significant portion of their time carrying out the work program in the public sector. A challenge will be to develop a professional cadre with network-standard skills to deliver on the public sector agenda. In this effort, the public sector group will also work closely with the social policy secretariat, where anticorruption efforts spanning both the private and public sectors are integrated for the Region as a whole.

Strengthening partnerships

The Region has appointed an external advisory group on governance and anticorruption to broaden our thinking on these challenges. The group includes senior figures from the Region, and has so far met three times with the Region's management team to discuss strategic directions.

The Bank is working in coordination with IMF's Fiscal Affairs Department and its Public Expenditure Division. For example, in Thailand, IMF consultants on tax and customs administration are working with our PSRL mission to implement jointly sponsored programs. In Vietnam, public expenditures efforts were coordinated through joint missions. In Mongolia, our fiscal TA program is coordinated with the Fund.

The Bank has collaborated loosely with the ADB, primarily in the common agendas of the financial sector. The potential upside to increased collaboration is great: the ADB routinely offers our client countries tens of millions of dollars in technical assistance grants, and in most countries without formal country donor meetings, this is implemented with little if any Bank involvement. Similarly, the Bank could work more closely in its projects and analytic work with the ADB. Impediments on both sides include distance, staff overload, and differing internal agendas.

The Bank is also collaborating with other partners in the region around specific projects, for example, with the UNDP, USAID and the Asia Foundation during the development of the anticorruption work in the Philippines.

Cambodia: Public Expenditure Review

Type of Activity: Analytic and Advisory Activity
Timing: Initiating memorandum February 20, 1998; Final report January 8, 1999

Summary of Contents

The Cambodia Public Expenditure Review (PER) undertakes, for the first time, a systematic review of the adequacy and effectiveness of public expenditures in Cambodia. Rather than narrowly focusing on expenditure issues, the PER takes a broader approach—it closely links public expenditure issues to revenue mobilization and governance problems because reforms to enhance the effectiveness of public expenditures need to be implemented in a comprehensive context. While the PER analyzes sector-specific issues for various sectors within the overall framework, it provides a more in-depth analysis of the health and education sectors because of their direct relevance to poverty reduction through human resource development. The PER was prepared as the main document for discussion at the Consultative Group (CG) meeting.

Innovative / Risky Elements

The PER tackles governance issues as a critical impediment to sustainable development in Cambodia, in particular through estimating the extent of revenue loss resulting from weak governance. It estimates foregone revenues with credible accuracy based on known information and assesses the potential for enhancing revenue mobilization, a prerequisite for effective expenditure policy in Cambodia. The PER also constructs, in close collaboration with government, a consolidated public expenditure database, encompassing expenditures incurred by the government, donors and NGOs, and analyzes the level and composition of this more complete picture of public sector expenditures with government. In addition, the PER assesses the implications of the institutional arrangements and management practices in the budget process on determining budget outcomes, and makes specific recommendations for reforming institutional procedures in view of Cambodia's weak institutional capacity. The Cambodia PER received a "best practice" rating from a QAG assessment panel.

Partnerships

The Bank team collaborated extensively with the Government in establishing and analyzing the consolidated public expenditure database. The IMF contributed the chapter on "Macroeconomic Framework, Resource Envelope, and Public Expenditures" in consultation with the Bank team. The UNDP socioeconomic survey formed the basis of the health and education sector sections, as did consultation with WHO, UNICEF and UNESCO.

Indonesia: Governance Partnership

Type of Activity: Grant-based Activity
Timing: November 1999. First Board meeting:May 2000
Loan Amount: $1 million, funded by IDF, Dutch & Australian governments

Summary of Contents

The Partnership's main objective is to help establish strong institutional building blocks for governance in Indonesia. It will function as a knowledge-sharing arena, a consensus-building forum, and a vehicle for strategy development and coordination of the various critical facets of the reform process. It will pursue this aim by:

- Generating and disseminating knowledge on good practice in governance from Indonesia and abroad,

- Coordinating the governance reform efforts of Government, donors, and civil society, and

- Funding initiatives to promote reform of governance in Indonesia.

The partnership will support activities in five key areas where governance reforms are urgently needed:

- Reform of democratic non-executive governing institutions;

- Regional autonomy and effective decentralization of government service delivery;

- Core executive public sector capacity building;

- Civil society strengthening; and

- Anticorruption initiatives.

The Partnership will help identify effective approaches by promoting a broad national consultation process involving participatory assessment and wide dissemination of results. The aim is to reach consensus on a realistic strategy to affect and monitor key reforms.

Innovative / Risky Elements

The governing structure of the Partnership is an innovative arrangement between the World Bank and the UNDP. The Partnership's activities will fall under two components: the Facility for Policy Dialogue and Analysis, and the Trust Fund to support capacity building for good governance. The partnership is not intended to be a permanent structure; it is seen as a transitional mechanism to engender a longer-term governance agenda that will eventually be sustained by national institutions. The phase-out plan will contain a plan for transferring the partnership's activities to Indonesian organizations. The Partnership will provide a mechanism to transfer knowledge and expertise on governance transitions and to catalyze the initial stages of an ongoing national governance debate, helping to bring together diverse groups in government and civil society. This approach can also serve as a potential model for other countries where independent support for embryonic national governance institutions is needed.

Partnerships

In this joint undertaking, the Bank has submitted proposals for financing to IDF and bilateral funding sources, while Trust Fund financing will be arranged by UNDP with Bank consultation. The Executive Board running the Partnership will comprise representatives from UNDP, the Bank, Government of Indonesia, and civil society.

Thailand: Public Sector Reform Loan

Type of Activity: Loan, Programmatic Structural Adjustment Loan
Timing: Board Approval: October 14, 1999; Reform program defined over a 3-year period
Loan Amount: $400 million for first stage of reforms

Summary of Contents

Thailand's PSRL seeks to improve public sector governance and enhance the efficiency, effectiveness, equity, and transparency of public resource management and service delivery. The reform involves both central agencies and line ministries such as education and health, which have embarked upon substantial reforms to deliver better services. Its core components include a more performance-oriented budget system, a flexible and effective civil service, and greater transparency. Reforms are being implemented in (a) expenditure management, (b) human resources management, (c) revenue management, (d) decentralization, and (e) cross-government accountability and transparency.

Innovative / Risky Elements

The PSAL framework of a three-year program of technical and financial assistance provided by the Bank, with flexible performance benchmarks, is ideally suited to the Government's reform program. However, improvements in the Thai economy have occurred both sooner and with greater depth than had been anticipated when the PSRL was presented to the Board. The Government's need for financing has diminished substantially while its commitment to the reform program remains strong. This presents an opportunity for redefining the Bank's role in supporting the Thai program with less emphasis on financial assistance and greater emphasis on technical assistance and facilitation, and monitoring of reform progress.

Partnerships

The Governments of Australia and New Zealand have provided significant technical assistance in support of the Thai reform program that has been well coordinated with ongoing Bank activities. The UNDP has been active in supporting decentralization and general governance issues, also in complementary ways.

Europe and Central Asia Region (ECA)

The Europe and Central Asia Region's strategy for public sector institutional reform reflects the formidable challenges stemming from the unique institutional legacy of the previous system and the institutional flux resulting from dramatic political and economic transition since the collapse of the Soviet Union. What distinguishes transition from reforms in other countries is the systemic change involved: reform must penetrate to the fundamental "rules of the game" that shape behavior and guide organizations. Reform programs in other countries often pale in comparison to the scale and intensity of the systemic transition from plan to market.

The Region's involvement in institutional reform is recent, and has intensified over the last two years. Key features of our recent work and forward-looking strategy are: (a) an emphasis on building in the users' perspective and strengthening public oversight, with the aim of focusing attention on outcomes and more importantly, generating external, demand-side pressures for reform in the face of powerful internal resistance and weak checks and balances on the state; (b)

diagnosing institutional dysfunction and developing quantitative performance indicators for benchmarking and monitoring progress; (c) an aggressive thrust on anticorruption in countries where corruption is blocking the process of policy and institutional reform and where entry points can be identified; (d) the establishment of a cohesive unit devoted to public sector reform with a balanced skill mix that can spearhead work on new dimensions (including "voice" and participation, and quantitative indicators); and (e) a recognition of the especially difficult and complex challenge of reform in ECA, our limited record of experience, and hence the imperative for managing expectations and actively learning from ongoing efforts.

Experience to date in the Region

The experience in the Region reflects an evolution of priorities from first-generation economic policy reforms with accompanying technical assistance to a greater focus recently on deeper institutional reforms.

The latter approach, however, is at an early stage, and the emphasis is on learning from early experience and refining the operational strategy in an iterative process.

Technical assistance: The early years. When the Bank began supporting ECA countries in the early 1990s, the most immediate challenge was to initiate the process of transition with extremely limited institutional capacity for policy design and implementation. These countries needed to implement quickly a series of policy measures to steer the economies away from heavy state intervention. At the same time, longer-term objectives of transition required building entirely different sets of institutions in both the public and private sectors.

At this early stage, the Bank concentrated on the more immediate policy reform measures with a strong emphasis on macroeconomic stabilization, liberalization, and privatization. The balance between economic policy and institutional reforms also reflected the belief that privatization, the creation of markets, and private sector development were essential for creating an effective *demand* for institutions and the required check and balance upon the state. During these years, the Bank's typical instrument was Institution-Building/Technical Assistance (IBTA) projects, which were designed to augment in the short run the weak institutional capacity of the client government to carry out the necessary policy and structural reforms. The IBTA projects were often the first Bank lending operations in these countries, and thus were designed with very limited country knowledge by Bank staff. They typically covered a wide range of reform areas without tight strategic linkages among them.

The performance of these TA projects seems to have been generally poor. According to a recent QAG review, the early ECA TA projects suffered from weak client commitment and turned into information technology projects with a limited prospect of sustainable impact on institution-building. A review of these projects' components also indicates that there was relative-

ly little variation across countries, suggesting country-specific factors were not adequately taken into account in their designs.[4]

Initiation of broader institutional reforms: The mid-1990s. In the mid-1990s the Region began to develop two types of approaches to supporting public sector institutional reform. The first addressed public resource management and aspects of administrative reforms in the context of adjustment operations. In the Kyrgyz Republic, a number of institutional improvements were accomplished, including a comprehensive modification of the Law on the Principles of the Budget, initiation of a medium-term financial planning process, inclusion of all public investments in the budget, and strengthening of the audit and public procurement systems. The Kazakhstan operation covered these areas, as well as public administration and CSR. The second type of approach aimed to support, in a focused manner, specific functions of the state, such as tax administration (Albania), public finance including the treasury system (Kazakhstan, Ukraine, Hungary), and legal systems (Russia) in order to build up both technical and organizational foundations for modern public administration.

Supporting deeper institutional reforms: The recent years. The last couple of years have witnessed a significant expansion in the scale, scope and depth of public sector institutional reform activities in the Region. The Region signaled its commitment and the importance of public sector institutional reform by setting up an enhanced unit on public sector institutional reform within PREM. Recent work has built upon reform efforts initiated during the mid-1990s, and is trying to deepen its approach to address more fundamental institutional reforms in *fiscal management* (effective linkage of policymaking and budgeting through the introduction of medium-term expenditure frameworks in Bosnia and Herzegovina), *public administration and civil service* (reforming cabinet decisionmaking, and instituting a merit-based civil service in Kazakhstan and Ukraine) and *legal, regulatory, and judicial reform* (an informed and consultative system of legal drafting in Russia, toward an independent and accountable judiciary in Albania, and inspectorate reform in Latvia). Furthermore, we are working to integrate work across these thematic areas and forge closer links to develop truly integrated approaches to public sector institutional reforms (more closely linking the core legal and judicial reforms with administrative reform by developing a system of administrative law in Azerbaijan, strengthening the accountability mechanisms in the management of financial and human resources in Estonia, and introducing performance and financial performance monitoring in Latvia).

As laid out at the beginning of this paper, we have begun to introduce new strategic elements in our work. These include an enhanced and explicit focus on diagnosing and reforming incentives governing public sector performance, strengthening "voice" and participation, and addressing corruption and checks and balances. To this end, we have made a significant investment in building our knowledge base through analytic work, and we have increased lending operations in both adjustment and accompanying TA.

Diagnosing institutional dysfunction and developing quantitative performance benchmarks. Recent ESW and lending work is seeking to develop quantitative indicators of public sector performance, and link these with hard measurements of associated institutional arrangements (including civil service, policy capacity, and expenditure management). These are then used for setting benchmarks for improvement and designing methods for monitoring whether they have been improved.

Within ESW, the Institutional and Governance Review for Armenia illustrates the Region's pioneering attempts to diagnose institutions in a systematic and rigorous fashion, and develop a program of actions to be supported by follow-up operations. This IGR examines quantitative indicators of public sector performance, and then focuses on the health sector as a microcosm to examine problematic outcomes, and the institutional weaknesses that help explain these outcomes, such as weaknesses in contracting mechanisms, civil service incentives, budget unpredictability, and arbitrariness in policy choice. This serves as the launching pad to examine cross-cutting issues in budget management, civil service and cabinet decisionmaking, and accountability and checks and balances on the Executive. The analysis will help us identify concrete entry points for reform to be supported by follow-up operations with explicit performance benchmarks.

Similarly, recent public sector reform loans explicitly develop quantitative benchmarks of public sector performance and associated institutional reforms that are monitored as an integral part of the operation. For instance, the Albania SAC and its companion technical assistance project develop performance and institutional reform benchmarks for each major component (policy formulation and coordination, legal and judicial reform, public administration, service delivery, and mechanisms for oversight). What makes this particularly powerful is the emphasis on public dissemination of these benchmarks and its monitoring by parliament and civil society.

In Azerbaijan, we deferred requests for immediate lending, and opted for an approach that aims to build consensus within government on reform priorities with a public sector strategy paper, and to involve nongovernmental stakeholders in workshops to foster ownership. The strategy paper covers a broad gamut of issues such as budget management, audit, procurement, public administration and civil service, and legal and judicial reform. The emphasis is not only on building basic systems, but also on enhancing transparency and accountability by institutionalizing beneficiary surveys on the quality of service delivery. We are in the process of initiating medium-term programmatic lending with supporting TA.

Our approach to single-purpose TA operations is also to tightly weave together quantitative performance benchmarks, associated institutional reforms, and the user perspective. In Latvia, for example, we have supplemented the necessary information technology for modernizing the tax system with explicit measures to improve the management of the organization, including institutionalizing appeals processes and feedback mechanisms such as taxpayer surveys as performance benchmarks. The Russia Treasury operation is similarly using expenditure tracking surveys and deviations between budgets and actuals both to diagnose the underlying institutional dysfunction and to set explicit performance benchmarks for assessing improvements in systemic reforms being supported by the project.

Enhanced emphasis on "voice" and participation. Closely related to the emphasis on benchmarking performance, the Region has begun to explore options other than strengthening internal systems and hierarchy, by strengthening citizen "voice." As mentioned above, "voice" options have become common features of Bank lending operations, such as public monitoring of institutional reforms and public sector performance in recent adjustment and investment operations. The public dissemination of anticorruption surveys in Albania, Georgia, and Latvia is explicitly designed to build public oversight of the governments' anticorruption programs and strengthen checks and balances. The People's Voice Program in Ukraine is another innovative attempt to build civil society participation and institutionalize service delivery surveys at the local level. The Bank-funded Urban Land Management Project in Albania is mobilizing slum residents into formal community associations that contribute monetarily to the provision of certain infrastructure in exchange for a right to regularize and legalize their informal land titles. Such operations can contribute to strengthening public sector institutions in at least two ways: first, the development of strong community associations (social capital) can result in effective partnership with the public sector for better service delivery; and second, the same community associations can serve as citizens' watchdog organizations to provide oversight of the state at the local level.

Given the relative weakness of civil society organizations in the region, the incorporation of user perspectives in reform design through surveys is a promising approach. We intend to expand its use, while refining the methodology and developing more varied choices of survey instruments. Simultaneously, the workshops and anticorruption activities that we are supporting are helping to mobilize local NGOs in Georgia, Latvia, and Ukraine, so that they can play a more active role as both watchdogs of government actions and as alternative means of public service delivery. Our emerging conditionality in adjustment operations is requiring governments to publicize the findings of user surveys and their accompanying action plans, as well as periodically and publicly to report on progress in implementing actions and to repeat surveys as benchmarks.

Anticorruption initiatives. Countries in transition rank particularly poorly with respect to corruption, and some governments in the region have requested Bank assistance in combating it. Our approach has been to encourage a firmly country-driven program with the Bank playing only a catalytic role. We have had dialogue with the highest levels of government, and encouraged them to set up high-level working groups, consisting not just of the Executive but also of other branches of government and civil society. One aspect of this catalytic role has been for the Bank to show cross-country empirical evidence that corruption is not just a law enforcement problem, but a symptom of underlying problems stemming from a distorted policy environment and weak institutions of restraint. This has led us to advocate a multi-pronged strategy for combating corruption, combining economic policy reforms

FIGURE 6 Results of Diagnostic Surveys

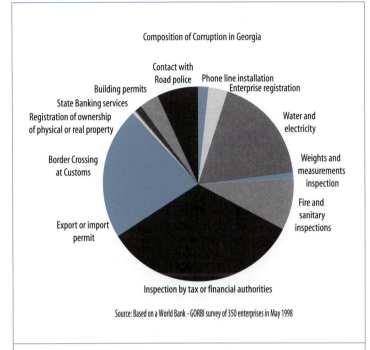

Composition of Corruption in Georgia

Contact with Road police
Phone line installation
Enterprise registration
Building permits
State Banking services
Registration of ownership of physical or real property
Water and electricity
Border Crossing at Customs
Weights and measurements inspection
Fire and sanitary inspections
Export or import permit
Inspection by tax or financial authorities

Source: Based on a World Bank - GORBI survey of 350 enterprises in May 1998

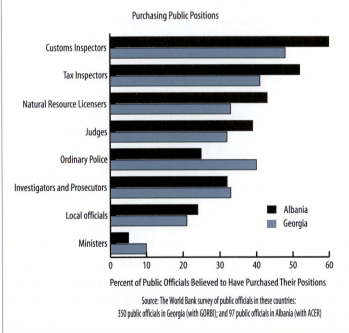

Purchasing Public Positions

Customs Inspectors
Tax Inspectors
Natural Resource Licensers
Judges
Ordinary Police
Investigators and Prosecutors
Local officials
Ministers

■ Albania
■ Georgia

Percent of Public Officials Believed to Have Purchased Their Positions

Source: The World Bank survey of public officials in these countries:
350 public officials in Georgia (with GORBI); and 97 public officials in Albania (with ACER)

(deregulation, delicensing), financial controls (audits, procurement), CSR, legal/judicial reform, and building public oversight and transparency.

To advance the anticorruption work, the Region has—in collaboration with DEC/WBI—pioneered the use of diagnostic surveys to identify the pattern and profile of corruption in particular countries. This has included administering three survey instruments: the first, for households ranking the extent of corruption and satisfaction with service delivery by public agencies; the second, for enterprises identifying activities and agencies for which they have to pay illicitly; and the third, for public officials asking how much they have to pay to purchase public positions (Figure 6). The results of these diagnostics have been presented in public workshops, often with powerful impact. They have helped to give concrete substance to the rhetoric of anticorruption, and helped generate a momentum in client countries to act on the specific patterns of corruption.

Recognizing the risk that governments may respond to such results and pressures by political scapegoating and firing individuals, we have emphasized the reforms to address directly underlying institutional dysfunction that create opportunities for corruption. For instance, the structural adjustment credit and supporting TA in Albania tackle two key sources of corruption: patronage in judicial appointments and the civil service. In particular, we are supporting measures to test the professional qualifications of all judges with less than 10 years of experience, and take appropriate actions against those that do not qualify. We are also helping the government to institute a merit-based civil service for the first time, through introduction of competitive and transparent recruitment processes. And to strengthen public oversight and transparency, the program requires government to publicize its anticorruption action plan (including the findings of the diagnostics on the nature and profile of corruption), as well as monitor and publicly report progress in implementing the action plan, together with NGOs.

In Georgia, the diagnostic work reveals excessive licensing and regulations as the principal sources of corruption. Our strategy has been to leverage the Strategic Compact funds for upstream country dialogue and consensus-building among the various stakeholders; to utilize the existing procurement IDF and the SAC III to put in place the legal and institutional framework for procurement, licensing and tax administration reform; and to follow up with a future operation that deepens and extends the institutional reforms so far achieved.

In Latvia, the diagnostic revealed that high-level corruption is quite serious. The Government has clearly acknowledged this problem, and asked for our support in developing a strategy to address these and other problems of governance. Together, we prepared a programmatic SAL, which included a comprehensive three-year plan for reform of public administration, budget management, the judiciary, and regulation of infrastructure monopolies and other firms. A key feature of this program is the strengthening of institutions to reveal and resolve conflicts of interest, which are at the heart of the problem of high-level corruption.

Finally, we are seeking to mainstream a concern for corruption by building anticorruption measures into the design of sectoral projects, such as the competitive restructuring of gas sectors or in the reform of health systems. As explained further below, progress in this area has been slow, but we are advancing.

The challenges ahead

Mainstreaming. The Region has made only limited progress in mainstreaming an institutional focus in recent years. The challenge is to learn about institutional reform in other sectors and help fine-tune and facilitate such reforms in conjunction with the broader public sector reform strategy. While ECSPE concentrates its activities on reforming and developing core government functions, parallel efforts at strengthening policymaking, regulatory and service delivery capacities in various sectors are imperative for the Region's work in institutional reform as a whole to have an ultimate impact on the ground.

Efforts to mainstream institutional issues are underway. The recent CASs on Azerbaijan, Albania, Bulgaria, and Russia for instance, accord a central role to governance and public sector institutional reform. These CASs not only support reform of the core public sector and cross-cutting anticorruption initiatives as a principal priority, but also seek to improve governance and public sector reform in the design of sectoral projects. The CAS for Azerbaijan seeks to introduce governance indicators (user satisfaction from service delivery and reduction of corruption levels) as core benchmarks.

Mainstreaming also requires giving attention to cross-cutting institutional issues. One such issue is the role of project implementation units (PIUs) in Bank-financed projects, and their impacts on institutional development. PIUs play useful roles in project management, particularly in those countries where the government's capacity to manage development projects is minimal. But there is now evidence that use of stand-alone PIUs often frustrates long-term institutional development by creating enclaves within the public sector and distorting incentives of the staff both within and outside the PIUs. The Region is conducting a systematic review of PIUs, with a view toward enhancing institutional development while still ensuring effective project implementation.

To support efforts at mainstreaming, we propose a three-part strategy of collaboration with country and sector units in the Region.

- *Country Focus:* ECSPE in collaboration with other sector units will work with a country unit to develop a comprehensive approach to institutional reform across major sectors in a given country. Such an effort could start with an IGR or a public sector strategy paper. Needless to say, strong leadership and coordination by the country director will be essential for such an arrangement to be effective. This strategy has been piloted in Latvia. Armenia and Azerbaijan also may be appropriate candidates for piloting this approach.

- *Sector Focus:* In addition, ECSPE will collaborate with a particular sector unit to develop a coherent sector institutional reform strategy across several countries. Given the progress made in the Armenia IGR, the health sector seems to be a promising area for such a collaboration. This collaborative effort will entail helping conduct institutional assessments for the particular sector (health) in a few key countries and participating in the design and supervision of institutional reform and development components of sector projects.

- *Thematic Focus:* The third modality is to pick a cross-cutting institutional issue—(for instance, public expenditure management)—and work with several sector units in several countries. ECSPE could provide support in assessing public expenditure management at the sectoral level and contribute to designing and supervising project components in this area.

Assessing political readiness for reform and building consensus. Institutional reform alters the incentives facing politicians, bureaucrats and other social elites. Thus, even if reform is necessary for development, the political leadership may not find it desirable. Even if the leadership desires change, the opposition may block implementa-tion. We first look for the credible commitment of the highest-level government officials as a necessary step to initiate a dialogue. For those countries with more tentative commitment, we ask the government to take an even tougher set of up-front actions to demonstrate its readiness.[5] Despite these attempts, it remains to be seen whether powerful losers from reform will nevertheless prevail in blocking institutional reforms that the Region is supporting.

Activities and instruments. We envisage an enhanced emphasis on ESW to improve continuously our understanding of "what exists on the ground" and to draw lessons from reform experiences. We expect the Armenia IGR to serve as a useful pilot for providing an analytically and empirically rigorous but practical document to inform our understanding of institutional realities and the sequence of operations to support. PERs will inextricably weave in institutional dimensions of public expenditure management as a regular feature. For example, the Macedonia Public Expenditure and Institutional Review will analyze not only the sustainability of the fiscal program, but also its institutional drivers, particularly the rigidity in the expenditure program and the decision-making process. Other ESW, such as the CEMs on EU accession countries, will also continue to have institutional chapters diagnosing realities on the ground relative to the requirements of accession.

An important ECA initiative that has contributed to our understanding of the problem of corruption in the post-communist world is the preparation of a report entitled *Anticorruption in Transition: A Contribution to the Policy Debate.* This report, which was released at the 2000 Annual Meetings in Prague, examines forms of corruption in transition economies, including the problem of "state capture" in some countries whereby powerful economic interests purchase decrees and legislation for their private benefit. The report traces the origins and consequences of corruption, and highlights the reforms that lead to improvement. While the document itself has been valuable for the audience at the Annual Meetings, the process of developing the report has afforded ECSPE an opportunity to step back and evaluate the state of knowledge about anticorruption reforms. Next year, we are planning an initiative that more broadly examines the performance of public sector, as well as private sector institutions, with the goal of developing a strategy to promote the mainstreaming of institutional reforms.

As for lending instruments, ECSPE plans to move more systematically and aggressively toward longer-term programmatic lending instruments (PSALs, and APLs), with disbursements conditional upon improvements in system performance. Presently, we envisage PSAL-type operations for Macedonia, Bulgaria, Armenia and Georgia. We expect these longer-term programmatic adjustment loans to be accompanied by supporting TA. We also envisage more operations like the Ukraine Public Sector APL, which will approach reform of institutions in key areas on a sequential basis over a period of time.

One of the lessons of experience is the importance of ensuring that adjustment and TA operations complement each other. Adjustment operations tend to bring high-level financial leverage to place appropriate institutional issues on the government's agenda and to induce necessary policy changes. But they do not allow the Bank to offer day-to-day input into the quality and nature of the technical assistance, which is still critical for supporting concrete actions for institutional reform and development. TA operations alone, on the other hand, run the risk of supporting discrete activities without an overall strategic program that is required for comprehensive and sustained implementation of the reform efforts. TA operations may also lack leverage to bring about difficult, yet necessary, policy actions. Furthermore, many countries in the region have been reluctant to borrow from the Bank for TA partly because other donors offer TA on a grant basis. As long as TA serves an important purpose of transferring our technical knowledge to the client countries, the Region needs to reflect further on how best to use TA in considering the appropriateness of some of the newly proposed lending instruments, such as PSALs.

Organization, staffing, and partnerships. The Region has set up a strong unit on public sector institutional reform. The group is staffed with specialists who, as a group, combine thematic specialization in core areas, analytic skills, as well as practitioner experience. The demand for public sector work from country units has increased rapidly, which has been reflected in the growth of ECSPE to around 30 staff, including some in the field. No further expansion is planned at this stage except in audit and tax administration, where we are seeking a sharing arrangement with other Regions or the network anchor. Rather than spread ourselves too thin, the objective is to consolidate, focus on existing commitments, and go deeper in existing areas with a view to achieving demonstrable success. The challenge is for the team to continue to function as a cohesive unit, sharing experiences and seeing reforms in our client countries through over a period of time.

A major goal of our strategy work is to solidify existing external and internal partnerships and build new ones. Only a comprehensive approach is likely to pay real dividends, and the Bank simply cannot do it all by itself, given the limitations of expertise and the constraints imposed by its role and mandate. Indeed, other multilateral and bilateral aid organizations, such as SIGMA, EU-Tacis, and EU-Phare, have considerable experience in assisting ECA countries in public sector reform. Close collaboration with the EU is an integral part of our strategy to support EU accession in general, and to strengthen public sector institutional capacity in particular. Close relationships should also be maintained with various public administration commissions and concerned foundations and NGOs, as well as relevant academic and other institutions.

Managing expectations and institutionalizing learning. Our work with public sector institutional reform is at an early stage. Reform in this area is complex, often politically very difficult, and takes time. The Soviet legacy and the dynamics of the transition make our tasks even more challenging. One central challenge is to manage the expectations of quick fixes. Another is to institutionalize a learning process to adapt and fine-tune our operational strategy as we proceed. We have yet to see whether our emerging knowledge base, the design of our operations, and the implementation of reforms indeed yield intended results. It will be critical to build evaluation and performance monitoring into our work. We are using both the Bank-wide and the cluster thematic groups to engage in a learning process. However, results of learning are not always easy to measure, and therefore expectations about outcomes should be appropriately modulated.

The importance of these lessons have also been disseminated in the Prague 2000 report *Anticorruption in Transition*, which highlights the magnitude of the challenge and the importance of managing expectations.

Armenia: Institutional and Governance Review

Type of Activity: Analytic and Advisory Activity
Timing: Fiscal 2000

Summary of Contents

The Armenia IGR focuses on:

- Country-level empirical diagnostics, detailed examination of specific potential targets of reform, and the resulting implications for strengthening public institutions consistent with the political realities that emerge from the analysis. The IGR is examining: (a) the current status of public sector performance and development of key public institutions and (b) the underlying causes.

- The hypothesis is that the two critical institutional issues confronting Armenia are the unbalanced development of policy capacity, and underdeveloped institutions of accountability. The IGR attempts to draw conclusions for expected future outcomes, providing policy recommendations, especially on sequencing reform for achieving sustainable institutional development. The policy recommendations cover core institutional and governance-related reform areas such as public expenditure management, public service reform and decisionmaking processes.

- Moreover, the IGR emphasizes the importance of explicitly addressing institutional concerns to improve sectoral policymaking and service delivery (using the health sector as an example).

Innovative / Risky Elements

The Armenia IGR is the pilot IGR for the ECA Region.

- It takes into account the broader political and institutional context, as well as exogenous shocks that influence or constrain reform opportunities. An assessment of the political economy behind institutional constraints and opportunities has been a crucial input into the IGR. This considerably expands the boundaries of work so far since it explores political economy issues.

- It emphasizes the importance of institutional reforms and issues for sectoral policymaking and implementation, an area that has been neglected so far. The IGR is an important step in mainstreaming institutional concerns into the Bank's broader agenda, as it shows that institutional reforms should be an integral part of any sectoral reform agenda and that institutional dysfunction, if not taken into account, can affect or even counter sectoral reform approaches.

- It is a pioneering attempt to develop quantitative tools for assessing public sector performance and a range of specific assessment instruments and approaches for replication in other countries.

Partnerships

During the preparation of the IGR all development partners including UNDP have been consulted. It is expected that the IGR will form the basis for subsequent operational work in this area. Since institutional reforms require substantive technical assistance, this will involve close coordination with UNDP.

Latvia: Governance PSAL

Type of Activity: Loan
Timing: 2000 – 2003
Loan Amount: $100 million (tentative)

Summary of Contents

To support the Government of Latvia in its reform process, the Bank has prepared a Governance PSAL. The PSAL considers a 3-year reform horizon, emphasizing in the first year, the design of the reform program and in subsequent years, its implementation. A special set of benchmarks consists of achievements in anticorruption at the legislative and executive level and in the judiciary, including specific actions to target conflict of interest and to support the separation of powers. Further benchmarks measure achievements in introducing greater efficiency and transparency in the public sector. They include: (a) strengthening the institutions that coordinate and monitor public sector and anticorruption reform; (b) supporting the development of instruments for multi-year planning and control, including budget management and performance monitoring; (c) reforming the institutional structure of the public sector; (d) strengthening the incentives and accountability of public sector employees; (e) rationalizing the interaction between the public and private sectors by streamlining the system of regulation and fostering privatization; (f) introducing mechanisms for the public to provide feedback on the performance of the public sector as well as to litigate against the state; and (g) increasing the access of public to public sector information.

Innovative / Risky Elements

One of the most innovative and politically challenging elements of this agenda is the reform of public sector agencies. In a number of developed countries, a decision has been taken to devolve some public sector functions to autonomous agencies. These agencies are designed to operate based on private sector principles that combine flexibility in personnel and budget management with adequate accountability mechanisms. The types of functions that are best delegated to agencies are those functions whose performance is most easy to monitor using quantitative indicators. Unfortunately, GoL has devolved a broader set of functions to autonomous agencies, most of which cannot be easily monitored because appropriate accountability mechanisms were not put in place. Agencies favor this status for this reason and because the restrictive system of public sector pay, as well as other regulations, do not bind them. The overuse of autonomous agencies has resulted in much informality, waste, and abuse, and is believed to be an important source of corruption in the system and of loss of control over budget resources. The PSAL agenda includes establishing a legal framework for the creation and transparent operation of agencies, and implementing it within a two-year framework. The success of this reform is closely linked to success in other parts of the PSAL agenda, most notably the reform of public sector pay and promotion practices.

Russia: Russian Federation Treasury

Type of Activity: Loan
Timing: Fiscal 2000-06
Loan Amount: $200 million

Summary of Contents

The project has been designed as a response to the Government's request for assistance in developing a modern treasury. While the proposed project will address the core requirements for establishing treasury functions, the design of the program has been developed from an assessment of broader institutional weaknesses in the budget management system. As core support for treasury development, the project will provide technical assistance, computer equipment and software and training to enable the Government to design and implement procedures and systems, related regulations and training programs for budget execution, treasury operations and cash management. Design of the project also includes institutional review of the treasury function, its interdependence with other functions of budget formulation and audit, and subsidiary components of the project are expected to provide support in these areas. The investment is designed as an APL. A broad set of monitoring indicators capture not only effectiveness of treasury controls, but also other aspects of the budget system, especially budget formulation and audit, which are essential for the treasury reform to lead to substantial improvements in budget performance and transparency. The indicators will be used in adjusting the focus of later phases of the program to ensure support for any emerging weak areas in the broader program.

Innovative / Risky Elements

Implementation of the treasury system in Russia is a key requirement for strengthening public expenditure control and the transparency of the fiscal system. The project follows other experience in the Region and elsewhere in supporting treasury development, but locates such support within a broader budget management agenda and proposes to use some recently developed monitoring tools in order to identify primary bottlenecks in the program. The project and the treasury development program are linked with the wider country program. First, implementation of the treasury program is included as a key element in CAS triggers. In line with the new guidelines proposed for adjustment lending, the counterpart funds from SAL3 and other adjustment loans are tracked to ensure disbursement into an account under treasury control and supporting only public expenditure funded from the Treasury Single Account, thus reinforcing support for treasury development and encouraging rapid expansion of the scope of the coverage of the treasury system.

Latin America and Caribbean Region (LCR)

The Bank began its public sector and institutional reform operations in LCR in the early 1980s, primarily to support structural adjustment and economic liberalization. Most early operations focused on strengthening core government functions so that countries could cope with economic crises. By the late 1980s and early 1990s, public sector operations adopted a "modernization" approach, aimed at developing technical building blocks to improve the agility and effectiveness of public sector management.

A mixed reform record over the past two decades has made the particular challenges posed by LCR public sectors more apparent than they were originally. In light of a growing recognition of the complexities of public sector reform, LCSPR operations are beginning to tackle broader and deeper institutional issues. The institutional focus is reflected both in the Bank's involvement in new lending areas (decentralization and subnational government reform, judicial reform, anti-corruption), and in new approaches to project design and implementation ("voice" and participation; "exit" and competition; change and better enforcement of internal rules and regulations) even in traditional

public sector reform areas. Work in these new areas with new approaches requires stronger, broader and deeper commitments for sustainable implementation and challenges the Bank to become more strategically selective. More preparatory analytic work will be crucial for gauging the likelihood of success in these more difficult areas.

Salient characteristics of the Latin America and Caribbean Region

Following World War II in the region, activist governments led a push for economic development through industrialization. One of the most notable side effects of the predominant import substitution model of industrialization was the dramatic growth in the region's public sectors. At the onset of the debt crisis in the early 1980s, inefficient public sectors with large numbers of public employees were closely involved in a broad range of economic activities.

The LCR stands out in the developing world because of its particularly strong reform history, driven by democratization and the debt crisis. With the consolidation of democracy in the 1980s, civil society voiced strong demands for change, including more transparency, opportunities for participation, and less corruption among government leaders. At the same time, as poor performance by most governments led up to, and even exacerbated, the debt crisis of the early 1980s, political leaders were obliged to recognize the need for reform.

Initially, political leaders focused on macroeconomic ("first-generation") reform, and in some countries such as Argentina, Bolivia, Mexico, and Peru, governments led or dominated by technocrats embraced and pushed market-oriented reforms. As governments made progress in implementing these reforms, however, attention shifted to structural and institutional ("second-generation") reform issues.

The deep institutional reforms now on the agenda are much more difficult to implement than the economic policy reforms that have been successfully carried out to date by a number of LCR countries. These public sector reforms require much broader and firmer societal and political support, not just the endorsements of government technocrats. The region's relatively well-developed and well-organized civil society and private sector are key to reforms, sustaining the commitment to reform, and playing more active partnership roles in strengthening public sector institutions.

Experience to date in the Region

Early-mid 1980s: Fiscal adjustment focus. The Bank began its involvement in public sector and institutional work in LCR in the early 1980s to support fiscal adjustment and economic liberalization. During the 1980s, paired operations of structural adjustment and technical assistance took place in several countries.[6] These operations typically addressed improving "public sector efficiency" in economic management, and reforming industrial and sectoral policies in such areas as agriculture and mining. Some TA loans were implemented without accompanying SALs.[7] These projects also concentrated on strengthening the core government functions in economic management (investment planning, budgeting, debt management, public enterprise management), and on supporting the government's policy management capacities to promote economic liberalization. In limited instances, bold reform attempts were made, such as the (unsuccessful) introduction of a senior executive service (SES) in the 1982 Peru Public Sector Management Project or the introduction of a performance budgeting system in the 1984 Jamaica Public Administration Reform Project.

Late 1980s—Early 1990s: Public sector modernization. Once strong fiscal pressures subsided between the late 1980s and the early 1990s, many of the Region's public sector operations began to adopt what may be called a "modernization" approach. The fundamental objective of modernization has been to improve the efficiency, effectiveness, and transparency of financial operations through the adoption of coherent procedures and norms supported by modern information technology. These projects invested heavily in improving the performance of existing bureaucratic institutions by modernizing the legal framework for government functions such as financial and personnel management, by updating management tools through new computer and information systems such as an integrated financial management system or a computerized taxpayer registry, and by developing more streamlined operational procedures. Training government personnel on the new tools and procedures was a central component of these projects. A series of public financial management operations in Bolivia, Colombia, and Guatemala, as well as some tax administration projects fall into this category.

Mid-1990s—Today: New areas. In the 1990s, representative governments consolidated, and economic stabilization programs enjoyed considerable success.

These advances led client governments to seek Bank support for changes in new areas. Since the mid-1990s, the Bank has begun to get involved in judicial reform, decentralization,[8] and anticorruption efforts.

Beginning with the Venezuela Judicial Infrastructure Project in 1992, the Bank has developed a judicial reform portfolio in LCR composed of six projects; four more are currently under preparation. Early projects, like the modernization projects discussed above, were focused on providing technical solutions that offered quick answers to the most pressing issues facing the courts, such as rationalization of internal procedures via automation and streamlined case management techniques to reduce delays. Today, attention is shifting to some of the underlying aspects of judicial performance, such as judicial culture, informal rules and procedures, incentive systems for judges, and connections between the judiciary and the surrounding political-economic environment.

The Bank has also responded to a marked increase in demand for support for several aspects of decentralization, and has begun to incorporate decentralization issues into CASs and PERs. The first operation, a 1990 Provincial Development Project in Argentina, focused on subnational government borrowing. Bank operations also support sectoral decentralization, usually in social service delivery and the provision of safety nets.[9] Another area of increasing importance is capacity building for subnational governments. For example, LCSPR is working with WBI to provide management training for Mexican mayors, while projects in Chile (1994, 1998) and Bolivia (1996)[10] support the preparation and implementation of municipal development plans. Finally, the Bank is providing advice to some countries (in country dialogues) on defining a legal and constitutional framework for decentralization.

One of the newest public sector institutional reform activities is support for client countries' anticorruption agendas through specific components in some ongoing projects. For example, Judicial Reform Projects in Guatemala and Venezuela support the fight against corruption by improving procedures for court supervision and discipline of judges; increasing transparency through publication and dissemination of Supreme Court jurisprudence; revising incentive systems for judges, and improving remuneration for judiciary personnel. The Public Financial Management Project in Colombia is financing a study of vulnerability to corruption in the country's Tax and Customs Administrations. LCSPR is also involved in new anticorruption operations in Argentina (IDF), Ecuador (IDF) and Bolivia.

Regulatory reform is another area that is intimately linked with institutional issues. The Region's first experience with regulatory reform was as part of a privatization operation in Argentina in 1991. The project, which created a regulatory agency for the telecommunications sector, has been one of the Bank's less successful regulatory reform operations, largely because of political resistance to genuine reform. The telecommunications agency lacks independence, has typically been slow in making decisions and resolving conflicts, and has not been very transparent in its performance. A more successful example is the Bank/PHRD-supported Peruvian INDECOPI (Competition Agency) created in 1992. The broad range of areas (anti-trust, dumping, patents and trademarks, etc.) covered by this agency lends itself to effective coordination of competition policy. Another key to INDECOPI's relative success is that it created its own appeals court, bypassing the Peruvian judicial system and making conflict resolution much more flexible.

New approaches. Since the mid-1990s, the Bank has also begun to introduce more ambitious approaches to traditional areas of public sector reform. For example, in the area of revenue administration, some of the newer projects explicitly aim at improving the sector's governance structure by establishing autonomous or semi-autonomous revenue administration agencies.[11] In the area of administrative and civil service reform, some recent operations adopt New Public Management approaches of inter-agency contracts and perform-ance-based incentives to facilitate reform implementation and improve agency performance.[12]

Another set of relatively new operations has explicitly incorporated "competition" options in project design and supports private participation in public service provisions, particularly in the areas of public utilities and transport services.[13] The Public Sector Modernization Projects in El Salvador, Honduras, and Venezuela all include components that support private participation in public service delivery ("competition"). In education, Colombia is experimenting with voucher programs, and has also received substantial Bank support, both lending and nonlending, to further its decentralization in the education sector at the national, departmental, and municipal levels.

Finally, there have been new efforts to incorporate more participatory ("voice") approaches. Such an approach has been particularly successful in El Salvador's Bank-supported EDUCO program, which introduced community-managed schools in rural areas and is now being expanded to include marginal urban areas. Beneficiary surveys and other participatory approaches have also been adopted in some recent operations including some judicial reform projects.[14]

The record and lessons of experience. Despite relatively long operational experience, the Bank has not conducted systematic evaluations of public sector and institutional development operations across LCR. Although in many cases the projects are still too recent to evaluate for their sustainable impact, LCSPR has begun systematic evaluations of selected operational areas, including judicial reform and financial management projects, to draw the lessons that can be learned from our experiences to date. The limited evidence we have so far indicates that our record is likely to be mixed.

Many of the projects in the 1980s suffered from implementation difficulties and limited sustainable impact. When the Bank began supporting public sector institutional reforms in the region, most client countries, with the exception of Chile, were still grappling with the tasks of implementing "first-generation" reforms (macroeconomic stabilization, and market liberalization). Unstable macroeconomic conditions and relatively weak, incipient democratic regimes did not provide an environment conducive to implementing public sector institutional reforms in the region. This was especially true in some countries to which the Bank offered early support.[15]

The mixed record applies equally to what we call "modernization" approach operations. The series of financial management projects provides a useful illustration. Often eschewing the broader strategic goals of institutional reform of the budget system, the projects focused on developing the technical building blocks of financial management: creating properly functioning accounting, cash management, and budget sub-systems capable of recording and reporting government finances accurately and rapidly. In some cases, this "building-block" approach has borne fruit in the form of greater efficiency and transparency in financial management, as manifested in the very successful installation of well-functioning integrated financial management systems in Argentina and Guatemala. But in other cases, inadequate attention to political and bureaucratic constraints has frustrated implementation and limited project impact, as in Bolivia and Ecuador. Evidently, the apparent success of these projects owes much to the existence of a conducive environment, including sustained government commitment and limited bureaucratic resistance. The challenge for the Bank is to evaluate these diverging experiences more systematically and assess conditions under which a "building-block" approach tends to lead to more fundamental institutional reform.[16]

The challenge ahead

As LCR countries move toward improving public sector institutional performance by way of either modern administrative framework and management tools, or the introduction of performance-oriented management practices, much remains to be done to redefine the role of the state and reshape its organizational structure, in the ongoing work on decentralization, in the restructuring of incentives, and in the introduction of competition and "voice." These more complex reform efforts require strong underlying constituencies to succeed, and the Bank must learn to be more strategically selective. More strategic selectivity can be ensured by investing more in upfront analytic work.

Deeper institutional reforms of core government functions. Most of the Bank's current lending activities in LCR support country efforts in "traditional" public sector management operations that concentrate on core government functions. The Bank is now moving toward addressing a deeper institutional reform agenda concerned with the rules and incentive structures that affect public sector performance. For example, in the area of public financial management, the Bank intends to go beyond a narrow technical focus on integrated financial management system operations and begin to address the need to reform budget institutions. This would require attention to linkages between policymaking and budgeting functions of the state, including the role of the legislature and executive policymaking bodies in the public expenditure management process.

In the area of personnel management, the greatest challenge is to develop merit-based bureaucracies in highly politicized administrative environments, and where conditions are ripe, to push for more performance-oriented public management. The Region is experimenting with performance-oriented management approaches in a few countries, including Bolivia, where an ambitious ten-year reform program support-

ed with an Adaptable Program Loan (APL) is being prepared. The main objective of this Institutional Reform Project is to professionalize pilot agencies by introducing merit-based personnel management practices, and by encouraging these agencies to move toward a more performance-oriented management culture. In Jamaica, the Bank is supporting the establishment of UK-style autonomous executive agencies on a pilot basis. The goal of creating executive agencies is to empower managers by granting them considerably enhanced autonomy in managerial, financial, personnel, and operational management, in exchange for strict accountability for predetermined performance targets.

Emphasis on combining internal rules, "voice" and competition. Given the relatively developed civil society and private sector in LCR, the Bank should be able to rely more on both participatory and competitive approaches. Already some of the new operations, such as the 1998 Guatemala Judicial Reform Project, and the 1998 Peru Urban Property Rights Project, utilize participatory approaches for project design and implementation involving NGOs and project beneficiaries (the indigenous population and urban slum dwellers). These approaches appear particularly suited to improving citizens' access to public services.

Privatization and other means of introducing competitive pressure to the provision of public services are other ongoing agenda items in many countries. Our initial experiences in this area have so far been favorable as evidenced by the relative success of the 1996 Honduras Public Sector Modernization Project. While the bulk of the Bank operations in public enterprise reforms, privatization and regulatory reforms are now handled by the FPSI Sector Management Unit, it is important to ensure that reform efforts in these areas and reforms of core public sector functions mutually reinforce each other rather than introduce inconsistency and contradictions.

The Bank is also paying greater attention to the challenges and new questions raised by decentralization throughout the region. All elements of public sector reform will affect or be affected by the changing configurations and divisions of power generated by decentralization. As decentralization progresses, more service delivery functions are devolved to subnational levels. Therefore, any effort to improve public sector performance in a way that directly benefits the population would have to take into account the roles and capacities of subnational governments. Better coordination is needed between projects to support central government reforms and those that strengthen subnational government capacities. One way to mitigate this problem would be to design a project that links institutional reforms at the central and the subnational levels. Another approach would be to design projects based on a common analytic framework of broader institutional issues that affect both levels of government.

Strategic selectivity. These new lending areas are more politically sensitive and technically difficult, and therefore call for greater strategic selectivity. Strong, sustained political commitment and societal support are essential for these interventions to succeed. For example, as judicial reform has become more popular in the region, courts and political leaders are eager to finance buildings, computer equipment, new laws and training centers, but few envision, let alone support, the sorts of changes in behavior required to make judicial output more efficient, predictable, equitable, and subordinate to transparent rules. A judicial reform project in Peru designed in 1995-96 was postponed repeatedly because of lack of government compliance with effectiveness conditions. The Government cancelled the project in 1998, after it passed a new law that constrained the Judicial Council's freedom to discipline judges.

Similarly, the current attention to anticorruption induces a number of well-intentioned governments to request our support but presents us with the risk of entering to provide assistance where understanding of the nature of the problem is limited, and true political commitment is absent or unsustainable. This is an area where there are few, if any known means to solve problems in the short term, but where countries have strong desires to see progress and may be particularly impatient. This can translate into undue pressure on the Bank to seek quick solutions, when a more appropriate approach may be a carefully designed multi-faceted institutional reform program that tackles the weaknesses of the public sector institutions in the long run.

When strong constituents of reform do not exist, we must either devote much of our initial effort to building effective demand for reform, or if that is not feasible, we should decline assistance until a better opportunity arises. Strategic selectivity can be ensured by investing more in upfront analytic work.

Greater emphasis on analytic work and learning. To date, the amount of sector work in the public sector and institutional development area has been limited, and the treatment of these issues in PERs has often been cursory and superficial. In both cases, analytic work has rarely had an impact on the choice or design of Bank reform projects and operations. Clearly, more needs to be done to increase and improve our analytic work on public sector institutional issues.

Given the technical difficulty of public sector institutional reforms, the Bank's future strategy emphasizes rigorous analytic work in order to learn more about the performance of Bank operation and the particular challenges of the region. Future analytic work should focus on three main areas: country-specific institutional assessments; operationally relevant research and analysis of institutional and public sector reform issues; and systematic evaluations of our past and ongoing operations to draw appropriate lessons of experiences.

To aid in country-specific institutional assessments, the Bank is developing and applying new diagnostic tools, such as the Institutional and Governance Review (IGR), recently piloted in Bolivia. In addition, the

Region is developing a framework for mini-IGRs to diagnose institutional problems in those countries where a full IGR cannot be implemented for whatever reason. These mini-IGRs could be offered as part of a menu of products in support of anticorruption activities. Both full IGRs and mini-IGRs will address fundamental institutional issues including rule compliance within the public sector, and the political economy factors that affect performance of government bureaucracies.

The Region will become more active in operationally relevant research programs dealing with institutional behavior and public sector reform in collaboration with DECRG and PRMPS. Such research will address issues such as the pervasive bureaucratic informality and weak rule of law within the public sector. Many Bank reform measures currently rely on new rules and organizational structures to change public sector behavior. Needless to say, weak rule compliance seriously undermines the efficacy of any rule-based solutions.

Finally, the Bank will need to do a better job of learning from experience. So far the Region has not been able to develop an effective system of self-learning and knowledge management. To address this issue, LCSPR has launched a knowledge management program, with a focus on distilling and disseminating lessons of experience from past and ongoing operations. While attempting innovative approaches to institutional reforms, the Bank should make better use of experimental instruments such as Learning and Innovation Loans to increase the likelihood that the proposed reform finds a "good fit" with the country's political and institutional surroundings, and to ensure that the Bank can draw appropriate lessons in a timely manner to improve design of subsequent operations. To date, two Learning and Innovation Loans (LILs) for judicial reforms are underway in LCSPR (the 1997 Venezuela Supreme Court Modernization Project was the first LIL Bank-wide).

Bolivia—From Patronage to Professional State: Institutional and Governance Review

Type of Activity: Analytic and Advisory Activity

Timing: Concept paper review: March 11, 1999

Decision draft review: February 29, 2000. Document in final stages of completion.

based on the country's own political and institutional realities, and propose several measures that are both realistic and yet critical for improving public management in Bolivia.

Summary of Contents

Institutional and Governance Reviews (IGRs) are a new type of analytic instrument being piloted Bank-wide in the Public Sector. IGRs are intended to be an in-depth analysis of a country's public sector institutions with explicit emphasis on political economy issues (wherever and to the extent it is feasible). The Bolivia IGR was designed to provide analytic input into refining the design of, and formulating an implementation strategy for, the Institutional Reform Project (IRP), which aims at introducing a merit-based civil service and performance-oriented public management in selected government agencies. The Bolivia IGR identifies several key political-institutional factors (particular constraints presented by the country's coalition politics) that influence public administration (personnel and financial management), reviews past institutional reform efforts in the country (successful efforts to build autonomous regulatory agencies), and offers operational recommendations (sequencing for gradual introduction of advanced public management techniques such as results-oriented budgeting). The recommendations emphasize the importance of political feasibility

Innovative / Risky Elements

The Bolivia IGR's innovative aspects include the explicit political analysis used and the conscious effort to avoid prescribing "international best practice" in favor of a "good fit" for the country's political and institutional realities.

The potential risk was a possible disconnect between the Review's recommendations and the design of the Institutional Reform Project (IRP), which was already at an advanced stage of preparation when the IGR work began. This potential risk has been mitigated through close coordination and communications between the IGR and the IRP teams. The politically sensitive nature of the topic continues to be a risk that needs to be recognized as we enter discussion with the Government and consider options for public dissemination.

Partnerships

The Bolivian counterpart was involved from the beginning as peer reviewer and potential consumer of the report, but there were no other institutional partners for this work.

Guatemala: Financial Management Reform (1999 President's Award for Excellence)

Type of Activity: Technical Assistance Loan
Timing: Board Approval: May 1995, Closed: June 1999
Loan Amount: $9.4 million

Summary of Contents

This project attempted fundamental reform of the government's budgeting, accounting, cash management, procurement, and auditing sub-systems, with ongoing reforms in debt management and public investment. The sub-systems are fully integrated through updated laws and regulations, coherent and consistent accounts classifications and administrative procedures, and a powerful single relational database information technology system providing on-line, real time information to managers and stakeholders.

The project, a model throughout Latin America, has had tangible impact on government transparency, efficiency, and effectiveness. Specific results include: (a) widespread reduction in prices paid for goods (medicines and school supplies); (b) significant improvements in social sector ministry performance; (c) elimination of government payment arrears; (d) replacement of government checks with electronic funds transfers; (e) reduction of average payment time to suppliers from 3 months to 72 hours; (f) sharp reduction in number of government bank accounts, permitting more sophisticated cash management; (g) presentation of proposed budget to the Congress on CD ROM including information on executed budget to within four days of budget submission; (h) availability of proposed and implemented budgets online to legislators, private citizens, and other stakeholders, with budget execution data updated biweekly; (i) decentralization of budget formulation, execution, and payments to line ministries; (j) incorporation of physical and other performance indicators into the budget; and (k) provision of immediate, detailed information on all recorded financial transactions, through a unique relational database, providing an audit trail and reduced scope for corruption.

Innovative / Risky Elements

The project team insisted that the project be viewed as a complete and coherent system affecting and integrating all key sub-systems in terms of concepts as well as information technology, rather than piecemeal or based on information technology alone. It supported the government's decision to build a new graphics-based software system specifically designed in conjunction with the conceptual design of the various sub-systems. The project has involved working closely with national accounting trade associations and universities to promote understanding of the new system and to facilitate the training of new accountants on the new public sector financial management system. Finally, it has become the backbone of state modernization, closely involved in tax administration reform, improvements in human resource management, and municipal development (in a third loan under preparation).

Partnerships

Close cooperation with USAID in Guatemala City, and with UNDP, which has acted as procurement agent for the project.

Guatemala: Judicial Reform Project

Type of Activity: Lending
Timing: Board Approval: October 22, 1998
Effective: April 22, 1999 Closing: June 30, 2004
Loan Amount: $33 million

Summary of Contents

As part of Guatemala's peace process after 36 years of civil war, the Supreme Court of Justice and the Judiciary Branch, with contribution from the Judicial Sector Strengthening Commission and civil society, have initiated a judicial reform program to overcome the failings of the past and move toward improved administration of justice in the country. This Bank-supported program aims at creating a more *effective, accessible* and *credible* judicial system that would foster public trust and confidence and improve consistency and equity in the application of law. In order to meet its objectives, the project is implemented through the following four components: Strengthening Institutional Capacity of the Judiciary Branch, Providing Anticorruption Support, Strengthening Access to Justice, and Improving Social Communications.

Innovative / Risky Elements

The singularity of the program lies in the fact that the project has been developed using a collaborative, participatory assessment. In the project preparation phase, judges and justices of the peace, instead of disregarding the criticism from civil society, initiated a broad stakeholder consultation. Key players not only in the judiciary, but also in the indigenous community, the NGO sector and the media were heard in order to identify critical areas for reform and start a process to regain public confidence in the system. The program can be seen as a flagship case of a post-conflict judicial reform initiative that is implemented through extensive participation from wide-ranging constituents of the government as well as the civil society.

Partnerships

The Modernization Program was developed in 1997/98 with the participation and support of international organizations, such as the World Bank, IDB, UNDP, USAID, MINUGUA, the Governments of Sweden, Japan, Switzerland, Canada and others.

Peru: Institutional Development of the Ombudsman's Office

Type of Activity: IDF Grant Activity
Timing: February 1999 - February 2001
Loan Amount: $500,000

Summary of Contents

The Grant has supported the following activities:

- provision of technical assistance and training (including advisory services, strategic workshops, and evaluation studies) for the institutional strengthening of the Ombudsman's Office, in the areas of: (a) institutional image and media relations; (b) internal organization and methods, and budget control; (c) assessment of local governments and pension plans; (d) supervision of the provision and regulation of public services; and (e) poverty and senior citizens issues;

- logistical support and strategic planning for the administrative modernization of the Ombudsman's Office aimed at promoting the decentralization of its services, in particular through the development of basic integrated management systems for the central and departmental offices;

- carrying out workshops, forums and training programs aimed at improving coordination between State authorities and civil society; and

- carrying out a dissemination campaign about the Ombudsman's Office activities, including the preparation and distribution of materials and regional workshops.

Innovative / Risky Elements

The Grant has supported the independence of the Ombudsman's Office. The strengthening of the Office's role in the defense of citizens' rights is expected to have spillover effects in the entire state system. The activities selected for IDF support have assisted in building civil society capacity for demanding and monitoring access to the state apparatus through greater awareness about the rule of law and the role and functions of this new institution, an essential element of a better system of checks and balances provided by the 1993 Constitution.

Partnerships

Comisión Andina de Juristas (major NGO active on governance issues); Instituto de Defensa Legal (major NGO active on human rights); Instituto para Democracia y Buen Gobierno (new NGO active on governance issues).

Peru: Urban Property Rights Project

Type of Activity: Technical Assistance
Timing: Board Approval: August 6, 1998
Amount: $38 million

Summary of Contents

The main idea of this project is to help poor city dwellers by formalizing the property they own (getting the state to recognize on-the-ground realities of ownership). Formalization will allow the poor to enjoy the fruits of greater security of ownership. The project will thus encourage more investment in property, more real-estate sales, and more use of property as a security for borrowing—all this reflected in considerably higher property values. The formal rules, organizations, and processes of Peru's regime for real property rights have never worked for poor people. The project is supporting greater security of ownership though a radical and systematic approach to institutional reform which involves simultaneously tackling legal, administrative, and technical problems:

- *Legal reform*: a "bottom-up" reform (requiring a consultative approach which ends up in adapting laws to the reality on the ground).

- *Administrative reform*: new organizational arrangements (independent, but accountable agencies) to break the former stranglehold of corrupt and incompetent agencies and build sustainability into the reform process.

- *Technical reform*: the design and implementation of a low-cost, low-technology, and participation-intensive process that "mass-produces" formalized ownership through an area-based titling approach

and an "industrialization" of the formalization process.

The project also helps lay the groundwork for the development of instruments to support the use of real estate as security in financial transactions.

Innovative / Risky Elements

This operation is an application of a "second-generation" reform that originated in the early 1990s. The Bank was involved, through technical assistance, from 1992. The project provides an approach to the reform of service delivery and to the problem of informality and can serve as a model for other countries and sectors. This has been a controversial reform, in large part because of the legal changes and its quasi common law approach to formalizing property rights. The controversy has receded as a growing number of countries have sought to adopt similar reforms. The project has a high political profile because it provides tangible assets to poor people. In this sense, conferring property ownership is used as political currency. This has often been the case with this type of project, but unlike the past, this project will provide mechanisms that will lead to effective property formalization on the basis of technical criteria.

Partnerships

The project concept was developed a decade ago by a local NGO, the Instituto Libertad y Democracia. The Bank and the ILD worked closely together to pilot the concept.

Middle East & North Africa Region (MNA)

The Middle East and North Africa (MNA) Region is characterized by large public sectors, centralized governments, and limited political participation. In addition, for the most part, systems of accountability in the region need strengthening. Forces for change remain modest, and the impetus comes principally from the governments themselves. The Bank's track record in supporting institutional changes has been variable, with respect to the degree of attention institutional issues have received and the success achieved in public sector reform work. Nevertheless, the Bank is broadening its analytic work, and efforts to promote "voice" and competition have met with relative success. Looking ahead, the MNA Region anticipates putting in place internal processes that will ensure that institutional concerns are mainstreamed within Bank work, tightening the link between lending and institutional reform, and making good use of windows of opportunity for advancing discussions of corruption and service delivery.

Salient characteristics of the MNA Region

"Statist" traditions took root early on in most MNA countries,[17] giving rise to large public sectors, highly centralized governments, and dominant executive branches operating against a backdrop of limited political pluralism in most countries. These fostered significant progress, but access to basic social and infrastructure services still lags behind that of many comparable developing countries. Institutional arrangements have in many cases been geared to absorbing significant sections of the workforce (mainly at the central level of government) more than to ensuring lean, merit-based public administrations. In several countries this hiring held at bay a potentially explosive problem of unemployment. However, the consequence has been that the region has the largest public sector wage bill compared to GDP of any region, without commensurate public sector performance.

Accountability mechanisms. As discussed in Part I, improving public sector performance depends in part on strengthening mechanisms of accountability. As in much of the developing world, the role and functioning of legislatures in MNA countries is often weak, and judicial systems tend to be overloaded relative to means and capacities. Most MNA countries have established traditions and systems of public financial management, although supreme audit institutions are often not independent of the executive and do not always publish the results of their activities. In those countries where they are independent, their effectiveness can be limited by the absence of effective sanctions. There is also a limit to which executive branches of government present ex-post budget outcomes to legislatures in a systematic, timely, and transparent manner. More generally, accountability and transparency are sometimes impaired by restrictions of information dissemination on public officials and agencies.[18]

External feedback on public sector performance and "voice" and participation mechanisms (including the media and NGOs) have also been constrained, although there are signs that "voice" and participation mechanisms are strengthening in some countries. In Morocco, for example, the trend toward greater political openness over the past two years has been accompanied by increased activity on the part of NGOs and civil society groups with respect to such issues as gender, corruption, and social inequality. In Yemen and the West Bank and Gaza, new, more flexible NGO legislation is being adopted.

Competition and service delivery. Competition—ranging from outright privatization of state-owned enterprises in market-driven activities to contestability in the provision of various services traditionally delivered exclusively by the public sector—has had a slow start in the MNA Region. While several MNA countries, including Egypt, Tunisia, Morocco, and Algeria launched privatization programs in the late 1980s or early 1990s, the approach was cautious and gradual

because of political constraints. As a result, of the more than $162 billion worth of state-owned enterprises sold worldwide in developing countries during the period 1988-96, only about three percent was in MNA countries. The share of MNA countries in infrastructure privatization and private provision of infrastructure (PPI) projects was similarly small. Meanwhile, deficiencies in public provision of a variety of goods and services—notably infrastructure services—became increasingly apparent, as provision failed to keep pace with rapidly growing populations.[19]

Recent trends are encouraging, however. Over the past few years there has been a clear secular shift in the role of the state in several MNA countries from one of "player" to one of "referee." Privatization, and particularly PPI, appear to be gaining momentum. In Egypt, Jordan, Lebanon, Morocco, Tunisia, the West Bank and Gaza, and several of the Gulf Cooperation Council (GCC) countries, competitive bidding for the provision of certain infrastructure services is being successfully put into practice.[20] At the same time, as more and

FIGURE 7 Institutional Quality

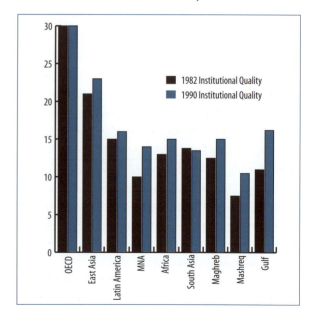

more MNA countries turn to PPI, the need for regulatory strengthening and clarity is becoming more pressing.

Institutional quality and anticorruption. Broadly based cross-regional measures that attempt to capture the quality of public sector institutions, such as the Index of Overall Institutional Quality (Figure 7)[21] suggest that although MNA countries lagged behind other developing countries in the early 1980s, by 1990 they had improved and closed the gap. Performance in the Mahgreb exceeded that in the Mashreq, while—because of strong performance on rule of law and freedom from the risk of expropriation—the Gulf Countries had the highest institutional quality measure in the MNA Region.

The typology and extent of corruption and its effect on public sector performance in MNA countries has yet to be systematically investigated. In-depth diagnostic survey work of the type initiated in several Bank clients (notably in ECA, AFR, and LCR) has not yet been carried out, although (depending on client demand) efforts in this direction are envisaged in Lebanon, Jordan, Morocco, West Bank and Gaza, and Yemen.

Momentum for change. In most MNA countries, the forces and momentum for reform (and specifically far-reaching reform of public sector institutions), while rarely absent, remain modest. The modest momentum for reform comes from the selected governments that are experimenting with political opening.

Over the coming decade, the EUROMED association agreements with the European Union (EU) are likely to act as a catalyst for further reform. The EUROMED initiative framework, which encompasses virtually all MNA countries in the southern Mediterranean rim, mirrors the three pillars of the EU's pre-accession program in ECA—free trade, structural reform, and financial assistance. The parallelism with pre-accession is weak in that the time frame for the Mediterranean Free Trade Area is around 2010, the nature of the structural reform content is expected to become better defined only as the process deepens, and the amount of financial assistance is much smaller. Nevertheless, the EUROMED framework is expected to provide gradually accelerating momentum for a broad range of institutional and policy reforms, including reforms relating to governance and the role of civil society.

Experience to date in the MNA Region

As in other Regions, the Bank's track record of support for public sector reform in MNA countries is mixed.[22] The CASs have focused on institutional reforms to a limited (and varying) degree. Capacity building efforts have been more successful than attempts to change existing institutional incentives. Nevertheless, the Bank is building a substantial pipeline of new analytic work. Efforts to stress the importance of "voice" have proven catalytic, efforts to improve competition have been successful, and dialogue on corruption is slowly being advanced in response to new windows of opportunity.

Country Assistance Strategies. At the overall program level—as reflected notably in the Country Assistance Strategy (CAS)—the focus on public sector institutional reform needs has been variable. A review of CASs from fiscal 1994-98 for Egypt, Algeria, Morocco, Tunisia, Jordan, Yemen, and Lebanon indicates significant diagnostic focus on specific areas of public sector institutional reform in these countries. Prominent themes include civil service reform, privatization and increased competition in service delivery, public expenditure management, and decentralization of project management (especially in relation to Bank portfolio implementation). Some of the CASs reviewed (for example, Egypt, Algeria and Morocco) focus on broad supportive changes in formal rules (notably the legal, regulatory, and administrative frameworks) to foster market competition and encourage private provision where appropriate. Institutional changes that broadly address incentives in order to create an enabling environment for private provision are discussed in specific terms in the Egypt and Morocco CASs. However, most CAS documents did not attempt a broad, systematic diagnosis of governance in the country. As a result, potentially key areas of institutional dysfunction (for example, political patronage, procurement practices, and checks and balances and accountability mechanisms) have received little focus.

Bank activities. Over the past several years, specific Bank activities in MNA countries (lending operations, ESW, and technical assistance) have addressed a broad range of public sector institution-building needs, with variable success. With respect to core public sector institutions, such as the civil service, the focus of Bank lending has been on capacity building, including the provision of training and equipment and advice on systems.

By and large, however, Bank support has been less successful in changing the *incentives* driving public sector performance through reforms of institutional arrangements.[23] A recent OED evaluation of Bank Civil service reform interventions rates only 10 percent of completed interventions, and 17 percent of still ongoing and recently completed interventions in the MNA Region as satisfactory.[24] In particular, downsizing and reform of institutions were unsuccessful in the completed interventions (although they are improving over time), while capacity building efforts that attempted to improve principal-agent relationships were successful 50 percent of the time.

Experience in the Region with ESW focusing on core public sector institutions has been similar. A recent OED evaluation of the impact of public expenditure reviews (PERs) rates such work in the MNA Region as marginally satisfactory, lower than other Regions and on par with SAR.[25] While the PERs perform relatively well in terms of quality and timeliness, they receive a poor rating in terms of cost

efficiency and especially impact on client behavior and donor coordination.[26]

New analytic work. Experience notwithstanding, the Region has recently begun to build up a substantial pipeline of analytic work on public sector institutions, both through Bank ESW and through support for research activity in client countries. Examples of recent Bank work include: (a) region-wide analysis of the links between public sector institutions and economic performance, and of the role of the public sector as regulator; (b) country-specific diagnostic work on budget and related public sector institutions (for example, in Jordan, the West Bank and Gaza, and Yemen); and (c) country-specific analysis of accountability in public sector institutions (for example, in Jordan, Yemen, and West Bank and Gaza). The Bank also helped create, and is providing substantial support to, the Economic Research Forum (ERF), a network of in-country think-tanks and university departments. ERF has already conducted substantive research on the role of the state in MNA countries—one of the four major themes in its work.

Bank support for "voice" and participation. Recent Bank support for "voice" and participation mechanisms through specific in-country activities is noteworthy and has had catalytic value. Service delivery survey work has been conducted in the West Bank/Gaza and in Jordan, introducing the concept of client feedback. Similarly, Bank support for the formulation of a gender strategy for Morocco, which has involved broad consultation through in-country focus groups, has helped illustrate "voice" and participation mechanisms at work. More generally, the Bank has been instrumental in building up a broader network among the countries in the region on gender-related issues, and the social assessments of Bank projects conducted in several countries have ensured broader stakeholder participation in project design. The Bank's efforts in building up the ERF and EDI's launch of the Mediterranean Development Forum in 1997 (now planned as an annual event) have helped strengthen regional mechanisms for collaborative research and discussion. This in turn has helped to bring key policy and institutional issues, including those relating to public sector performance, to the center of the agenda. Finally, both the Bank and the Fund are supporting the strengthening of the watchdog function of journalists in the region through training in economic policy issues.

Competition. Several recent Bank activities have supported reductions in the State's role as service provider through divestiture or increased competition in service delivery, with relative success. Examples include support for: (a) setting up the Technical Privatization Office in Yemen; (b) contracting out the management of the Gaza City water and wastewater system; (c) NGO delivery of social services in the West Bank and Gaza; and (d) independent power generation in Morocco.

Anticorruption. Bank involvement in explicitly addressing corruption in MNA countries has been limited, owing in large measure to client government reservations. Apart from WBI seminars on integrity in government in Jordan in fiscal 1996 and discrete focus on the issue in ESW and project work (for example, in the West Bank and Gaza and in Yemen during fiscal 1998-99), there has as yet been no in-depth work aimed at diagnosing and combating corruption (through diagnostic survey work and broadly based in-country discussion).

However, windows of opportunity for anticorruption work are appearing in some countries. In Morocco, the *alternance* Government, in part responding to mounting pressure from civil society, has approached the Bank for assistance. An in-country anticorruption workshop to which WBI and the PREM anchor contributed was held in June 1999, with broad attendance from government and civil society. An anticorruption consultative group comprising senior figures from government, NGOs, the private sector, and donors has since been established to develop and monitor

implementation of an anticorruption institutional and policy reform agenda. In addition a PHRD grant that will be used to prepare a good governance project, centered on improved transparency and efficiency of service delivery and improved internal and external controls over the administration, has just been approved. In Yemen, the Public Sector Management Adjustment Credit (PSMAC) supports a reform program to improve governance by packaging several micro-level measures to increase transparency and integrity in the public administration.

More systematic public sector reform. The trend in recent (fiscal 1998-99) Bank work toward a more holistic approach to the medium-term policy and institutional development agenda in several MNA countries is promoting more systematic focus on public sector institutional reform needs. The selection of the West Bank and Gaza and Morocco as pilots for the CDF is encouraging broader assessments of governance—a key component of the CDF—in these countries. Background work to this end has already begun. A similar trend is taking shape in Yemen, where work on the PSMAC has drawn up a road map of needed public sector institutional reforms, as well as in Jordan.

The challenge ahead for MNA

A key element of the regional strategy is to strengthen mechanisms that can help mainstream a focus on public sector institutional concerns at the overall country program level. Emphasis will be placed on regional mechanisms for upstream CAS discussions reviews, and on seeking broader input through the Public Sector Board early on. The regional country strategy process also needs to be strengthened through regular consultations with Country Directors to evaluate how we are addressing key institutional imperatives that have been identified in line with the annual budget and work program cycle.

The mainstreaming process will be facilitated in the pilot countries where work on the CDF—which includes broadly based governance assessments—will underpin CAS preparation. The same is true of other MNA countries (Jordan, Yemen) where a more holistic approach to the medium-term policy and institutional development agenda is being adopted. To facilitate mainstreaming beyond such countries, the Region needs to move to a CDF-type approach even in countries that are not presently pilots.

The Bank's recent efforts to ensure broader in-country consultation in CAS/CDF preparation in the MNA countries also needs to be continued. In-depth discussion involving civil society, the private sector, and other stakeholders in addition to a broad range of public officials is proving effective in highlighting weaknesses in public sector institutions and pushing the boundaries of the dialogue on the subject.

Within the CAS framework, the Bank's choice of nonlending and lending activities and instruments in the MNA countries needs to be geared to putting public sector institutional concerns at the center of the development agenda, subject to the constraint of political feasibility. In particular, nonlending work needs to address still-significant gaps in the Bank's diagnostic knowledge of public sector institutions (broadly defined) in MNA countries, as well as assist in key areas of public sector institution-building where lending vehicles are unsuitable.

The recent trend toward greater institutional focus in public sector-related ESW (for example, in the fiscal 1999 West Bank and Gaza Public Expenditure and Jordan Public Sector Reviews) needs to be broadened. There is a near-term opportunity in Morocco, where work on a broad diagnostic assessment of public sector institutions and governance (along the lines of the prototype Institutional and Governance Reviews) had been commissioned by the Country Director as input into the CDF. In Tunisia, where the Bank has concluded a review of the performance of key public sector

institutions as part of a Social and Structural Policy Review, an opportunity for sustained Bank support for reform may arise.

On corruption and public service delivery, the Bank needs to remain responsive to windows of opportunity to conduct survey work and in-country activities involving civil society as well as public officials. The Bank will also move toward a more systematic use of social assessments, where survey methodology can provide extensive data on institutional dysfunction. In addition, the Bank plans to continue supporting such mechanisms as the ERF and the MDF and to build up local networks of expertise on public sector institutions—a subject on which detailed in-country knowledge is essential and more efficiently tapped through local expertise. Finally, targeted capacity building initiatives (for example, the April 1999 WBI/Arab Planning Institute course on economic management for civil servants in the region; various IDF-supported programs to strengthen expenditure and revenue management) will continue to be pursued.

The Bank is progressively tightening the link between lending and progress on *overall* policy and institutional reform in several MNA countries. It is envisaged that over the next few years the lending program in these countries will include PSAL-type programmatic instruments which map out the medium-term reform agenda for key public sector institutions. This approach is already being piloted in Jordan, where preparation of a fiscal 2001 Public Sector Reform Loan has begun. It has also moved in this direction in Yemen with the fiscal 1999 PSMAC, and to some extent in Morocco with the fiscal 1999 Policy Reform Support Loan. In the West Bank and Gaza, there are presently no plans for the use of programmatic instruments, owing in part to the still-nascent state of public financial management systems.

Future project lending is expected to build on demand-driven opportunities focusing on key public sector institutions and capacity building needs. Examples of such projects include: (a) a fiscal 2000 Civil Service Management Technical Assistance Project in Yemen; (b) a fiscal 2001 Institutional Development Project in the West Bank and Gaza (which will likely focus on the Palestinian Authority's core budgeting and financial management functions); and (c) fiscal 2000 Legal and Judicial Development Project in Morocco (which aims to develop an independent, competent, and professional judicial system and puts in place mechanisms that facilitate commercial transactions and resolve potential commercial disputes). At the same time, there is a recognition that implementation of projects with significant institution-building components is likely to be difficult and time-consuming, implying a need for realistic expectations on portfolio performance (disbursement rates).

Efforts are still needed to strengthen organization, staffing, and partnerships to ensure delivery of high-quality work on public sector institutions in the MNA Region. Under the present organizational structure, the thematic responsibility for public sector institutional concerns lies in the regional PREM unit (MNSED), with six to seven full-time-equivalent MNSED staff. Several tasks in the Region with a potentially significant bearing on public sector institutional reform are contracted to MNSED by the CMUs. In the first instance, the main focus needs to be on fine-tuning the organizational mechanism and providing resources for staff time to ensure in-depth upstream review and input into the country strategy process and into lending and nonlending tasks with a significant public sector component. Because the MNA Region is small, and the Chief Economist and MNSED Director functions are combined, efforts are being directed to put in place a mechanism where such upstream input is doubled up with the broader input and review functions carried out by the Chief Economist's Office.

Core staffing in the MNA Region is broadly adequate to address the present pattern of demand for public sector work. However, there is an emerging gap with respect to certain specialized skills in such areas as civil service reform and anticorruption survey work. Given present budget and staffing constraints, as well as the difficulty of predicting sustainability of demand for such skills in the Region, it appears preferable to address the skills gaps that arise by drawing on talent pools outside the Region (the PREM anchor, WBI and in certain cases other Regions) rather than recruiting individuals directly into the Region. Such an approach does, however call for reinforcing joint planning and consultation (through the Public Sector Board). There is also a need for training of MNA regional staff—primarily MNSED staff involved in public sector work. In the first instance, the focus will be on anticorruption awareness-raising (a workshop for regional staff organized by WBI was held May 1999) and on Institutional and Governance Review methodologies. Finally, focused partnerships can help ensure that the public sector institutional reform agenda in MNA countries is better defined and more effectively addressed. Aside from continuing to support and strengthen regional networks of think-tanks, universities, and civil society groups through such mechanisms as the ERF and MDF process, Bank efforts will be focused on developing more systematic contact and consultation with two sets of bodies. The first consists of key donors to MNA countries who have a strong track record of involvement in governance and public sector institution-building such as the UNDP, the European Commission, and USAID. Both UNDP and USAID are becoming increasingly active in conducting anticorruption assessments in several MNA countries,[27] and progress in moving the anticorruption agenda forward in such countries is sensitive to efforts to maximize complementarity in donor interventions at both the technical and political levels. The second set of bodies with which contact and consultation will need to be strengthened consists of NGO watchdog bodies in MNA countries.

Jordan: Public Sector Reform Loan

Type of Activity: Programmatic Loan
Timing: Fiscal 2001
Loan Amount: $120 million (tentative)

Summary of Contents

This project assists in comprehensive reform of the public sector, focusing on a well-performing civil service, improvements in service delivery and adequately functioning institutions of accountability (both horizontal and vertical) with a long-term focus on improved budgeting.

Innovative / Risky Elements

Innovation lies in a holistic approach that lays out a comprehensive medium-term public sector reform agenda, stressing inter-linkage among the various components. Support for implementation is through a programmatic instrument.

Implementation of the reform will be a lengthy process and requires coordination of critical steps in order to fulfil long-term goals. The Bank, other donors and the client country need to work together very closely to ensure success. Political commitment to the reform is essential. Although the reform agenda has been set by the client and is being pushed from the top in Jordan, buy-in from other levels needs to be ensured so that the process of reform can be successfully managed.

Partnerships

Collaboration with GTZ and IMF in budget reform.

Morocco: Institutional and Governance Review

Type of Activity: Analytic and Advisory Activity
Timing: Fiscal 2000-01

Summary of Contents

Beginning with a CDF governance matrix format, this IGR is a mapping out of the governance and public sector reform agenda in Morocco, including a focus on broader governance, accountability and anticorruption issues. The resulting strategy note will be developed into a full-fledged institutional review following discussion with authorities.

Innovative / Risky Elements

This IGR entails a holistic look at the public sector reform agenda, including attention to elements that previously received little (for example, horizontal accountability mechanisms, and anticorruption safeguards).

Close attention needs to be paid to the process set up by the government to conduct an analysis of governance issues. The Bank needs to support this work within the time frame set up by the Moroccan authorities.

Partnerships

Collaboration with UNDP in supporting the governance agenda through technical support for the anticorruption steering committee.

Yemen: Civil Service Modernization Project

Type of Activity: Loan
Timing: Board Approval: April 20, 2000; five year duration
Loan Amount: $30 million

Summary of Contents

This project is envisaged as the first phase of a longer-term reform process designed to make Yemen's civil service more cost efficient, effective and transparent. The objective of this process is to lay the foundation for such a reform by putting in place core personnel and financial management systems, to establish a mechanism to reduce the number of unqualified civil servants, and to initiate a restructuring process in individual ministries. To make this foundation as solid as possible, another objective of the project is to upgrade the management capacity in the civil service.

Innovative / Risky Elements

This project focuses on the very basics. In order to provide a "good fit," it is designed with the limited institutional capacity of the client country in mind, while at the same time seeking to increase this capacity.

The limited institutional capacity of the client country implies that the focus needs to be narrowed and the pace of reform measured, while working toward the long-term goals.

South Asia Region (SAR)

The 1990s witnessed increasing demand throughout South Asia for an effective, transparent, accountable, and responsive public sector. There are many reasons behind this phenomenon, including the global impetus that issues of good governance and institutional reform received in the wake of the so-called Asian crisis; the consolidation of democracy in Bangladesh and Nepal; economic liberalization—particularly in India but also elsewhere; the movement toward decentralization and an expanding role for subnational governments; improved economic and social performance, coupled with the growing middle class in many countries of the region; and increasingly innovative and assertive NGOs. With the exception of Afghanistan, these factors can be found in all the eight countries of the region (Afghanistan, Bangladesh, Bhutan, India, Maldives, Nepal, Pakistan, and Sri Lanka).

The South Asia Region has responded to these developments through country-level strategies for advancing reforms aimed at fundamentally changing public sector institutions. In support of this strategy,

and in collaboration with other multilaterals, bilaterals, and NGOs, the Bank has supported regulatory reform and privatization, as well as the reform of key government functions (for example, reform of service delivery in certain key sectors, civil service reform, financial management, tax administration, and legal reform). The Region intends to consolidate this approach and strengthen it with a new focus on supporting inclusive and accountable institutions, particularly at the local level, and more effectively integrating lessons of experience in our work.

Salient characteristics of the South Asia region

South Asia has the world's largest concentration of people living below the poverty line. Per capita income averaged $430 in 1998, and ranged from $1,171 (Maldives) to $210 (Nepal). With 1.3 billion people, Bangladesh, India, and Pakistan account for the bulk of the region's population and a quarter of the world's population.

All South Asian countries, except for Afghanistan and most recently Pakistan, have parliamentary democracies. India and Sri Lanka have maintained democratic governments since independence, although Sri Lanka has suffered a long and costly civil war. Pakistan and Bangladesh have alternated between periods of military dictatorship and democracy. (In Pakistan, a military government took over in October 1999, but much of the 1990s was spent under democratic rule.) Nepal has emerged from an absolute monarchy to a constitutional monarchy and parliamentary democracy, but has struggled to maintain political stability in recent years. Bhutan has been governed by an enlightened oligarchy. Most of the eight countries of South Asia share similar cultures and institutions shaped to some extent by their common political past and history of colonial rule.

Freedom of the press is well established, and while there is respect for basic human rights, these rights are difficult to enforce uniformly, particularly for the poor. Caste and gender prejudices have led to vested interests and have played an important role in electoral politics, policymaking, and in some instances, state capture. Affirmative action, which has sought to compensate for fragmentation in society, has significantly shaped the public sector through employment and access policies. The judicial system is highly inefficient, and in most countries it is also largely impartial and proactive at its top echelons. Although women are subject to extensive discrimination and exploitative child labor is common, strong women's movements have emerged, and the issue of child labor is on the public agenda. South Asia boasts some of the world's largest and most vibrant NGOs, including the Grameen Bank, BRAC, and ASA in Bangladesh, SEWA in India, and the National Rural Support Program in Pakistan.

Development is impeded in South Asia by the serious difficulties governments face in redefining their role, improving the functioning of core agencies and the delivery of key public services, and in addressing systemic weaknesses in public administration. Poor public management compounds the difficulty of redefining the role of government and transferring appropriate functions to the private sector, and therefore acts as a major obstacle to faster private sector development. Lax tax administrations, harassment of enterprises by the staff of regulatory agencies, slow judicial systems, and improper land registries all increase transaction costs for private citizens, enterprises, and the economy.

Surveys by Transparency International and other domestic and external organizations report deep-seated problems of politicized bureaucracies and both administrative corruption and corrupt actions as a result of state capture. On the positive side, they also highlight (especially in India and Sri Lanka) the independence of the senior judiciary, close compliance with court rulings, and effective recourse to the high courts for challenging government actions.

Reflecting the legacy of central planning, the public sector's influence in South Asian countries has been all-pervasive, a major source of employment covering many sectors of the economy, with entrenched bureaucracies often administering complex regulations that create a scope for corruption. Poor delivery of key public services is of particular concern, ranging from health and education to legal services and road maintenance. While formal institutional mechanisms exist for promoting public accountability (including oversight by parliamentary committees, auditor-generals, anticorruption agencies and legislation), in practice these have been ineffective. Informal "rules of the game" have evolved to cover many economic transactions, and have shaped the roles of the public and private sectors. Government employees are often perceived as aloof and unresponsive, viewing themselves more as public officials than civil servants.

In parts of South Asia, poor governance goes beyond corruption. In these parts, criminal elements, allegedly with powerful political patrons, extort tolls and run protection rackets, presumably a result of the ineffectiveness or the capture of the police and courts. The links to the political system make the problem difficult to tackle. Partial political reforms or dysfunctional politics in such instances do not allow civil society to enforce political contestability that would hold state officials accountable for civil liberties and public services.

Growing demands for institutional change

In almost all South Asian countries, political, social and economic developments have created strong impetus for improvements in public institutions, and their accountability, transparency, and effectiveness.

Political and social developments. The consolidation of democracy in Bangladesh, more recently in Nepal, and until recently in Pakistan, growing literacy, and urbanization have all importantly shaped the demand for institutional change. The influence of NGOs on improving governance, inclusion, and the delivery of key social services has grown rapidly, not only because of their increase in number, but also because of their innovative approaches to service delivery. These developments have already yielded important lessons for the Bank, even though there is still more to learn and integrate into our work.

Liberalization. Reflecting a changing global consensus, all South Asia countries have been gradually liberalizing their economies and reducing the role of the public sector since the late 1970s. They have progressed at different paces in this endeavor—Sri Lanka the fastest and Nepal the slowest, though South Asian countries as a whole still lag behind other parts of the world. Even in Sri Lanka, for example, trade protection is much higher than in East Asia or Latin America, the public sector continues to dominate the financial sector, public enterprises account for a larger share of GDP, private participation in energy and infrastructure

is negligible, and taxation is based on highly differentiated rates falling on narrow bases. Though partial, economic liberalization has nonetheless reduced incentives for state capture, increased competition, and made more evident the costs of ineffective provision of public services that reduce the competitiveness of domestic production.

Decentralization. Responding to grassroots pressures, and in parallel with market reforms, a process of decentralization took off in the mid-1990s in South Asia. Both India and Bangladesh have put in place the legal foundations for elected local governments. In India, economic liberalization has given way to the states' responsibilities that had been circumscribed by central planning. More powers to the states and local governments are expected to increase accountability. Though limited, there are early signs that service delivery is improving (Madhya Pradesh and West Bengal in India, local infrastructure construction in Bangladesh). Strong public pressure for more responsive and accountable local governments have also emerged in Nepal, Pakistan, and Sri Lanka—however, except for the Punjab province in Pakistan, little progress has been achieved in these countries.

Information technology. The spread of information technology, and India's emergence as a leading exporter of software, is beginning to have a significant impact upon public sector management. States like Andhra Pradesh have used computerization and business process re-engineering to radically improve the timeliness and quality of services (and, while doing so, to eliminate opportunities for graft and "speed money"). Other states, ministries and departments are utilizing information technology to greatly improve transparency, by putting forms and information on the Internet, or to enhance convenience and accountability by creating one-stop shops for service delivery.

High-profile corruption cases. Several recent high-profile legal actions—including against a former Pakistani Prime Minister and several Indian ministers—

have sought to censure corruption in high places and are also a reflection of the growing public demand for institutional change that addresses both administrative corruption and state capture.

Experience to date in the South Asia region

South Asian governments have both sought Bank support for strengthening the performance of public institutions and have also initiated reforms independent of Bank assistance. Our assistance for public institutional reform has had three main objectives:

- reorienting the public sector,

- establishing regulatory frameworks and agencies to enhance private competition and protect consumer rights, and

- reforming *key* government functions where there is a clear role for the public sector.

These elements have been pursued through sector lending and analytic services by each sector unit, in line with the regional strategy of mainstreaming this work in our country programs, the matrix organization, and the substantial decentralization of the Region.

While the Bank is engaged in extensive dialogue on these issues, political considerations in each country have often made leaders reluctant to pursue measures to reform the role of the state. Our work has therefore focused on country-level strategies for improving incentives for reorienting the public sector. For example, in India, our strategic approach and assistance are concentrated on states willing to reform, and where the nature of these reforms is expected to help improve institutions, including in power, irrigation, tax administration, and privatization (Box 22). In Nepal, the assistance strategy and lending program depend on reforms that will fundamentally change public sector

institutions, also including Bank assistance to local governments that are willing to reform. The Bangladesh CAS makes public institutional reform its central focus. Through a process of unbundling politically complex and time-consuming reforms, Bank assistance seeks to match client commitment and strengthen existing institutions or help create new ones, such as in banking, power, and the social sectors. In Pakistan, power sector reforms are leveraged by the lending program, and are likely to have substantial repercussions on how public institutions perform. In Sri Lanka, support for privatization is also leveraged by the lending program.

Reorienting the public sector. The Bank has encouraged governments to exit progressively from commercial activities and service delivery that can be carried out more efficiently by the private sector. South Asian governments have now opened most areas of the economy to the private sector, including areas that had been reserved for public sector investment for many decades. However, because of strong opposition from vested interests (principally unions and bureaucrats), privatization of state-owned enterprises has been slow, and government officials continue to dominate company boards. In India, the states have made more progress on privatization and in promoting competition in the private sector than has the central government.

Notable among the efforts to reorient the public sector are the institutional changes being made in the power sector, which are encouraging substantial private investment in power accompanied by a very different way of doing business (Box 23). The Indian states of Orissa, Haryana, and Andhra Pradesh are in the midst of major reform programs to privatize power utilities with Bank assistance, and several others (Gujarat, Rajasthan, Uttar Pradesh) have declared their intention to follow suit. The Bank has started a dialogue on the long-term reform of the power sector in Bangladesh, but the process is at an early stage. Privatization outside the power sector has also been initiated in Bangladesh,

BOX 22

Subnational Assistance for Governance and Public Sector Reform in India

The 1997 India CAS urged a "focus mainly on those states that have chosen to embark on a comprehensive program of economic reforms." Bank assistance to Andhra Pradesh represented the first such partnership. The Andhra Pradesh Economic Restructuring Project (APERP) is a multi-sector loan within a fiscal framework that shifts expenditures toward growth enhancing social and infrastructure investment, while containing growth of debt, public guarantees, and debt service expenditures. Sectoral components of the loan include support for strengthening rural irrigation, primary health and education services, rural roads development, and child nutrition. The APERP also supports the state's efforts to restructure and divest public enterprises, many of which constitute a major drain on the budget. The Bank continues to work closely with the Government of Andhra Pradesh to provide assistance and make available information about promising reform efforts in other countries.

Uttar Pradesh represents the second phase of this state-focused approach, based on a multi-year, multi-sector reform strategy that includes governance and fiscal reforms as core elements. The Bank's program in Uttar Pradesh brings together a diverse set of instruments, from adjustment to investment lending, and from poverty to judicial assessments. These are being delivered in an integrated manner, akin to the approach envisaged by the CDF, and through an overall Bank-Government dialogue rather than the traditional sector-specific approach. The governance reform program covers a broad spectrum of issues, including civil service renewal, expenditure management, public enterprise reform and privatization, decentralization, anticorruption, and financial management and accountability. These reforms to core systems and procedures of government are being closely integrated with policy and institutional reforms in key sectors such as power, irrigation, forestry, health, and roads, as part of a broad, multi-sector program.

Depending on client interest, this integrated approach to economic policy, governance, and institutional reform is likely to be adapted to other states in India. With the Bank's encouragement, Karnataka recently began developing a strategy for public sector reform involving topics such as right-sizing, public sector restructuring and electronic governance. Dialogue is just beginning with other states, such as Rajasthan and Orissa.

BOX 23

Power Sector Reforms in South Asia

South Asian countries are transforming their power sectors. Pakistan and several Indian states have pioneered this transformation, and important lessons have been learned in the process. The power sectors have been dominated by inefficient and poorly governed public utilities. The bulk of the rural population and many urban residents do not have access to electricity, even though they can pay for it. Load-shedding and power outages have added greatly to business costs. Public power utilities have been subject to political pressures to set tariffs that subsidize the well-off, and to hire staff even while poor pay makes it difficult for the utilities to retain qualified employees. These factors, coupled with laxity about dealing with electricity theft, have led to the accumulation of huge losses. The utilities relied on the government to provide investment capital and to cover operating costs.

Starting in the early 1990s, donors and multilateral institutions began holding back their support for the power sector in the absence of fundamental reforms. At the same time the private sector started to display considerable interest in investing in power generation. The growing demand for better services, growing financial requirements, and the failure to find resources elsewhere led political leaders to consider reform.

In the early 1990s, Pakistan was among the first to attract private investments for new generating plants. In the process, mistakes were made

and lessons learned. Pakistan paid insufficient attention to financial and economic consequences and failed to fully implement planned reforms of the publicly owned utility, a process that should have preceded the entry of private capital in generation. These reforms include:

- Unbundling power plants from the power system;

- Creating a separate transmission company that can operate at arm's length from generators and distributors;

- Unbundling distribution into several utilities to facilitate regulation and create quasi-competition in natural monopoly settings;

- Creating an independent regulatory body, supported by adequate legislation, so that pricing is determined on the basis of objective criteria.

The process of power sector restructuring in South Asia has been far from easy, given the interest of stakeholders, unions, workers, and managers. Experience demonstrates, however, that involving workers' representatives early in the restructuring exercise can facilitate the process. Compensation for honest losers from the restructuring is also needed. More difficult to overcome is the resistance of those who wrongfully benefit from corrupt practices.

Nepal, Pakistan, and Sri Lanka. Each is now active in creating the minimum consensus and conditions to allow privatization to proceed. In Sri Lanka, the Bank helped privatize public enterprises ranging from tea estates and the national airline to the post office and telecommunications. In Pakistan, the Bank has supported privatization of public banks. Bank support for privatization in Bangladesh has, however, not been very successful, and a large structural adjustment credit (for jute mill privatization) had to be cancelled.

Establishing regulatory frameworks and agencies. Recognizing that without a competitive environment privatization cannot be effective and could result in abuses, the Bank has given considerable attention to helping governments establish effective and appropriate regulation. The dangers of inadequate regulation have been clearly demonstrated in South Asia's banking systems. In Bangladesh and Nepal, poor banking supervision and enforcement have allowed unrecoverable loans to accumulate to high levels, often through fraud. In India, Pakistan, and Sri Lanka, progress has been made with Bank assistance, but their respective banking systems continue to be dominated by inefficient public sector banks. Appropriate regulation is also needed to protect the public interest from environmental and other hazards.

Together with its support for privatization, the Bank is also supporting the establishment of independent regulators in power, telecommunications, the environment, irrigation, and water management. Reforms in power have focused on regulatory agencies (in several states in India, Pakistan, and Bangladesh) that can oversee the privatization of generation and distribution. In telecommunications, the Bank has supported

---

BOX 24

Transforming Water Management in Pakistan

Pakistan's agricultural production comes predominantly from irrigated agriculture. Consequently, the efficient management of irrigation and drainage is crucial in the Indus Basin, the world's largest integrated irrigation network. For decades this responsibility was entrusted to a federal agency, the Water and Power Development Authority, and four Provincial Irrigation Departments, all of which acquired reputations of being rigid, centralized bureaucracies. Little effort was made to involve farmers in irrigation management. There was mounting criticism of the agencies' wastage of resources, low operational efficiency, unresponsiveness to stakeholders, and poor financial sustainability.

This situation has been changing substantially in recent years with water management reforms supported by several IDA-financed programs, notably the National Drainage Program. Water users' associations have been set up with delegated authority to operate and maintain irrigation canals. These users' associations, the changed mandate and structure of the Authority and the Irrigation Departments and measures to increase their operational efficiency and financial sustainability, and the extensive use of public awareness campaigns to build public support have been key to the reforms. The private sector's role in service delivery has also been enhanced by contracting out operation and maintenance.

the entry of private operators and a transfer of regulatory functions to independent agencies. Progress in this direction has been most marked in Sri Lanka, where service has improved substantially. Irrigation reform has been based so far on the formation of water-user associations in charge of the maintenance of distribution canals and cost recovery. In Pakistan this has led to a radical transformation in the way the sector is managed (Box 24).

Reforming key government functions. Overstaffing, poor compensation, inadequate training, and civil service incentives that discourage initiative have been identified as important reasons for poor public sector performance. Administrative practices and laws inherited from colonial regimes have remained largely in place, and little has been done to modernize them. Given these serious systemic problems, it is not surprising that reforms have generally progressed slowly, with considerable resistance to change from powerful

vested interests (corrupt politicians, union leaders, civil servants, and business monopolists) that perceive reform as disadvantageous. The difficulties encountered are well illustrated by the case of Bangladesh (Box 25). Progress hinges critically on public sector downsizing that would release funds to be used for paying better salaries and for funding increased operations and maintenance—an approach that is opposed by public sector unions. The Bank has helped to meet the cost of staff redundancies in a number of cases (jute mills in Bangladesh), but there has been no concerted action so far by any government to create a smaller, higher-paid, well-trained, and better-performing civil service. Given the importance of improving key government functions, and notwithstanding the difficulties, the Bank's efforts in this area are extensive and diverse, covering budget systems and financial controls in most countries; civil service reform in Sri Lanka, Pakistan, and some Indian states; land records in Sri

---

BOX 25

Addessing Public Sector Management Reform in Bangladesh

In 1996 the Bank completed a study, *Government That Works: Reforming the Public Sector,* with the participation of senior Bangladeshi government officials and local researchers. The report laid out a candid assessment of governance issues and proposed a comprehensive set of reforms in the hope that the new government, which took office after the June 1996 elections, would be willing to act. Indeed, the Minister of Finance circulated the report to his Cabinet colleagues and to Members of Parliament. Subsequently, following a workshop attended by senior officials and some political

leaders, a number of priority measures were endorsed by Cabinet.

However, none of the substantive measures were implemented over the next three years, even though the need for reforms was apparently accepted. This experience serves to underline the political difficulties in supporting public management reforms from the top. It highlights the need to pay much more serious attention to the incentives faced by all stakeholders, both formal and informal, and to find ways to build public support for reform that go well beyond senior officials and the elite in society.

Lanka; tax administration in Pakistan, Bangladesh, and several Indian states; a public sector modernization project under preparation in Bangladesh; legal reform in Bangladesh and Sri Lanka; and procurement procedures in several countries. Assistance has been provided through both structural adjustment loans and technical assistance. Extensive domestic public debate, helped in some countries by reports by the Bank and other donors, has helped to fuel growing public pressure for reform of public administration, and the topic is now very much on the political agenda. In Pakistan, for example, the Bank has issued a major report on reforming the civil service, which will be a basis for further dialogue. This is also the case with the Bank's study on the state of Uttar Pradesh in India, which discusses governance as a central focus of our assistance.

We recognize that there will not be quick results, but rather a long and difficult process of change that will need to be pursued with persistence and patience. Partnerships with other donors—for example DFID, UNICEF, and USAID in India for the state-focused work, and with ADB and OECD for power reforms in Bangladesh—are important in this process of long-term change.

The challenges ahead

Using the lessons from the Bank's extensive assistance in South Asia to address public sector weaknesses, we are now moving to more strategic and systemic work on institutional development, public administration and governance. We realize that new approaches and new skills are required to become more effective. Our strategy will assist privatization and deregulation where the role of the public sector needs to be redefined; mainstream public institutional concerns in our sector lending and nonlending services; form partnerships with NGOs and others in civil society to foster the demand for institutional change; and ensure that insti-

tutional concerns are central to our country dialogue. Our aim will be to help governments, both at national and subnational levels, strengthen the core functions of public administration and to support the building of inclusive and accountable institutions for improved service delivery. We see the need to build partnerships with other donors and across sectors to tackle this task in more coordinated ways. Through operational learning, we will identify and disseminate good practice that fits local conditions.

There can be little dispute that the two crucial factors underlying the performance of institutions are the incentives that drive the behavior of the main stakeholders and the absence or presence of accountability frameworks. Our work has often proceeded under the assumption that the key to performance lies in formal organizational structures and rules, without full consideration of informal practices and their impact on development outcomes. We have tended to advocate technocratic, "best practice" solutions based on global experience, while ignoring the underlying social context in which the institutions are rooted and which shape the informal rules. An IGR recently completed in Bangladesh examines these issues as part of its assessment of institutional performance. The challenge ahead is to understand better this local reality, to listen better, and to help design "best fit" solutions that combine worldwide "best practice" and local "good fit". Ultimately, the solution to these problems must be home-grown—coming from within each country's administration, NGOs, and civil society and responding to a growing public demand for reform. The Bank can and should foster this growing demand by helping to make available promising practices, particularly those derived from within the region, and by placing the issues firmly and openly on the table through good analytic studies and dialogue with governments and civil society.

Nurturing inclusive and accountable institutions. There appears to be a growing consensus in South Asia that decentralization is one of the most promising strategies for greater inclusion of citizens in governance and development and for bringing government closer to the people. In India, the 1992 constitutional amendments provide for the establishment of stronger elected local authorities. Bangladesh is in the process of creating a three-tiered system of elected local government. These changes could have profound implications for the way public services are delivered and create opportunities for citizens to participate more directly in the process.

Unless effective accountability is ensured, the benefits may be captured by local elites. Consequently, the links between local NGOs, community-based organizations, and elected bodies need to be nurtured to achieve inclusive and accountable arrangements, and to give "voice" and representation to vulnerable groups. The Bank has already begun and will intensify a dialogue on center-state relationships and support for local government administrations (in Sri Lanka, Bangladesh, Pakistan, and several Indian states). We plan to undertake a number of studies to enhance our understanding of these issues and to improve the design of future Bank-supported operations. This work will also address the need to create more effective systems for monitoring and measuring accountability and inclusiveness.

Improving accountability mechanisms will be a general goal, not limited to local government settings. For example, we are very interested in seeing countries improve overall financial management accountability in the public sector. CFAAs have been started for almost all countries in South Asia. These will go hand in hand with our efforts to help improve countries' anticorruption efforts and will include support for civil society institutions, such as local chapters of Transparency International. Related to this effort is support for diagnostic surveys on service delivery and corruption that will generate hard data on what is actually happening as experienced by households and enterprises.

Operational learning. Recognizing the complexity of institution-building, we see a need to be much more cautious than in the past in advocating the transfer to South Asia of institutional models developed in other countries and contexts. Instead, there is an imperative to learn more from in-country experience. Furthermore, in supporting new initiatives, much value is to be gained from a highly participatory approach in order to arrive at appropriate project designs. This approach will be applied not just to village and municipal level programs (including school boards and community management of health facilities), but also to efforts to reform core public administration functions such as tax administration, public expenditure management, and personnel management. We are also proposing to undertake a review of the experience with institutional development activities in Bank projects to strengthen our understanding of what works and what does not at the project level. Such operational learning will be important since much of the South Asia Region's assistance for institution-building will continue to be incorporated in its sector projects. This will build on closer coordination and knowledge sharing between sector units, including the PREM and social development units.

Organization, staffing, and partnerships. To enhance attention to the institution-building, public management, and governance dimensions of our work, new staff are being hired with specialized expertise, particularly in core public sector reforms. At the same time, there is no intention at this juncture to create a separate public sector group in SASPR, as the Region sees institution-building as an integral part of all sector units' work, requiring staff with requisite skills and orientation to deal with these issues in each sector. To facilitate learning across sectors and countries, the Region is considering setting up a small working group on governance and public sector management involving staff from both sector and country units. In the area of financial management, we have already recruited specialist staff for Bank offices in the field. A new chief financial officer has joined recently and will help guide the Region's financial accountability framework.

The fuller recognition of the need to understand social, cultural and political aspects of our work will require the social development unit to give attention to wider aspects of governance and the management of the core functions of the state, as well as to intensify its work at the local level. Success in addressing institutional weaknesses will depend on both a multi-disciplinary and a cross-sectoral approach. It will also depend on more fully integrating "best practice" and the knowledge generated elsewhere in Bank and the networks, and integrating the services of WBI more closely in our work.

Since many development agencies are active in assisting South Asian countries with institution-building, public management, and governance, we are placing strong emphasis on donor coordination, especially at the country level. The aim will be to agree on common approaches and to ensure that we draw on each other's strengths to deliver the best possible support to our clients in South Asia.

India: Uttar Pradesh Fiscal and Governance Reform

Type of Activity: Loan/Credit

Timing: Approved: April 2000; Single-tranche operation

Loan/Credit Amount: $250 million ($150 million IDA and $100 million IBRD)

Summary of Contents

Uttar Pradesh is India's most populous state and one of its poorest. It has experienced prolonged economic stagnation, fiscal crisis, and collapse in its development programs. There has been little progress against its massive poverty (41 percent poor) in recent decades. This Loan/Credit supports the government of UP's reform program aimed at addressing the fiscal crisis and improving governance. It is a single-tranche loan, the first subnational adjustment loan in India and also the first in a sequence of three or four loans to support fiscal and governance reforms. The operation is part of a State Assistance Strategy that seeks to support the state's efforts to turn around its economic and social performance. That state strategy includes support for reforms in the power, water and irrigation, health, education, roads, urban and rural sectors. The proposed loan/credit will support the initial phase of the state's program to restore fiscal sustainability and reform governance, critical as they are to accelerating growth and reducing poverty. The actions triggering the presentation of the operation to the Board emerged from the economic policy dialogue with the government of UP spanning the last 18 months during which this operation was prepared.

Innovative / Risky Elements

This operation, designed to support CAS objectives and part of the UP State Assistance Strategy, is key in an ongoing effort to improve the fiscal situation and introduce structural reforms in Indian states. The operation reinforces recent initiatives by the Government of India to stimulate such reforms. Expected direct benefits include: (a) improved fiscal situation; (b) improved governance; (c) higher growth and reduced poverty; (d) contribution to reduction in the overall public sector borrowing requirement; and (e) encouragement of similar reforms in other Indian states. The major risks are: (a) possible reversal of reforms caused by political resistance; (b) lack of adequate institutional capacity; and (c) significant unanticipated decline in central government transfers to the state.

Partnerships

The Bank has initiated a dialogue on UP within the donor community and has briefed various development partners about its assistance strategy. Given UP's massive population and poverty, there is both room and need for a much stronger effort by development agencies there. Over time, following the reforms supported by this operation, many opportunities for collaboration are expected to open up in a new context of reform and restructuring. Some of this has already begun, for example in the power sector, where the Bank typically works alongside bilateral cofinancing. Bank staff are also keeping the IMF briefed on the status of these reform efforts.

Development Research Group (DRG)

Over the last few years, the World Bank's Development Research Group (DRG) has increasingly focused its research on institutions. Operational staff and policymakers in developing countries are seeking advice not just on the design of economic policies, but also on the design of institutions that lead to the adoption of good policies and to better implementation of policies. Furthermore, our research, reflected in Policy Research Reports such as *The East Asian Miracle, Bureaucrats in Business,* and *Assessing Aid,* provides evidence of the importance of institutions and points to ways of reforming institutions to achieve faster economic growth, more efficient public enterprises, and more effective foreign aid.

Research questions

This emphasis on institutions is exemplified by DRG's work on the public sector. Both the questions asked and the research method used reflect the fact that public sector reform involves an understanding of, and changes to, the underlying "rules of the game" that determine incentives and information in the public sector. The research questions address three main issues:

- **How and why are good policies adopted?** Building on the work in *Bureaucrats in Business,* DRG has been studying the incentives for policy reform in several areas, such as reform of public enterprises and reform of fiscal policy. The research has led to the development of a political database, as well as a set of indicators for operational staff to use in gauging their country's propensity for reform.

- **How should the public sector be organized?** DRG research, which contributed to and drew from *WDR97,* examines core public sector reforms aimed at improving the effectiveness of government. A first-level question is which activities should be in the public sector? Our research on privatization informs the decision of when to privatize, and also looks at problems in contracting, and post-privatization regulatory and competition policy. We also examine private participation in the health and education sectors.

For the set of activities in the public sector, DRG research focuses on how public sector institutions can make them more effective. A major institutional development is the decentralization of responsibilities to lower-level governments. The research examines the impact of decentralization on economic performance, and how different institutional settings affect this impact. A related area is the research on budget institutions and their effect on the outcome of public expenditures. This research has led to a significant shift in emphasis of Public Expenditure Reviews (PERs) from budget allocations to the underlying institutions that govern public spending.

- *How can public services be delivered more efficiently?* Inasmuch as the major role of government is to deliver services to the public, DRG research has focused on improving service delivery in a number of sectors, as well as some cross-sectoral issues. In education, a series of impact evaluation studies examines different forms of local autonomy to schools. In health, a study shows how provider-payment schemes affect health outcomes. In environment, the Policy Research Report, *Greening Industry*, documents how public information campaigns can complement pollution-control programs, especially in weak administrative environments.

The two most important cross-cutting issues are the research on anticorruption and on participation. Building on the synergies with operational work, the anticorruption research has provided both empirical foundations for anticorruption strategies, and diagnostic tools for implementing the strategies. On participation, DRG research provided the first empirical justification for favoring participation in projects, and continues to support and evaluate this widely used method of project management.

Research method

Since so much of the Bank's work is in the public sector, DRG's research program on the public sector is closely linked with operations. Most of the research questions derive from consultations with operations, mainly through the Public Sector Board and other sector boards (all of which have DRG representation). Furthermore, much of the research, such as the anticorruption and public expenditure work mentioned above, is carried out in collaboration with operations. DRG also works in close collaboration with the World Bank Institute on both research and dissemination in many areas (anticorruption and public expenditures being good examples).

In addition, DRG research in general, and public sector work in particular, involve partners from academic institutions in developed and developing countries. For instance, the research on decentralization involves collaborators from Asia, Africa, and Latin America. In this way the public sector research also serves as a vehicle for building policy research capacity in developing countries. Recently, DRG researchers have lent their expertise in developing research networks in our client countries, such as the African Economic Research Consortium and the Middle East Economic Research Forum. Finally, DRG's standard practice of making its data available has benefited the policy community inside and outside the Bank, especially on public sector issues such as public expenditure, foreign aid, and corruption.

Current work program

DRG's current work program reflects both a heightened emphasis on public sector issues and an increased focus on the institutional dimensions of those issues.

Decentralization, competition and regulation, effective schools, and the delivery of health services are major components of this work program. New initiatives on NGOs, crime and violence prevention, agency credibility, and privatizing telecommunications in Africa all contribute to the common goal of helping our clients improve public sector performance. Given the increased emphasis on institutions and political economy, DRG has recruited two non-economist social scientists to broaden its methodological scope. We expect to recruit one or two more, especially in political science. Two major data initiatives, one on firms and the other on subnational data, will buttress the research on public sector reform. The firm-level data are already being used to examine corruption issues, while the subnational data will contribute to the work on decentralization.

A strategy for public sector research

The coming years will see a consolidation of DRG's public sector work in two ways. First, anticipating the *World Development Report* on "Institutions and Development" in 2001/2002, the Group is preparing a series of Policy Research Reports, each of which will examine particular institutional questions in depth. The PRRs on decentralization, education, regulation and competition, and health mentioned earlier are all part of this series.

Second, public service delivery is rapidly becoming the most important development issue in the post-adjustment era. It is also an area in which the Bank has perhaps the most cross-country experience of any organization in the world. Building on its current research on public service delivery, DRG plans to develop this topic into a major, if not the major component of its portfolio, with a view toward providing the development community with an in-depth document on public service delivery in three years.

Indonesia, Venezuela, and Russia: Special Governance Zones

Type of Activity: Research and Knowledge Transfer

Timing: March 2000 - March 2002

Summary of Contents

Building on the worldwide experience with special economic zones, this project seeks to establish "special governance zones" (SGZs) in countries where comprehensive, system-wide governance reform may not be feasible. The SGZ is a well-defined area (for example, a municipality) within a country where high standards of governance and anticorruption are met. The SGZ serves both as a means of testing anticorruption strategies on a small-scale, as well as a showcase which, if successful, could be replicated elsewhere in the country.

This project is currently being piloted in Russia, Indonesia and Venezuela, with the Bank providing (in addition to the idea) analytic support in setting up surveys to monitor progress in anticor-ruption, and in designing the appropriate governance strategies.

Innovative / Risky Elements

The idea is new, although it draws from two well-known ideas: special economic zones, and anti-corruption diagnostics. The risks include the possibility that the zone may not be replicated anywhere in the country, and of course that it may not be truly corruption-free. There is also a risk that the project may be seen as another requirement from the World Bank.

Partnerships

Harvard University's Center for International Development, and local institutions in Indonesia, Russia and Venezuela.

Global: Fiscal Decentralization

Type of Activity: Policy Research Report
Timing: June 1999 - June 2001

Summary of Contents

With over 80 countries reforming their intergovernmental fiscal relations, this policy research report looks at the promises and pitfalls of fiscal decentralization. Based on cross-country and case-study evidence, we find that decentralization promotes efficiency and equity only under certain circumstances—mostly having to do with well-functioning institutions at the local level. Furthermore, decentralization can jeopardize macroeconomic stability, by creating incentives forsubnational governments to over-borrow. The report identifies ways of managing decentralization so as to avoid the pitfalls and fulfill some of the promises.

Innovative / Risky Elements

Politically sensitive—some countries are decentralizing for political reasons. Risks include the report being ignored by policymakers.

Partnerships

Extremely productive partnerships with local researchers in case study countries (Argentina, Brazil, China, Colombia, India, Nigeria, South Africa) and with OECD-based researchers.

World Bank Institute (WBI)

Partnering with the rest of the Bank Group, with outside organizations, and with numerous stakeholders within client countries, WBI takes an integrated approach to capacity building and improved public sector performance. This strategy is predicated on a number of central premises that are described in detail below.

Going beyond public sector malfunction (the 'symptom') to assist countries in integrating institutional, regulatory and economic reforms (the 'fundamentals'). The basics of reforms within the public sector, such as traditional civil service reforms, are still very important, and are prominent in WBI's strategy. However, broader reforms, including the way in which the public sector relates to the economy and to the private sector, are also crucial for improved public sector performance. Using a governance and capacity building approach, WBI has a clear focus on poverty reduction and works with PRSP countries, as it is becoming clear that misgovernance has social costs and that the poor are often discriminated against in the provision of basic services. The poverty-alleviation focus goes hand in hand with a sector focus, whereby the governance

and public sector management reform program targets, among other things, the banking sector, the energy sector, the health sector, and the environment sector. Thus, management of public finances, corporate governance and business ethics, regulation of privatized infrastructure, financial sector regulation, and competition policy are also emphasized in order to affect lasting, welfare-improving institutional change, and as exemplified below, they are integrated with each other. A key component of the governance and anticorruption program is the poverty-alleviation and sustained-growth focus, backstopping much of the operational research findings within our group that fits into the World Bank program, and increasingly linking with other parts of the Bank on the CDF and the PRSP countries.

Emphasizing rigorous empirical analysis. WBI's activities increasingly focus on in-depth analysis of the empirical evidence on public sector institutions. Significant efforts are going into building a major data bank on institutional indicators, a previously underdeveloped area, and to the analysis of this evidence for use in designing our work program. New approaches to measuring and improving public service delivery as well as in-depth diagnostic tools on governance and anticorruption (based on new survey tools for public officials, enterprises, citizens, and now, consultants), were developed in collaboration with DEC and ECA and are now being extended to Africa, Latin America and Asia. The resulting diagnoses are proving important determinants of the scope and sequencing of governance reforms. In partnership with EBRD and ECA, a very innovative approach has emerged based on data from a specially designed survey—the 1999 Business Environment and Enterprise Performance Survey (BEEPS), which allows the unbundling of the measurement of influence and corruption into specific components, as well as empirically examining a number of key questions regarding state capture for the very first time. The findings of this empirical work have major policy implications, pointing to a departure from the conventional public sector management approach to combat corruption and improve governance.[28]

Emphasis on setting in motion a collective action process, where WBI facilitates coalition-building and bottom-up participatory processes for institutional change. The focus is on clients in the field, moving beyond mere participation and assisting the creation of coalitions between civil society, parliamentary groups, private sector and key government stakeholders, bodies empowered for collective action and sustainable institutional change.

Building partnerships. Much more focus is being put on partnership arrangements as key elements for leveraging activities and increasing their impact:

- partnerships within countries (for example, the Centers for Regulatory Reform discussed below; survey institutes carrying out diagnostics, other NGOs, etc.),

- partnerships within the Bank Group, where now we expect to have a partner (usually in operations; also with the network anchors and DEC) in virtually every activity; and

- partnerships with other international or regional institutions such as the Commonwealth Press Union and the Parliamentary Center (Canada).

Moving beyond conventional training courses to knowledge dissemination, policy advice and consensus-building activities. The demand for expert policy and technical advice from high-level policymakers is significant, and rising. Thus, technical advice and high-level policy seminars responding to specific requests from countries and Bank Regions are becoming increasingly important. Further, moving away from conventional lecturing to interactive and action-oriented courses allows participants to prepare and internalize a program of institutional change within their own countries. A prime example is the "core course" program on Controlling Corruption and Improving Governance. The pilot program started in June 1999 in Washington, followed by six weeks of distance learning activities through simultaneous video conferencing to seven capitals in Africa, capped by the final stage at the 9th International Anticorruption Conference in Durban, South Africa, where the seven Africa teams presented their governance programs. Responding to an ever increasing number of requests from client countries, advisory services on participatory processes consistent with the CDF and the substantive action programs to improve governance and address corruption will continue to be provided. These services are linked to the new and participatory Anticorruption Core Course mentioned above, which has a focused and well-structured approach to the formulation of a governance program by the country stakeholders, including fundamental components of institutional changes, such as reforms in: (a) judiciary and legal institutions; (b) procurement and financial management; (c) customs and tax institutions; (d) civil service reforms; and (e) regulatory reform and corporate governance/business ethics.

Scaling up the governance program. The integrated program on Governance and Anticorruption will be scaled up, building on the Core Course experience with seven African countries, the municipal/decentralization program with partners such as Monterrey Tech, and the Campo Elias case that aimed at disseminating lessons on establishing credible, efficient, and transparent municipal governments in Latin America. This program involved joint participation among WBI, the city's mayor, and civil society with the purpose of providing the municipality with the tools to implement an integrated action plan for institutional reform. It was designed to create a transparent local government by enhancing credibility and accountability, promoting citizen participation, and encouraging government and civil society to share responsibility for service delivery.

Utilizing new tools and instruments and knowledge dissemination. Further development and use of distance learning techniques as well as electronic interface techniques is underway. Examples include video conferencing support to the African Parliamentarians Network Against Corruption and the Development Forum virtual conference on curbing corruption. New approaches to the implementation of participatory workshops, with the media present, followed by particular focus groups and teamwork, are also being piloted. A consolidated Media Development and Accountability program will be developed in fiscal 2001. A more recent undertaking is related to e-governance, with the relaunching of the governance website as a true learning tool that incorporates lots of training materials and data, as well as operational research elements.

Innovating and taking managed risks. Focusing on the knowledge side of the Bank permits WBI to work on areas which, when associated with lending, would be more controversial, such as: encouraging civil society participation to promote citizen "voice" and participation, workshops with the media and parliamentarians, the dissemination of research findings on civil liberties, corruption, democracy and development, and new empirical diagnostic work. But knowledge in this area is still evolving; there is not a single "best practice" model, but at best "good fit," and we will learn from the

mistakes and successes while innovating and taking judicious risks.

The interrelated themes for improved public sector performance

Public sector management reforms. To achieve objectives on the ground, the program has a major focus on establishing sustainable institutional development, and is fully consistent with the governance program. All public sector management work starts from an assessment of the role, structure, and efficiency of the state in particular country circumstances. The approach used in each key area is grounded in economic theories of institutions and has been designed to provide participants with a coherent view of a system, such as a personnel system or budgeting system. This work is done with all institutions that shape the way public functions are carried out and is aimed at building sustainable institutional development.

Large deficits, poor resource allocation, and inefficient delivery of public services have caused many countries to reform their public expenditure management systems. Many developing and transitional countries are facing similar or more severe problems and have developed their own adaptations of some of these reforms. But in general these reforms, and in particular the conditions under which they might work, are not very well understood. The public sector management work focuses on developing and offering training and dissemination programs to improve the functioning of government at all levels and thus to enhance its performance. These efforts include the following:

A core program on *Public Expenditure and Management,* which will be delivered through distance learning. Three deliveries are being contemplated this fiscal year. The program will provide a forum through which these reforms and their applicability can be discussed and will have an increased focus on the PRSP. The reforms build on innovations and research in the area of the new institutional economics, which focuses on the impact of rules, norms, and procedures, both formal and informal, on budget outcomes. They consider in an integrated way the three key budget objectives of aggregate fiscal discipline, strategic resource allocation, and operational efficiency, and emphasize their linkages. The development of new lending instruments such as PSALs, which will allow a longer-term focus on institution-building, will increase the emphasis on reforming public expenditure management systems. This core program is undergoing a major update which will include an in-depth treatment of public sector management reform with much more emphasis on PRSP countries.

Civil service reform traditionally looks at personnel management, improved organizations and structures, and general capacity building. Consideration is being given to commencing work in the area of managing the senior civil service as a key lever in public management reform. Furthermore, it is proposed to develop a regional course in the area of performance management (sometimes referred to as results based management). This fits within WBI's recent emphasis on deepening a rigorous, empirically oriented approach to the analysis of institutional variables, outcomes, and performance. The course would assist countries in developing performance measures and evaluation techniques, and linking them with decisionmaking processes—of which the budget is a major vehicle.

Municipal performance programs. The focus is on policy as well as intergovernmental fiscal relations and urban-management issues. The rapid urbanization rate throughout the regions implies that much of the public sector management challenge into the next decade will reside with the city managers, to respond to the new challenges posed by globalization, decentralization, and urbanization/localization. Issues of city governance, financial management, private sector involvement, and land markets have taken on a new meaning within modern municipal management and policy-making frameworks. The main objective of the program is to provide tools to city managers to improve local government management and efficiency in the provision of local services.

The LCR municipal initiative. It focuses on two complementary approaches to developing credible and transparent municipal governments in the LCR Region: (a) carrying out national-municipal accountability diagnostics (NMAD) to map the different institutions from the perspective of the political and fiscal framework, and to define how the national structures affect the incentive framework of municipal government for a more open, accountable, and transparent government; and (b) developing pilot programs at the subnational and municipal level to document and codify practical advice. The concept of municipal transparency will be introduced to local governments as a means of enhancing accountability and credibility. Pilot interventions are taking place or will take place in Venezuela, Guatemala, Honduras, Chile, and Bolivia to promote initiatives for a transparent government.

An innovative program, "Challenges in Urban and City Management," has been developed by three groups within WBI, the Urban Department, and thematic groups. It is a distance learning-based activity—complemented by an electronic space—and looks at several disciplines including: governance, municipal finance, environmental management, and intergovernmental fiscal relations. Another important dimension that is taken into consideration is the critical role of urban and subnational issues in the context of the CDF, and workshops are offered on subnational capital markets development, credit ratings, and bond issuing.

Another major new initiative is being designed to offer local government capacity building training, knowledge, and expertise based on distance learning programs. The program will respond to the increasing pressure put on governments at the subnational level to perform new roles in their communities as a result of globalization, decentralization, urbanization, and the reform of government, involving changes in roles of the public and the private sector. The clients will primarily be subnational local governments in sub-Saharan Africa, South and Southeast Asia, and possibly Latin America.

Core Courses: These are two-week Urban and City Management core courses for city managers and researchers who could help replicate the course in different parts of the world. The pilot (including ten modules) took place in Toronto, in May 1999. It focused mainly on LCR. The courses have been replicated in Buenos Aires and Brasilia, Montreal (for West Africa), India, East Asia, MNA, and ECA. The courses are delivered in conjunction with partners, including, University of Toronto, CUI, Buenos Aires, and University of Montreal.

Workshops, courses, and policy services: There are three workshops per year focusing on urban services for the poor and urban upgrading. The objective is to draw from the experience of practitioners, Bank staff, and academics to review the framework conditioning urban growth and access to formal and informal housing, evaluation of current policies (land, regulation, pricing, fiscal and judicial systems), and development of new strategies.

Distance Education and Partnerships: Distance learning (DL) is a component of the overall program. It comprises DL replication of the above programs based on the material being developed:

- The urban management series (12 sessions of two hours) will address questions related to urban and city management with the expertise of mayors and scholars (first session: Urban Challenges in the Next Century);

- A network of practitioners and course participants being developed to serve the core course and the workshops; and

- A learning space, prepared to assist the students of the core course, to be connected with the Urban Help Desk presently managed by the Knowledge Network.

Comprehensive framework for Bank Assistance to Cities: WBI, in conjunction with each Region, has prepared a three to five year strategy for urban and local government development which includes capacity building and knowledge management as one of its components.

Governance and anticorruption. WBI has been at the forefront of the Bank's anticorruption efforts. A particularly powerful approach has been adopted, which combines in-depth empirical diagnostic surveys and a technocratic approach to institution-building with, from the outset, a participatory, coalition-building focus that promotes collective action. Corruption diagnostics and governance indicators allow a data-driven, empirical approach to national anticorruption strategies. The work on worldwide indicators and operational research, which is done in full collaboration with DEC, will allow the linking of the operational research, indicators, diagnostics, and surveys (now completed or underway in more than 20 countries), with action program work in the countries. Such a systematic approach to measuring governance, its determinants, and its consequences for economic and social development allows governments and civil society to encourage institutional change. However, qualitative data which are relevant for measuring some aspects of governance need to be coupled with quantitative indicators, such as surveys. These surveys shed light on the political economy and institutional causes of governance failures and point to specific reforms; they also illustrate the social costs of corruption. The use of these data and surveys by stakeholders and their dissemination through participatory workshops have helped mobilize broader coalitions for action, and spurred institutional reforms.[29] Through such an approach, a broader group of stakeholders than the Bank's more traditional clients in the executive branch are empowered. These stakeholders, who include parliamentarians, the media and civil society leaders, are critical players in national efforts to curb corruption. They also play an important role in developing and maintaining political commitment to governance reforms. While there is no blueprint for curbing corruption, WBI activities include:

- Governance and anticorruption surveys and in-country diagnostics,

- Public awareness and support to coalition building,

- Action Planning (National Integrity) Workshops,

- Investigative journalism, media development and accountability,

- Promoting integrity at the municipal level,

- Strengthening parliamentary oversight, and

- Judicial reform program.

In addition, the Institute's approach focuses on a comprehensive, holistic approach to national anticorruption programming, emphasizing the need for a collaborative partnership between the state (legislature, executive, and judiciary) and civil society (including the media and the private sector) and at the same time, drawing on international "best practice" and experience. Increasingly, it is recognized that a critical component of anticorruption programming has been lacking in the Bank's involvement: the political dimension. In addition to working with parliamentarians (noted above), WBI's work is now focusing on such issues as press freedom, access to information, and media accountability.

This approach is designed as an integrated and systemic process where empirical analysis and coalition-building are key. It has the following components:

- *Inclusion and Coalition-building*—the participation of civil society, government, parliament, the private sector and the media, coupled with top-level political support and commitment to a transparent and participatory process.

- *Empirical Diagnostic Tools*—surveys of households, businesses, public officials, and consultants are utilized to measure the prevalence as well as the social and economic costs of corruption, shifting the focus of the policy debate to institutions rather than individuals and helping to establish reform priorities.

- *National Workshops and Task Forces*—in-depth survey results and analyses are then utilized by task forces working in key areas during a national workshop to develop a consensual anticorruption strategy and action plan. Workshops include participants from all branches of the state, political parties, civil society, and professional groups. They are widely publicized and are open to the media.

- *Strategies and Action Plan*—workshops help define the anticorruption and institutional reform strategy and action plans, assign responsibilities, and develop a timetable for action. In close collaboration with civil society, the government carries on the implementation, strengthening its credibility by taking timely action in an open manner.

- *Strengthening Institutional Capacity*—customized training workshops provide the tools and skills for a free media, a supportive environment for the private sector, and for an efficient, accountable, and transparent state (civil service, judiciary and legislature).

- *Continual Learning*—continually improving the methodology for capturing the most relevant data and translating survey evidence into reform priorities, and supporting the implementation of the reform agenda, emphasizing sustainability, prioritization, and sequencing, are key.

Recent WBI programs and development in anticorruption. As anticorruption issues have become mainstreamed within the Bank, so WBI's work is moving from awareness-raising to closer integration with operations, thus ensuring that WBI activities complement other Bank activities and provide tailor-made policy advice and assistance in response to requests from client countries. In this context, the collaboration with the PREM network and regional staff is a priority. From a start in just two countries, namely Uganda and Tanzania in fiscal 1994, the program is now being delivered in over 20 countries, and our partnership base has grown significantly as well (domestic and international NGOs, other IFIs, bilateral donors, etc).

Fiscal 2001 Program. WBI is continuing its collaboration with DEC, PREM and other partners, to continue to develop new and innovative approaches to curbing corruption. It is working with operations to deepen the work in Africa, LCR and South Asia and expand its work in South East Asia, francophone Africa and MNA. It is extending and refining anticorruption and diagnostic work, continuing to encourage the inclusion of both state and civil society in anticorruption programming, supporting and encouraging the establishment of parliamentary oversight and investigative journalism networks, and developing new seminars and workshops for the private sector, watchdog agencies, and the judiciary. It is using the WBI's distance learning (video conferencing and internet conferencing) facilities to complement traditional face-to-face workshops and seminars and will continue to emphasize the dissemination of lessons learned.

The Legal and Judicial Dimension. WBI, in collaboration with LCSPR and LEGLR, has been preparing anticorruption components designed to increase the transparency of the judicial process in Guatemala, Venezuela, and Bolivia. These components are part of a larger project that integrates other elements oriented to reform the judicial system. The anticorruption components involve: (a) diagnostic of the problem of corruption in the judiciary system; (b) preparation of the implementation strategy, and working meetings with local counterparts, international and local experts; and (c) preparation and presentation of policy matrices and short papers to be included in the programs of judicial reform. Furthermore, WBI in collaboration with PREM, LEG, and the *Autonoma* University of Madrid is expected to deliver a course on anticorruption measures in judiciary reform projects.

Corporate Governance.

- *Course on Corporate Governance, Business Ethics and Corruption:* The Joint Vienna Institute's new Comprehensive Course has a module on Corporate Governance and Private Sector Development with a segment focusing on business ethics. The pilot delivery of this module will provide an initial input for the design of an integrated course: government policy and regulatory framework for private sector development, corporate governance, strategic management framework and competitiveness, strategic restructuring, privatization and post-privatization issues, business ethics and anticorruption, environmental issues in enterprise restructuring and privatization.

- *Corporate Social Responsibility and Business Ethics:* The main objective is to develop an integrated program of learning in this field that will be used at the country level in the design and implementation of appropriate policy measures and initiatives aimed at creating an environment that supports sound corporate responsibility and business ethics practices. The program will thus strengthen the effort to promote in-depth transparency and sound societal values, and fight poverty and corruption. In particular, state capture will be looked at very carefully in this program. State capture refers to the capacity of firms to shape and affect the formation of the basic "rules of the game" (laws, regulations, and decrees). State capture—as well as administrative corruption and influence—has distinct causes and consequences. One of the negative aspects is the very large social cost associated with pervasive state capture. The BEEPS survey mentioned above and the analysis and findings on state capture offer significant methodological improvements over existing governance and corruption indexes in that it relies on the direct experience of firms rather than on external elements.

Competitiveness and competition.

- *Enhancing Country Competitiveness and "Vision of the Future" Integrated Approach*: Many developing and transitional countries are at present facing the challenge of global conditions with little time to design a new, more appropriate development strategy. Experience from several countries demonstrates that building a consensus around a country's vision of its future can be an effective means for generating and disseminating knowledge among different segments of society. Through this consensus-building and utilization of other countries' "good fits," new development ideas are generated. The two pillars of this approach are the concepts of country competitiveness and a vision of the future. The competitiveness focus offers a useful rigorous framework to address the issue of strategic thinking and *visioning* at a company, country, and regional level. To assess a country's competitive advantage, local experts are trained to master the methodology developed at the Harvard Business School.

- *Competition Policy*. A dynamic and competitive environment, underpinned by sound competition law and policy, is an essential characteristic of a successful market economy. It is also a means to increase transparency and involves a major rethinking of the role of the state. The main goal of this course is to upgrade the analytic understanding and problem-solving capability of participants on competition policy measures that directly impact enterprise conduct, market structure and public sector performance. The course is intended to sharpen the implementation and enforcement skills of competition policy practitioners with a focus on priorities for developing and transition economies. Offered worldwide in fiscal 1999, it has been offered to South and East Asia in fiscal 2000 and will be con-

tinued with an increased focus on the linkages between competition and regulation and on corporate governance.

- *Regulation of privatized monopolies*. Private participation in the provision of utility and transport services is spreading rapidly in many countries. Governments now have to focus on developing new skills as regulators of the private providers, and therefore on the governments' changing role. The main goal of the program is to strengthen the capacity of national and subnational governments to take on these new skills. While most of the program is designed to help academics and the regulators of newly privatized infrastructure monopolies to be as effective as possible in dealing with technical topics, the program looks at ways to minimize corruption and poor governance, paying particular attention to issues such as state capture by the private sector (the propensity of firms to manipulate the "rules of the game" or regulations to their own advantage) or corruption in procurement. Transparent and professional regulation is one of the safest ways to reduce governance dysfunction. It also ensures that all consumers, particularly the poorest, benefit from the changes brought by increased public-private partnership in the infrastructure sector.

Financial sector regulation and fraud. The objective of the Bank Group Finance and Banking program is to provide a full range of tailored activities that complement the operational and policy agenda, and respond to the increasing demand for training in financial sector topics. Another goal is to explore and develop the governance dimension of financial sector health. Underlying the training program is the notion that a functioning financial sector should have a governance process and transparent business environment, and maintain enhanced levels of accountability and transparency. This includes the process by which those in authority are selected, monitored, and replaced; the capacity of the government to effectively manage its resources and implement sound policies; and the respect of citizens and the state for the institutions that govern economic and social interactions among them.

The East Asia crisis has amply demonstrated that the weaknesses and failings of the financial system were not solely attributable to poor policies, but had, at the root of the crisis, poor government and poor private governance.

Africa: Core Courses on Controlling Corruption Toward an Integrated Strategy

Countries: Benin, Ethiopia, Ghana, Kenya, Malawi, Tanzania, Uganda
Type of Activity: Workshop
Timing: Fiscal 1999-2000

Summary of Contents

The 1st phase of the course in June 1999 involved participants from seven countries who were invited to Washington DC to share the latest methodologies for addressing corruption. The focus of the workshop was to share information and to enable the participants to prepare action programs for their countries. The workshop covered, among other areas: mobilization of stakeholders—government, civil society, and the private sector; diagnostics and problem identification; strategy development; action-plan development and implementation; and an analysis of the pros and cons of existing anticorruption programs. The 2nd phase (a three-month distance learning phase) focused mainly on: financial management, the rule-of-law, customs reform, and civil service reform, although other subjects ranked as important by participants were also discussed. Building on the action plans developed in Phase 1, the teams were responsible for developing country-specific strategies in the aforementioned areas.

In Phase 3 (Durban), the teams presented anticorruption strategies and action plans summarizing the approaches each team had developed over the previous four months. The workshops reached consensus that successful anticorruption programs require: (a) strong political will, from political leaders and other stakeholders; (b) a holistic approach, treating corruption as a symptom of deeper, systemic governance problems; (c) rigorous diagnosis and analysis of governance issues in-country; (d) customized programs for specific needs; (e) a focus on high priority areas; (f) anticorruption strategies anchored within countries' existing institutional reform programs; (g) collective action by all stakeholders; and (h) coordinated and timely support from the international community.

Innovative / Risky Elements

This was an attempt to try a different approach (combining the sharing of tools and techniques with participant involvement in working out a shared commitment for concrete institutional change) in an area in which, to date, it has been difficult to achieve sustainable results. The participatory nature of the program helped teams understand the importance of building coalitions, and how this, in turn, improves the implementation of institutional reforms. The current challenge for the World Bank is to effectively facilitate and support the implementation of the action programs developed by the country teams.

Partnerships

UNDP will most likely be a partner in upcoming activities.

Venezuela: Corporate Responsbility and Business Ethics

Type of Activity: Learning Program
Timing: June 2000 - December 2001

Summary of Contents

Corporate responsibility and business ethics issues are closely related to both corporate and national governance. Putting these issues together can provide a better understanding of how to localize governance systems to meet the needs of a specific country. It also provides a basis for analyzing the needs of a diverse group of stakeholders in a systematic way and what is needed to build sustainable competitiveness at the country, industry, and firm level. A framework for ethical leadership is essential to excellence in both private sector and public service. This framework encompasses not only financial expertise or strategic thinking, but also personal integrity, upholding and promoting values and a code of conduct, and behaving in an honest, ethical and professional way. Also, and most importantly, state capture will be looked at very carefully in this program. State capture refers to the capacity of firms to shape and affect the formation of the basic "rules of the game" (laws, regulations, and decrees). Even though state capture, as well as administrative corruption and influence, have distinct causes and consequences, one of the negative aspects is the very large social costs associated with pervasive state capture.

The objectives of the program will be achieved through a combination of research, high-level roundtables, electronic discussion forums, video conferences, workshops, conferences, training of trainers courses, and assistance in designing and implementing country and company-specific programs.

A pilot delivery of this global initiative, which was launched by President Wolfensohn at the Global Economic Forum in Davos, took place in June 2000 in Sarajevo, with participants from Eastern Europe.

Innovative / Risky Elements

Anticorruption issues are presented in a fully integrated approach within national and corporate governance, and corporate responsibilities and business ethics. For the first time, client countries, Part I countries, and Bank staff worked jointly to address these issues, bringing various perspectives on the role of the government, civil society, private sector and international institutions, within the context of sensitive topics such as value systems and leadership. Moreover, journalists were invited to participate in the conferences. For the next deliveries, the issue of state capture will be thoroughly explained and discussed, so as to sensitize the audience to the very negative social and economic impact of this phenomenon.

Partnerships

World Bank: Office of Business Ethics and Integrity, Leadership Development Group, Global Corporate Governance Program. Others: Center for International Leadership, Merck, PriceWaterhouseCoopers, World Business Council for Sustainable Development and many other partners from 10 countries (Bosnia, Bulgaria, Croatia, Macedonia, Poland, Slovakia, Austria, Norway, Germany, and USA).

1   The review sampled about two-thirds of all Bank projects with civil service components undertaken during this period. So, even if the sample was biased toward African examples, the preponderance of effort in the African region is clear.

2   See *World Development Report 1997: The State in a Changing World,* Chapters 2 and 3.

3   Financial Times March 15, 1999.

4   While these TA operations fell short of the standard of "good" institutional reform projects, the urgency of reforms and the precarious institutional foundations in the region necessitated them as the pragmatic stop-gap measures, which inevitably placed less emphasis on medium-term institutional development.

5   Minimal commitment may be demonstrated with willingness to conduct a diagnostic survey to identify and make transparent the profile of corruption. Assessments of political commitment were conducted in Albania, Georgia and Latvia.

6   Operations include Jamaica (1982), Costa Rica (1985), Panama (1983), Trinidad & Tobago (1989) and Uruguay (1987, 1989).

7   Stand-alone TA projects include Public Sector Management Projects in Argentina (1986), Brazil (1986), Chile (1985), Ecuador (1985).

8   It is true that the Bank has been involved in various areas of urban and municipal development since the mid-1980s.

9   For example, social fund operations in Bolivia (1993) and Peru (1994) are trying to link operations of Social Investment Funds with overall decentralization policies.

10 Chile 1994 and 1998 Municipal Development Projects; Bolivia 1996 Rural Development Project.

11 Guatemala (1997), Jamaica (1996).

12 Bolivia (1999), Ecuador (1994), Jamaica (1996).

13 El Salvador (1996), Honduras (1996), Venezuela (1998).

14 For example, the 1998 Guatemala judicial reform project supports consultations throughout the project design including not only the coordination of different donors, but also members of civil society and most importantly indigenous organizations, law schools, the legal profession, the private sector and the media.

15 Peru (1982), Argentina (1986), Jamaica (1984), and Brazil (1986).

16 In collaboration with PRMPS, LCSPR is beginning to conduct case studies of PSM reforms in both Bolivia and Ecuador. The piece on Ecuador was used as material at a workshop on Budget Reforms in 1999. The piece on Bolivia will form part of a larger research program on the Institutional Sustainability of IDA Lending with funding from the Dutch Trust Fund.

17 Active Bank borrowers include Morocco, Algeria, Tunisia, Egypt, Yemen, Jordan, Lebanon, and Iran, although the program with Iran remains very limited. Of these, only Yemen falls below the operational cutoff for IDA terms. The Bank also funds projects in the West Bank and Gaza Strip, thus far on IDA terms, from its specially-created Trust Fund for the West Bank and Gaza. Demand-driven, reimbursable technical cooperation takes place with the Gulf Cooperation Council countries and with Malta. In Syria, limited Bank activity (ESW, IDF) restarted in the wake of an agreement on an arrears workout plan. There is currently limited Bank activity in Libya and Iraq. The principal focus of this annex is on the low- and lower-middle income MNA countries (Algeria, Egypt, Iran, Iraq, Jordan, Lebanon, Morocco, Syria, Tunisia, Yemen, and the West Bank and Gaza).

18 "Civil Service Reform: A Review of World Bank Assistance," OED, (p. 7).

19 For example, in 1993 kilowatt hours of electricity produced per capita amounted to 0.73 in Tunisia, 0.66 in Algeria, and 0.41 in Morocco — well below the 2.44 average for comparator countries. Even today, distribu-

tion losses in the region's power networks remain in the 13 to16 percent range. Similarly, while most lower-middle income countries averaged nearly 10 telephone lines per 100 people in 1994, Tunisia had only 5, and Algeria and Morocco only 4, and waiting times for telephone connections continue to be measured in years in most MNA countries. About half the region's roads are in poor condition, as maintenance has failed to keep up with traffic levels. For example, Yemen's highway agency allocates less than 5 percent of its annual budget to preserving primary and secondary roads, while the needed maintenance would require about ten times as much funding.

20   Several countries in the Region have recently begun to experiment with management contracts, build-operate-transfer/own, divestiture, and other arrangements for private participation in infrastructure service provision. Contracts have been awarded to private operators for water and sanitation services in Gaza, solid waste and telecommunications in Lebanon, wastewater and power in Oman, and a port terminal in Yemen. Other projects already initiated or in advanced stages of preparation include power projects in Egypt, Morocco, Tunisia, and several Gulf countries; water/sanitation projects in Egypt, Lebanon, Morocco and Tunisia; telecommunications in Jordan, Morocco, Tunisia, and the West Bank/Gaza; and concessions for toll roads in Jordan, Lebanon, Morocco, and Tunisia and for port services in Oman, Morocco, and Tunisia. For further discussion, see J. Page, J. Saba, and N. Shafik, "From player to referee: the changing role of competition policies and regulation in the Middle East and North Africa," paper presented at AMF/AFSED seminar, March 1997.

21   See: J. Page and L. Van Gelder, "Missing Links: Institutional Capability, Policy Reform, and Growth in the Middle East and North Africa"; paper presented at the conference on "The Changing Role of the State of the Middle East and North Africa," at the School of Orien-

tal and African Studies, London, May 6, 1998 (which draws on data from Political Risk Services, International Country Risk Guide; cited in Easterly, 1997).

22   It should be noted that MNA as a distinct Regional Vice Presidency has been in existence only since late 1991.

23   This general remark notwithstanding, there are of course numerous instances where Bank lending has helped bring about positive change in the incentives underlying internal workings of the public sector. The breadth of examples ranges from the creation of otherwise absent coordination mechanisms among key government agencies in order to ensure adequate preservation and management of cultural heritage assets (Tunisia and Morocco), through the development of more transparent arrangements for inter-governmental fiscal transfers (Morocco), to the streamlining of customs declarations procedures (Yemen).

24   "Civil Service Reform: A Review of World Bank Assistance," OED, 1999 (p. 35).

25   "The Impact of Public Expenditure Reviews: An Evaluation," OED, 1998.

26   MNA Region PERs evaluated are those for Egypt (1993), Morocco (1994), Lebanon (1995), and Yemen (1997). The last was evaluated only for quality, timeliness, and cost-effectiveness—not for impact.

27   USAID recently completed an assessment of corruption in Lebanon and plans shortly to conduct similar assessments in other MNA countries while UNDP recently commissioned an assessment of financial accountability and transparency in Jordan.

28   Please refer to our website at *www.worldbank.org/wbi/governance* to look at the Policy Research Paper "Seize the State, Seize the Day."

29   Please refer to our website at *www.worldbank.org/wbi/governance.*

Annexes

Lending for Public Sector Reform in Fiscal 1997-99

To increase our understanding of the extent of Bank lending for public sector and institutional reform, we reviewed all 815 lending operations approved by the Board in fiscal 1997-99.[1] (We are currently reviewing loans approved in fiscal 2000.) In each operation all Public Sector components were identified. The following categorization was used:

- **Public Expenditure and Financial Management Reform (FM)**—including budgeting, accounting, auditing, cash management, debt management, procurement, aid management, financial evaluation, financial planning, and financial management.

- **Public Enterprise Reform (PE)**—including efforts to restructure, rehabilitate or privatize public enterprises, reform management in individual enterprises or industrial subsectors, or reform the policy framework for public enterprises.

- **Tax Policy and Administration (TP&A)**

- **Administrative and Civil Service Reform (CSR)** including civil service downsizing, pay reform, organizational restructuring, rationalization of functions, personnel management (recruitment, training, retraining, career development, etc.).

- **Legal and Judicial Reform (LEG)**

- **Regulation of the Private Sector (REG PRIV)**

- **Sectoral Institutional Development (ID)** institutional reforms within specific sectors, including changes in the role of the public sector, capacity building, and related technical assistance and training.

- **Decentralization (DEC)**

- **Multi-purpose (MULTI)** loans with institutional reforms that span more than one of the above components.

Table 5 shows the number of projects with a public sector reform component in a given category. (Some loans have components in more than one area.)[2] Over 96 percent of all operations (fiscal 1997-98) include at least one public sector component. Most of these are sector-specific interventions, although there is also significant, and growing, activity in the various areas of core public sector reform.

We also estimated the total amount of funds going to institutional reform (as broadly defined) and to technical assistance (more narrowly) for projects funded in whole or in part by the World Bank in fiscal 1997-99. The Bank's *total lending for public sector institutional reform* (equivalent to the lending amount in all components identified in Table 5 below) is estimated at about $5 billion to $7 billion per year (see Figure 8), split approximately evenly between adjustment lending and investment lending. As shown in Table 6, spending *on technical assistance alone* is estimated at

TABLE 5 Number of Public Sector Components in Fiscal 1997-99, by Region

Region Fiscal 1997	FM	PE	TP&A	CSR	LEG	REG PRIV	ID	DEC	MULTI	Total Public Sector (a)	Total Fiscal 1997 (b)	Percentage of operations with Public Sector Component (a/b)
AFR	10	7	7	5	16	4	43	15	11	48	49	98%
EAP		2			1	1	37	4		37	37	100%
ECA	7	3	3	1	6	7	60	1	7	67	67	100%
LCR	2	3	2	5	12	3	48	13	5	51	52	98%
MNA	1	2	4		6	1	17	4	2	17	17	100%
SAR	1	1		1	4		18	6		19	19	100%
Total	21	18	16	12	45	16	223	43	25	239	241	99%

Region Fiscal 1998	FM	PE	TP&A	CSR	LEG	REG PRIV	ID	DEC	MULTI	Total Public Sector (a)	Total Fiscal 1997 (b)	Percentage of operations with Public Sector Component (a/b)
AFR	9	5	3	4	15	1	52	14	3	58	59	98%
EAP	8	2	4	1	6	1	33	6	1	41	45	91%
ECA	17	7	8	1	18	4	49	5	6	65	69	94%
LCR	12	3	5	8	24	2	51	23	9	63	68	93%
MNA	4		1		4	1	14	4	1	17	20	85%
SAR	2	3	1	1	3	1	22	8		24	25	96%
Total	52	20	22	15	70	10	221	60	20	268	286	94%

Region Fiscal 1999	FM	PE	TP&A	CSR	LEG	REG PRIV	ID	DEC	MULTI	Total Public Sector (a)	Total Fiscal 1997 (b)	Percentage of operations with Public Sector Component (a/b)
AFR	21	8	9	15	18	18	47	26	13	61	63	97%
EAP	13	8	1	8	14	10	45	14	5	51	53	96%
ECA	18	13	7	11	38	17	43	10	5	63	72	87%
LCR	16	3	6	12	22	6	44	16	14	55	57	96%
MNA	8	4	2	7	8	5	13	5	2	20	21	95%
SAR	7		4	3	5	6	18	8	1	21	23	91%
Total	82	36	29	56	104	61	210	79	39	272	289	94%

Note: Totals do not add correctly due to rounding

TABLE 6 Cost of Technical Assistance (TA) in Fiscal 1997-99, by Region (in $ million)

Region and Years	Cost of TA	Total WB Lending	Total Project Cost	TA as % of Lending
AFR 1997	284.951	1608.6	3338.4	17.7
AFR 1998	443.57	2748.8	6095.6	16.1
AFR 1999	362.7	2166.8	5636.6	16.7
97-99	**728.5**	**4357.4**	**9434.0**	**16.7**
EAP 1997	279.22	4866	13442.9	5.7
EAP 1998	316.82	9623.2	13984.4	3.3
EAP 1999	417.975	9463.7	12529.6	4.4
97-99	**596.0**	**10109.8**	**27427.3**	**5.9**
ECA 1997	353.94	5039.9	6545.1	7
ECA 1998	323.17	5189.4	9614	6.2
ECA 1999	366.4	5332	6354.7	6.9
97-99	**677.11**	**10229.3**	**16159.1**	**6.6**
LCR 1997	682.1	4535	9598.6	15
LCR 1998	809.73	6021.1	18672.1	13.4
LCR 1999	413.45	5541.1	14476.6	7.5
97-99	**1491.83**	**10556.1**	**28270.7**	**14.1**
MNA 1997	63.76	914.8	3535.9	6.9
MNA 1998	79.87	961.2	2023.5	8.3
MNA 1999	90.8	1560.1	2319.3	5.8
97-99	**143.63**	**1876**	**5559.4**	**7.6**
SAR 1997	331.85	2008.7	2724.2	16.5
SAR 1998	536.03	3864.4	17878	13.9
SAR 1999	393.5	2562.2	4141.3	15.4
97-99	**867.88**	**5873.1**	**20602.2**	**14.8**
TOTAL 97	1995.8	18973	39185.1	10.5
TOTAL 98	2509.19	28408.1	68267.6	8.8
TOTAL 99	2044.82	26625.9	45458.1	7.7
TOTAL 97-99	**6549.8**	**74007**	**152910.7**	**8.8**

approximately 8.8 percent of total Bank lending. Africa devoted the largest share (16.7 percent) of its projects to technical assistance, and East Asia and the Pacific the smallest (4.1 percent). Of total World Bank lending for technical assistance, Europe and Central Asia accounted for the biggest portion (33.1 percent) and Middle East and North Africa the smallest (3.2 percent).

FIGURE 8 Lending for Public Sector Reform in Fiscal 1997-99

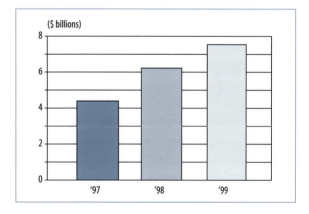

FIGURE 9 Technical Assistance as Percentage of Lending in Fiscal 1997-99

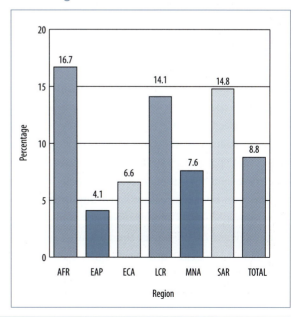

Instruments for Institutional and Governance Analysis and Assessment

Several types of diagnostic instruments are discussed in this strategy paper, all fitting under the general category of economic and sector work (ESW). While these instruments have different histories and somewhat different purposes, each is an important tool to help the Bank and client countries deepen their knowledge of governance settings and the constraints and opportunities these settings provide for development in general and Bank work in particular. Each is intended to provide strategic input into the Bank's CASs and lending programs and more broadly into the poverty-reduction strategies of our client countries.

Interrelated types of ESW

Public Expenditure Reviews (PERs) have traditionally been the most common analytic instrument for economic and sector work in the area of public sector reform; indeed, they are highlighted as key fiduciary analytic products in the Bank's recent review of the entire ESW program.[3] PERs vary significantly from country to country, but in general their focus has been primarily on budget structure and composition, with some attention paid to more general public sector issues. Reviews of PERs over the 10 years until 1998 showed that less than a quarter adequately focused on institutional issues such as budget management or incentives in the public service. Several recent PERs,

however, have made significant strides in this direction. For example, the 1998 PER for China focused heavily on the institutional setup for public expenditure management, including issues of decentralization, and the recent PER for Indonesia focuses primarily on institutional issues.

Current challenges (discussed in Section IV of the main text) include defining and streamlining the scope of PERs (particularly given increasingly tight operational budgets), improving consistency and overall quality, and enhancing the involvement and ownership of the client country. Information on budget allocations continues to be important (not only for the Bank but for the Fund and other donors also), but PERs will also focus increasingly on institutions for budget decisionmaking and implementation, and individual PERs may also look at specific expenditure topics of particular importance to the country. PERs will necessarily vary somewhat in scope, size, and timing, depending on country demand. In some cases, PERs may be undertaken annually but may have a rotating focus that covers individual topics only once every few years.

To improve the quality of PERs, the Public Sector Board is developing more thorough monitoring programs and stricter peer review procedures to complement the guidelines on scope and content. Half-day public expenditure clinics are now offered by the Thematic Group to teams about to embark on PER field missions. To enhance ownership, selected PERs are now undertaken by clients themselves with Bank assistance, with both client and Bank staff participating in any pre-mission training provided. In some cases there may be tradeoffs between objectives of quality, timeliness, and ownership. For this reason PERs (particularly if more narrowly defined in the new guidelines) must not be the only elements in the public expenditure program through which the Bank engages with clients; other forms of technical assistance, training, and analysis may also be appropriate as complements to PERs.

To enhance impact and relevance, PERs need to focus increasingly on how expenditure allocations are implemented in practice. As noted earlier in Section IV, recent innovations in tracking surveys can help monitor results on the ground.

Institutional and Governance Reviews (IGRs) are a broad family of analytic instruments now being piloted by the Public Sector Board (PREM network). They are designed to bring a greater focus on and understanding of governance arrangements in the public sector and their link to public sector performance. Four IGRs—for Armenia, Bangladesh, Bolivia, and Indonesia—were completed in fiscal 2000, and at least five more are underway. Numerous other initiatives in this family of products—including diagnostic anticorruption surveys of citizens, firms, and policymakers—are being undertaken in several other countries (see below). These efforts differ significantly from each other, because each is designed around specific country circumstances and needs of country teams and client countries. But they share the common goals of (a) focusing on performance by beginning with a problem (whether poor service delivery, corruption, or bad economic policies) and tracing its governance roots; (b) trying to use empirical methods and diagnostic toolkits (including analysis of political economy issues) to understand current governance realities in the country concerned; and (c) using this deeper understanding to help shape feasible and effective programs of institution-building for client countries and the Bank.

The pilot IGRs focus on major problems of government performance in one or more of three areas:

- Policymaking: How can governments reform their policymaking institutions so that policies more conducive to robust and equitable economic growth emerge?

- Service delivery: What governance problems underlie poor service delivery? How can governments reform institutions to improve public service delivery?

- Accountability: How can the accountability of public officials be enhanced and corruption reduced?

Anticorruption Surveys of citizens, private firms, and policymakers are often important inputs to IGRs. They can help uncover the extent and sources of institutional dysfunction in a country and are being used increasingly in the programs of the Bank. WBI and ECA-PREM pioneered the use of anticorruption surveys in the ECA Region in fiscal 1998 (see ECA and WBI strategies in Part II), and anticorruption surveys are being undertaken in numerous other countries in fiscal 2000-01. Results of the surveys inform a policy dialogue that aims to design effective anticorruption strategies. The availability of public information on the nature and extent of corruption has the added benefit of encouraging greater participation of civil society in governance and anticorruption efforts. The cost of these comprehensive in-country exercises implies that only a few countries can be surveyed each year, and there is no comparable worldwide dataset based on this in-depth approach. But carefully selected questions from these anticorruption diagnostics are being incorporated in worldwide surveys, such as the World Business Environment Survey (WBES).

Social and Structural Reviews (SSRs) are a new Bank ESW product focused on assessing major medium-term structural issues and intended to provide a more rigorous underpinning to the CAS and to downstream lending and ESW work in the country. SSRs are used to review medium-term development prospects (notably growth and poverty reduction) of Bank client countries and the extent to which their policies and institutional environment enhance or diminish these prospects (with this assessment based to the extent possible on specific performance indicators). One part of each SSR is an analysis of public sector performance.

Analytic toolkits to support ESW instruments

The development of standard diagnostic tools for assessing institutional settings has moved rapidly within the World Bank in recent years. By providing not only Bank staff but also country counterparts and partner organizations with frameworks and data to help them analyze domestic institutions in a comparative perspective, toolkits can help move donor support away from standard expatriate-led models of technical assistance. Toolkits are standardized approaches that:

- set out the principles that experience suggests should underpin public sector governance arrangements,

- provide methods for assessing the degree to which specific country arrangements are consistent with those principles, and

- present those assessments in a format that readily contributes to the dialogue between the government, donors, and civil society on reform priorities.

IGRs, PERs, and SSRs provide an opportunity to develop and test standardized toolkits for measuring government performance, delving into the institutional origins of that performance, and gauging prospects for sustainable reform. Among the toolkits currently being developed and tested are the following:[4]

Governance and Poverty Toolkit. This toolkit provides a framework to identify the multiple links between governance and poverty and to begin an assessment of the governance situation as input in the preparation of Poverty Reduction Strategy Papers (PRSPs). A draft of the toolkit is available on the Bank's external website at *www.worldbank.org/poverty/strategies.*

Public Expenditure Institutional Assessment. This assessment of budget institutions includes models for assessing formal public expenditure institutional arrangements and for assessing the capability of cabinet arrangements for social and sectoral policymaking. The toolkit has been piloted extensively, but is now being extended to assess the fit between budget institutions and the particular executive and legislature configurations. The toolkit has been piloted in Australia, Benin, Colombia, Ghana, Indonesia, Malawi, New Zealand, Thailand, and Uganda.

Civil Service Institutional Assessment. Learning from extensive work in assessing formal civil service arrangements in EU accession, this toolkit assesses both formal and informal institutional arrangements for public sector employment, including the impact of pay policy and the relations between national and subnational civil services. It examines the coherence and compliance with formal rules in relation to civil service policy and strategy, legislation and regulations, structure and career management, pay and employment, and performance management. The toolkit has been piloted in a range of EU accession countries, Bolivia, and Indonesia.

Assessment of Revenue Mobilization Capacity. This toolkit provides a model for assessing formal revenue institutional arrangements. It is under development with input from experts inside and outside the Bank. It incorporates an assessment of tax policy and accountability, including a review of revenue adequacy, shares of different revenue sources, stability, and vertical balance. In addition, it assesses service delivery performance, including the cost efficiency of revenue administration. Responsibilities for revenue policy and institutional incentives for clarity and comprehensiveness, including taxpayer consultative arrangements, are covered. The draft toolkit has been piloted in India.

Legal and Judicial Institutional Review. This toolkit is under development and will assess system performance in the deterrence of wrongful conduct, the facilitation of voluntary transactions, the resolution of private disputes, and the redress of governmental abuses of power. It will also assess how well the key institutions of the judicial system—the courts, the private bar, and the public prosecutors—are working.

Intergovernmental Relations Institutional Review. This toolkit, also under development with Bank-wide testing planned, will assess arrangements for fiscal decentralization, including expenditure and tax assignment by function and level of government, intergovernmental transfers, and subnational borrowing. It will also assess institutional arrangements for administrative decentralization and key dimensions of political decentralization.

Assessing Constraints on Service Delivery. This toolkit is designed to assess constraints on front-line service delivery. It helps locate where the constraints are—identifying the degree to which they arise from problems within the service-providing agencies, or from difficulties at other provincial or national levels. It diagnoses the nature of the constraints external to the service provider, including the degree to which poor performance is rooted in weak provincial and national arrangements for policymaking, for ensuring resource flows, and for ensuring accountability. The toolkit is being piloted in Ethiopia, Benin, and Argentina.

Commitment to Reform. This toolkit assesses the political desirability of proposed reforms, the political feasibility (including opposition to this project or to broader reforms inside or outside the government), and the sustainability of reform, including potential changes in key stakeholders.

Media Situational Analysis. This toolkit, to be piloted by WBI and EASPR, will examine the capacity of the media to play a significant role in curbing corruption. The toolkit will include such issues as press freedom, access to information, and media accountability.

Bank-Fund Collaboration on Public Sector Work

The Bank and the Fund share the common goal of helping member countries achieve sustainable development and reduce poverty. Recent reviews of Bank-Fund collaboration[5] have highlighted the need to strengthen cooperation between Bank and Fund staff in their work on public sector reform in order to achieve a better integration of policy and institution-building advice and more effective coordination of support for our clients' reform programs.

The two organizations' mandates and work programs in public sector reform overlap significantly, although specific roles may vary. In the area of revenues, for example, the Fund's Fiscal Affairs Department provides technical assistance to client governments on request, while the Bank lends extensively for information technology and policy support. In the public expenditure area, the Bank carries out Public Expenditure Reviews and provides policy advice, technical assistance, and project financing to support the development and implementation of public expenditure policies and financial management systems. The Fund includes public expenditure conditionality in Fund programs and provides technical assistance for public expenditure and financial management upon request. Both organizations are increasingly focusing on accountability and anticorruption concerns, including the size and pay policies of the civil service. Given the importance of these issues for both macroeconomic stability and social and structural reform, it is very likely that these overlaps in mandates and work

programs will continue—rather than focus on drawing boundaries, we prefer to focus on ways to share knowledge and improve communication and collaboration. Communication in some areas (such as financial management and tax policy) is quite strong, and we are building on a base of good will.

Work program review and regional discussions

The 1995 joint Guidance Note from Managing Director Camdessus and President Wolfensohn mandated annual consultations on public expenditure work between Regions and area departments, and these provide one forum to strengthen this collaboration. Consultations held in 1996 and 1997 focused on coordinating work programs to achieve a more timely availability of the Bank's public expenditure reviews and recommendations for Fund-supported adjustment programs. While no such consultations took place in 1998, the process was revived in 1999.[6]

As part of the annual consultation process, summary tables of country-by-country priorities in the public sector area (as reflected in their medium-term work program) were prepared by the two institutions. Since the Bank's approach to public sector reform has widened in scope, the topics of fiscal transparency and corruption, legal reform and judicial services, auditing, tax policy and administration, among others, were included in the 1999 consultations. In most meetings, these tables were the starting point of the discussion.

In addition to several country-level meetings, three meetings took place at the regional level to discuss the public sector work program of the two institutions. The general view of the Bank's country teams was that the two institutions should meet regularly and talk—not necessarily in a formal way—to discuss their involvement in a member country.

Discussions at the regional level indicate that cooperation between the two institutions is generally good, although it is sometimes hampered by different perspectives on substantive issues or on priorities for public sector work in member countries. The progressive shift in the focus of the Bank's public sector work toward institutional issues—for example, in PERs—has sometimes involved tradeoffs with other topics (including short-term budget analysis) of interest to Fund staff. The decline in the Bank's administrative resources also has consequences for Bank-Fund cooperation, requiring the Bank to be more selective in its undertakings, and Fund staff are aware of this constraint.

As part of the annual work program review, a survey was sent to each of the Bank's country directors asking specific questions on knowledge, staffing constraints, and cross-participation in Bank/Fund missions in public sector work. The survey results indicate that there is extensive exchange of information already but that room still exists for improvement. The Bank's needs for timely fiscal projections from the Fund appear to be adequately met across most regions. The Fund's needs for timely short notes from the Bank distilling the main recommendations of various sectoral reports appear to be partially but not fully met, in part attributable to the shrinking administrative budget in the Bank and competing priorities.

With regard to cross-participation in missions, responses for 95 countries reveal that Fund staff participated in Bank missions in 11 countries in 1997 (of which 10 were in the Africa Region) and 10 countries in 1998, again mostly in Africa. The number of countries in which Bank staff participated in Fund missions is significantly higher: Forty-four respondents (mostly in the AFR Region) in 1997 and 43 in 1998 report that Bank staff from their country team participated in Fund missions in the respective year.

Fiduciary issues and HIPC/PRSP collaboration

The recent intensive Bank-Fund collaboration on PRSPs and HIPC has also led to increased interaction between public sector staff of the two organizations. A Joint Bank-Fund Group on Public Expenditure Issues now meets regularly to review issues with regard to the tracking of poverty-related spending in HIPC countries, in part responding to the fiduciary concerns of all HIPC donors that debt relief translate into greater spending on poverty alleviation. The Joint Group is working with country team members in both organizations to determine what mechanisms are currently in place in HIPC countries to monitor public spending, and to design proactive work programs to help strengthen those mechanisms and improve underlying processes of budget formulation, execution, and monitoring. Staff of the two organizations are also interacting regularly to share information and ideas on the fiduciary framework needed in borrower countries to underpin the financial support offered by the Bank and the Fund (as outlined for the Bank in Box 12).

Conclusion

Bank-Fund collaboration on public sector work has improved through increasing exchange of information in recent years. There are—and will always remain—differences in opinion and in approach to public sector reform between the two institutions. The important thing is to avoid unnecessary duplication of work and conflicting advice to member countries. The consultative process, whereby different country teams at the Bank meet with their Fund counterparts at least once a year to discuss the coming year's work program, is a useful way to address this issue. Discussions at the regional level are also useful to solve major issues that affect the entire region as well as any unresolved country specific issues. Beyond that, cross-participation in missions, seminars, and conferences, and Fund staff membership in the Bank's public sector thematic groups (which is increasing) are other ways to improve collaboration. Finally, the PRSP and HIPC processes have recently stimulated increased collaboration in the area of public expenditure management, which is likely to prove very fruitful in many areas in the future.

Indicators of Governance and Institutional Quality

New global standards of governance are emerging.[7] Citizens of developing countries are demanding better performance from their governments, and they are increasingly aware of the costs of poor management and corruption. Attitudes are also changing in industrial countries where bribery is no longer viewed as a legitimate cost of doing business. Countries are asking for help in diagnosing governance failures and in finding solutions. This has led to new interest in measuring the performance of governments.

Governance indicators may be of two general types. *Descriptive* measures have limited normative content, and describe prevailing political and governance arrangements (for example civil service pay, the frequency of elections, organizational structure, size of government). *Evaluative* measures are normative, implying judgments about the quality of governance. These measures can be further divided into several subtypes:

- Several *objective fact-based measures* of the quality of governance and of public sector institutional arrangements have been identified and analyzed. Box 26 lists some examples, although this work is still in its infancy and this list will doubtless change substantially as work progresses.

- *Participant surveys* of interested parties reflect the views of citizens, entrepreneurs, foreign investors, public officials and others about the quality of governance in their own or other countries (see Table 7).

- Cross-country assessments are often based on the *opinions of experts* who are asked to rate the quality and effectiveness of government institutions (see Table 7).

The Bank has produced both descriptive indicators of institutional arrangements and evaluative measures based on survey data for many years. Cukierman and Webb[8] compiled a widely used set of indicators of central bank independence based on detailed descriptions of the institutions and regulations in many countries. More recently, Keefer and others have constructed a "Database on Political Institutions" to catalog detailed data on such factors as checks and balances by constitutional institutions, electoral processes, and other characteristics relevant to governmental decisionmaking. In 1997, the Bank commissioned a large cross-country survey of firms as an input to *WDR97*. This database has provided a wealth of information on the firms' perceptions of the quality of governance across countries. An updated Business Environment Survey is currently being conducted, and initial results are now becoming available for the ECA region. The Bank's internal Country Performance and Institutional Assessment (CPIA) is an example of a subjective assessment based on staff evaluations.

There are also many external sources of governance-related indicators. Risk-rating services—for example, Political Risk Services, Standard and Poor's, and the Economist Intelligence Unit—typically rely on panels of experts who rate countries (or institutions within countries) using a defined set of criteria. The use of common criteria provides some comparability across countries (and over time), but the ratings still depend on the experts' interpretation of the criteria and their subjective perception of each country. Other organizations (for example the Davos World Competitiveness Report, Gallup, and Political and Economic Risk Consultancy) rely on participant surveys. One advantage of surveys is that they reflect the opinions of many firms or citizens closely connected with the countries they are assessing. But many rely on voluntary responses and ask vague questions that may be misinterpreted by the respondent, limiting comparability across countries. Table 7 contains a listing of some of the major external surveys of governance indicators and notes on their methodology and country coverage.

Although the results of expert polls and participant surveys are unavoidably subjective, they are often the best available information on the less visible aspects of governance. Objective data on the prevalence of corruption are, almost by definition, difficult to obtain, leaving few alternatives to subjective indicators. In addition, perceptions of the quality of governance may often be as important as objective facts. While a country may have sound institutions according to objective criteria, the confidence of residents or investors is also required for good governance to result in good outcomes.

Common concerns with governance indicators are that they can be inconsistent, unreliable or affected by the biases of the observer. A country rated highly by one agency or panel of experts may be rated lower by another, even though both claim to measure similar attributes of governance. On the principle that more information is generally preferable to less, one solution is to aggregate indicators from several sources into an average or composite index—a poll of polls. This is the approach that Transparency International uses for its well-known "Corruption Perceptions Index" and that, within the Bank, Kaufmann, Kraay and Zoido-Lobaton

have used in constructing aggregate indicators of the quality of governance.

Finally, the Bank is now working with the Development Assistance Committee (DAC) of the OECD to develop a set of measurable indicators of governance and government performance that will be useful in coordinating donor approaches and policies in client countries. The DAC has been working to establish indicators that measure movement toward the meeting of major UN conference goals since the early 1990s. In *Shaping the 21st century: the contribution to development cooperation* (OECD, 1996) the DAC confirmed the goals and set out the areas of democratic governance that it saw as essential for achieving these goals. These areas include good governance (including public sector management, rule of law, corruption and military expenditure), human rights, democratization, and participatory development.

Since 1996, demand for measurements of progress has increased significantly, particularly from bilateral aid agencies. A DAC proposal to a joint OECD/UN/World Bank joint meeting on Agreed Indicators of Development Progress in February 1998 relaunched the initiative, and a further meeting in February 2000 confirmed that further work should be undertaken (recognizing that a consensus had not yet been reached). The DAC has asked the World Bank to lead this process in collaboration with the UK Department for International Development.

A major goal of this work is to identify a set of "second-generation" indicators with the potential for greater operational relevance than the existing broader indicators of the quality of governance. "Second-generation" indicators are intended to include more specific measures of public sector performance, as well as indicators of governmental processes and institutions. It is hoped that these will permit better testing of the links between particular public sector reforms (in the area of civil service pay) and outcomes (corruption and competence in the civil service).

BOX 26

Examples of Possible Indicators of Public Sector Institutional Performance

Examples of evaluative indicators (measures of performance outputs) based on objective data

- *Contract-intensive money (1 – currency/M2)

- *Budget volatility (from year to year, across functional classifications)

- *Waiting time for telephone lines.

Examples of descriptive indicators (measures of institutional "inputs")

Civil service

- *Merit-based civil service

- *Numbers of civil servants in comparison with international practice

- *Civil service pay (comparisons with the private sector)

- Civil service pay (vertical compression)

- Civil service pay (horizontal compression)

- Percentage of political appointees in the civil service

- Turnover rates for civil servants.

Tax and Public Expenditure Management

- Delays in auditing of public accounts

- Revenue predictability

- Variance between appropriations and actual spending.

Legal Framework

- Percentage of private land formally titled.

Intergovernmental Relations

- Extent of central government "bail out" of local governments

- *Elections at subnational levels

- *Subnational share of government expenditures

- Vertical imbalance (subnational expenditure minus revenue shares).

*Note: * Indicates that data for the measure currently exist*

TABLE 7 External Polls and Surveys on Governance

Source	Publication	Nature	Country Coverage
Business Environment Risk Intelligence	Business Risk Service	Poll	50 mostly developed countries
Wall Street Journal	Central European Economic Review	Survey	27 transition economies
Standard and Poor's DRI/McGraw-Hill	Country Risk Review	Poll	106 developed and developing countries
European Bank for Reconstruction and Development	Transition Report	Poll	26 transition economies
Economist Intelligence Unit	Country Risk Service & Country Forecast	Poll	114 developed and developing countries
Freedom House	Freedom in the World	Poll	172 developed and developing countries
	Nations in Transit	Poll	28 transition economies
Gallup International	50th Anniversary Survey	Survey	44 mostly developed countries
World Economic Forum	Global Competitiveness Survey	Survey	a. 54 developed and developing countries b. 23 African countries
Heritage Foundation/ Wall Street Journal	Economic Freedom Index	Poll	154 developed and developing countries
Political Economic Risk Consultancy	Asia Intelligence	Survey	11 Asian countries
Political Risk Services	International Country Risk Guide	Poll	140 developed and developing countries
Institute of Management Development	World Competitiveness Yearbook	Survey	46 primarily developed countries
Transparency International	Corruption Perceptions Index	Poll of polls	85 developing and developed countries

Note: Poll stands for "polls of experts" and Survey for "survey of entrepreneurs" (except Gallup, which is a survey of citizens).

The Links Between Governance and Poverty Reduction: The Empirical Evidence

Until the last several years, research on the performance of governments tended to focus on their management of the macro economy. Numerous studies used budget deficits, tax rates, or the rate of inflation to establish a link between government policies and development outcomes. For example, Fischer (1993) used the fiscal deficit, inflation rate, and foreign exchange premium as measures of the policy environment and found that good policies are conducive to faster growth. Similarly, Burnside and Dollar (World Bank 1997) reported a strong connection between a policy index and the effectiveness of aid. Deficits, inflation, and tax rates reflect the consequences of government policies. But they do not tell us why some governments choose good policies while others do not. Studies employing institutional indicators can illuminate the underlying sources of efficient policies (Cukierman et al. [1994] and Clague et al. [1996]).

The development of governance indicators has allowed scholars to conduct empirical studies of the impact of good governance on development and poverty reduction. Although governance indicators, often marketed as political risk information, have been available for some time, the systematic study of the relationship between quantified measures of governance and development outcomes is recent. Table 8 contains an annotated bibliography of scholarly research on the subject.

Indicators of the quality of governance can also be used to test the impact of institutional performance on economic outcomes. Collectively, these studies provide overwhelming evidence that good governance is crucial for successful development, as measured by high per capita incomes. Per capita income is a strong predictor of poverty rates, infant mortality, and illiteracy, suggesting that good governance improves the well-being of the poor. Recent studies examining the link between governance and poverty more directly confirm that good governance is important for poverty reduction.

Although not a comprehensive review, the summary below provides an overview of the evolution of research on governance and development, and of the alternative governance indicators used in this work, and reports the major empirical findings to date. It is organized more or less in chronological order according to the type of governance measure relied upon.

Indicators of civil liberties. The earliest studies use indexes of political freedoms and civil liberties as proxies for institutional and governance-related determinants of growth.

- Kormendi and Meguire (1985) used the civil liberties index from Freedom House as a proxy for "economic rights, such as freedom from expropriation or the enforceability of property rights and private contracts," and found that civil liberties were positively associated with investment rates, and—

through increasing investment—growth rates in per capita incomes.

- Scully (1988) used the civil liberties and political freedoms indexes as measures of nations' "institutional framework," finding they were positively related to income growth.

- Isham, Kaufmann and Pritchett (1997) found that rates of return on World Bank-financed projects in various developing countries over the 1974-93 period were higher in nations with greater civil liberties. The political freedoms index proved to be unrelated to project performance. The authors interpreted their findings overall as evidence for the view that "increasing public voice and accountability" improves government performance.

- A later set of studies investigating the relation of regime type to growth interpreted the Freedom House indexes as measures of representative government. Barro (1996) and Helliwell (1994) found that the indexes were positively related to growth only if variables such as educational attainment and investment rates are omitted as explanatory variables, and concluded that any beneficial impacts of representative government on growth may operate through these factor accumulation channels. Barro, Helliwell, and Burkhart and Lewis-Beck (1994) all concluded that the positive relation between income levels and democracy is mostly attributable to the former's impact on the latter rather than the other way around.

Political violence frequencies. Barro's (1991) classic empirical study on the determinants of growth tested the effects of coups, revolutions, and assassinations, which he interpreted as "adverse influences on property rights." These political instability measures were significantly and negatively related to growth rates and to private investment's share of GDP over the 1960-85 period. Alesina et al. (1996) showed that political instability and economic performance are jointly determined: coups lead to worse economic performance, but slow growth in turn increases the likelihood of coups.

Investor risk ratings. Beginning with Mauro (1995) and Knack and Keefer (1995), numerous studies have used governance indicators taken from "political risk" ratings provided by firms for sale to investors. These studies have found that the quality of governance is important for growth and investment rates, the effectiveness of foreign aid in promoting growth, and the prevention of inefficient patterns of government expenditures.

- Mauro (1995) used nine indexes produced by Business International (now part of the Economist Intelligence Unit), measuring such attributes as efficiency of the legal system, efficiency of the bureaucracy, corruption and various categories of political stability. He found that higher scores on these indexes are associated with lower investment and growth rates.

- Knack and Keefer (1995) used an index constructed from five International Country Risk Guide (ICRG) variables that reflect the security of private property and the enforceability of contracts: "Corruption in Government," the "Rule of Law," "Expropriation Risk," "Repudiation of Contracts by Government," and "Quality of the Bureaucracy." They created a second index from similar ratings provided by Business Environmental Risk Intelligence (BERI). Adding these indexes to a Barro-type growth regression, Knack and Keefer found that the quality of governance was positively associated with investment and growth rates.

- Knack and Anderson (1999) disaggregated income growth by income quintiles, and found using the ICRG and BERI indexes that income growth for the poor is particularly sensitive to the quality of governance.

- Examining time-series variation in income growth and in these risk indexes, Chong and Calderon (2000) found strong evidence for two-way causality: growth increases the values of the ICRG and BERI measures, but institutional quality as measured by ICRG (and BERI) values increases growth rates.

- Building on the work of Burnside and Dollar (1997, 1998), the World Bank's Policy Research Report, *Assessing Aid* (World Bank 1998), found that the impact of aid on growth and on infant mortality depends on governance. Aid has little impact in countries with poor economic policies and institutional quality, as measured by inflation, budget deficits, trade restrictiveness, and the ICRG index used by Knack and Keefer (1995). However, aid is associated with higher growth and lower infant mortality in countries with favorable policies and institutions.

- Using the same ICRG index and a measure of trade openness, Hall and Jones (1999) concluded that cross-country differences in incomes and productivity are "determined primarily by the institutions and government policies that make up the economic environment within which individuals and firms make investments, create and transfer ideas, and produce goods and services." They attempted to correct for possible endogeneity of institutions and policies to income levels by using as instruments the share of the population speaking European languages.

- Using corruption indicators from BI and ICRG, Tanzi and Davoodi (1997) found that corruption is associated with higher rates of public investment and with lower productivity of public investment.

- Also using corruption indicators from BI and ICRG, Mauro (1998) found that corruption was associated with reduced spending on education, a sector in which it is more difficult for public officials to collect large bribes.

- Evidence on corruption and foreign direct investment (FDI) is mixed. Using the BI corruption index, Wei (1997) found that differences in corruption are as important as differences in tax rates in explaining inflows of foreign direct investment from 14 source countries to 45 host countries in 1990-91. Using indexes from BI, ICRG and other sources, Alesina and Weder (1999) found no relationship between corruption and inward FDI over the period 1970 to 1995 for larger samples of developing nations.

Surveys of investors. An alternative approach to expert-provided ratings is to administer survey questionnaires to entrepreneurs and business managers.

- A survey focusing on the credibility and predictability of government policy was designed and administered in about 30 countries by Borner, Brunetti and Weder (1995). The survey was later expanded and administered for about 3,600 firms in 67 countries as part of *WDR97*. Entrepreneurs were asked for their subjective evaluation of aspects of their country's institutional framework, including security of property rights, predictability of rules and policies, reliability of the judiciary, problems with corruption and discretionary power in the bureaucracy, and disruptions caused by changes in government. With this information, a central governance question could be answered: "How good are governments at providing credible rules that will nurture the development of markets?" The survey showed that entrepreneurs in some parts of the world live in constant fear of policy surprises and that the institutional framework is not well enough entrenched to withstand changes in government without serious disruption. *WDR97* concluded: "Good policies by themselves can improve results. But the benefits are magnified where institutional capability is also higher—where policies and programs are implemented more efficiently and where citizens and investors have a greater certainty about government's future actions."

- Using corruption indicators from the *WDR97* survey, Campos et al. (1999) found that investment was more strongly affected by *uncertainty* associated with corruption than by the *extent* of corruption.

- Other survey-based governance indicators used in development studies are obtained from two organizations that evaluate economic "competitiveness." The World Economic Forum, with assistance from the Harvard Institute for International Development, issues an annual Global Competitiveness Report (GCR), which relies heavily on a survey of about 3,000 business executives. The survey covers between 50 and 60 countries, and includes items on bribery and corruption, tax evasion, and the reliability of the judicial system. Using corruption data from the GCR (and from TI, ICRG and other sources), Johnson, Kaufmann, and Zoido-Lobatón (1998) and Johnson, Kaufmann, McMillan, and Woodstuff (1999) found that corruption propels firms into the unofficial economy, undermining public finances and rule of law in a country.

- The Institute for Management Development produces a similar competitiveness index for its annual World Competitiveness Yearbook (WCY). Ratings are based on a survey of several thousand "businessmen around the world." For the 1996 yearbook, 3,162 "national and expatriate businessmen" representing both "local and international companies" responded to a survey covering nearly 50 countries. Several items included in the survey inquire about confidence in the administration of justice, security of persons and property, government "transparency," the adequacy of the "legal framework," and bureaucracy, the occurrence of "improper practices such as bribing or corruption" in the public sector, and the frequency of tax evasion. Using the WCY

corruption measure, Ades and Di Tella (1997) found that active industrial policies promote corruption, and that corruption in turn reduces the positive impact of active industrial policy on investment rates.

Aggregations of indexes. Aggregating several indicators that purport to measure similar aspects of governance is likely to improve accuracy, on the principle that more information is usually preferable to less. The best-known aggregations, described below, incorporate indicators based on expert assessments as well as those based on surveys of investors.

- Transparency International (TI) annually updates its "Corruption Perceptions Index" by aggregating corruption ratings produced by experts (such as ICRG) and from surveys. The index was first published in 1995, covering 41 countries with data aggregated from as many as seven sources per country. The 1999 index covered 99 countries, with information from up to 14 sources.

- Kaufmann, Kraay and Zoido-Lobaton (1999a, 1999b) constructed six aggregate indexes from numerous indicators collected from 14 different sources, including ICRG, BERI, Freedom House and others. The aggregate indexes are "rule of law," "graft," "voice and accountability," "government effectiveness," "political instability and violence," and "regulatory burden." Kaufmann et al. (1999b) showed that countries scoring higher on these indexes of rule of law, graft, voice and accountability, etc. tend to have lower infant mortality and higher literacy rates, as well as higher per capita incomes. They used the exogenous instruments used by Hall and Jones (1999) for their governance indexes to correct for possible reverse causality from income levels to governance.

TABLE 8 Empirical Studies of Governance and Development: An Annotated Bibliography

Authors	Methodology	Main Findings
Ades, Alberto and Rafael di Tella. 1996. "The Causes and Consequences of Corruption: A Review of Recent Empirical Contributions. " *IDS Bulletin* 27(2).	Review of empirical contributions of causes and effects of corruption.	Corruption negatively affects investment, and corruption is associated with the lack of competition in the product market and with less independent judicial systems.
Ades, Alberto and Rafael di Tella. 1997. "National Champions and Corruption: Some Unpleasant Interventionist Arithmetic." *Economic Journal*, 107, 1023-1042.	Cross-country regressions using 32 countries, with subjective indicators of corruption and industrial policy from the *World Competitiveness Yearbook*.	Active industrial policy is associated with increased corruption, which offsets part of the effects of an active industrial policy in increasing investment rates.
Alesina, Alberto and Beatrice Weder. 1999. "Do Corrupt Governments Receive Less Foreign Aid?" *NBER Working Paper* No. 7108.	Cross-country regressions for up to 90 countries, exploring the relationships between aid, foreign direct investment, and corruption.	Foreign direct investment over the 1970-95 period is reduced by host-country corruption levels, using one corruption indicator, but no relationship is found when using any of six other corruption indicators.
Alesina, Alberto; Sule Ozler, Nouriel Roubini and Phillip Swagel. 1996. "Political Instability and Economic Growth." *Journal of Economic Growth*, 1(2): 189-211.	Cross-country regressions for 113 countries for the 1950-82 period using annual data.	In countries and time periods with more changes in government (peaceful or otherwise), growth is lower. Slow growth in turn increases the likelihood of coups, but not of peaceful changes in government.
Barro, Robert. 1991. "Economic Growth in a Cross Section of Countries." *Quarterly Journal of Economics*, 106, 407-433.	Cross-country growth and investment regressions for 98 countries for the 1960-85 period.	Coups, revolutions, and political assassinations are associated with slower growth and lower investment rates.
Barro, Robert. 1996. "Democracy and Growth." *Journal of Economic Growth*, 1(1): 1-27.	Cross-country growth regressions, examining the impact of democracy (as measured by the Freedom House indexes) on growth.	Democracy is positively related to growth through factor accumulation: democracy is not significant when education and investment are included in the regression. A curvilinear relationship best fits the data, with partly democratic countries exhibiting the fastest growth rates.

Authors	Methodology	Main Findings
Brunetti, Aymo, Gregory Kisunko, and Weder. 1997. "Institutional Obstacles to Doing Business: Region-by-Region Results from a Worldwide Survey of the Private Sector." *Policy Research Working Paper No. 1759*. World Bank, Washington, DC.	Conduct a survey of business establishments around the world to construct an index of the "credibility of rules," composed of "the predictability of rule-making, subjective perceptions of political instability, security of persons and property, predictability of judicial enforcement, and corruption." Cross-firm and cross-country regressions are used to test the relationship between the credibility index and economic growth.	Credibility promotes investment and economic growth.
Burkhart, Ross and Michael Lewis-Beck. 1994. "Comparative Democracy: The Economic Development Thesis." *American Political Science Review*, 88: 903-910.	Time-series cross-sectional regressions analyzing the relationship between income levels and democracy, as measured by the Freedom House indexes.	The positive relationship between per capita income levels and democracy is mostly attributable to the effects of income on democratization; democracy has little effect on income levels.
Burnside, Craig and David Dollar. 1997. "Aid, Policies, and Growth." *Policy Research Working Paper No. 1777*. World Bank, Washington, DC.	Panel regressions measuring the relationships between aid, policies, and growth for 56 countries over six, four-year time periods.	Aid has a positive impact on growth in developing countries with good fiscal, monetary, and trade policies. Aid does not appear to affect policies systematically either positively or negatively.
Burnside, Craig and David Dollar. 1998. "Aid, the Incentive Regime, and Poverty Reduction." *Policy Research Working Paper No. 1937*. World Bank, Washington, DC.	Panel regressions explaining the impact of aid on growth in developing countries.	Aid spurs growth and poverty reduction only in a good policy environment. In developing countries with weak economic management, there is no relationship between aid and change in infant mortality. Where economic management is stronger, there is a relationship between aid and the change in infant mortality.
Chong, Alberto and Cesar Calderón. 2000. "Empirical Tests on the Causality and Feedback Between Institutional Measures and Economic Growth." *Economics and Politics* (forthcoming).	Geweke decomposition is used to test the causality and feedback between institutional measures from BERI and ICRG[*] (such as contract enforceability, nationalization potential, infrastructure quality, bureaucratic delays, and a composite index of the above four) and economic growth.	Improving institutional development promotes economic growth in developing countries. Causality also operates in the other direction, with growth leading to higher ratings on the ICRG and BERI indexes.
Chong, Alberto and Cesar Calderón. 1997. "Institutional Change and Poverty, or Why is it Worth it to Reform the State?" Mimeograph. World Bank, Washington, DC.	Cross-country regressions using measures of risk of expropriation, risk of contract repudiation, law and order, corruption in government and quality of bureaucracy for institutional development, and measures proposed by Foster-Greer-Thorbecke (1984) for poverty.	Improvements in institutional efficiency reduce the degree, severity, and incidence of poverty.
Chong, Alberto and Cesar Calderón. 1998. "Institutional Efficiency and Income Inequality: Cross Country Empirical Evidence." Mimeograph. World Bank, Washington, DC.	Cross-country regressions using a composite index of institutional efficiency based on measures of corruption of government, quality of bureaucracy, law and order tradition, risk of expropriation, and risk of contract repudiation.	For poor countries, institutional efficiency is positively linked with income inequality, and for rich countries it is negatively linked with income inequality.

*BERI stands for Business Environmental Risk Intelligence; ICRG stands for International Country Risk Guide.

Authors	Methodology	Main Findings
Clague, Christopher, Philip Keefer, Stephen Knack, and Mancur Olson. 1996. "Property and Contract Rights in Autocracies and Democracies." *Journal of Economic Growth,* 1(2): 243-276.	Cross-country regressions using time-series cross-section data, testing the impact of autocrats' time horizons, and the duration of democracy, on several measures of property and contract rights.	Property and contract rights are significantly associated with a proxy for the time horizons of autocrats (the log of years in power), and, in democracies, with the duration of democratic government.
Clague, Christopher, Philip Keefer, Stephen Knack, and Mancur Olson. 1999. "Contract-Intensive Money." *Journal of Economic Growth,* 4(2): 185-212.	Cross-country regressions testing an objective indicator of contract enforceability: "contract-intensive money" is the share of M2 not held in the form of currency outside banks.	"Contract-intensive money" is significantly related to growth, to investment, and to the size of contract-dependent sectors such as insurance.
Cukierman, Alex, Steven Webb, and Bilin Neyapti. 1994. "Measuring Central Bank Independence and Its Effect on Policy Outcomes." *International Center for Economic Growth Occasional Paper* No. 58:1-62.	Cross-country regressions used to develop four different rankings of central bank: legal independence, governors' turnover rates, responses of specialists to questionnaire on central bank independence, and an aggregation of the first two.	Legal independence is a statistically significant determinant of price stability among industrial countries, but not developing countries. The rate of governors' turnover contributes significantly to explaining inflation in developing countries and in explaining variations in inflation across the over-all sample of countries. An inflation-based index of overall central bank independence, combining legal and turnover information, helps explain cross-country variations in the inflation rate.
Cull, Robert. 1998. "How Deposit Insurance Affects Financial Depth." *Policy Research Working Paper No. 1875.* World Bank, Washington, DC.	Cross-country regressions in levels and differences.	Explicit deposit insurance is positively correlated with subsequent increases in financial depth if adopted when government credibility and institutional development are high.
Demirguc-Kunt, Asli and Enrica Detragiache. 1998. "Financial Liberalization and Financial Fragility." Development Research Group. World Bank, Washington, DC.	Panel logit regressions using rule of law, corruption, and contract enforcement as measures for institutional development as determinants of the probability of financial crisis after interest-rate liberalizations.	Banking crises are more likely to occur after financial liberalization. However, the effect of financial liberalization on the fragility of the banking sector is weaker when the institutions are more developed.
Dollar, David and Lant Pritchett. *Assessing Aid: What Works, What Doesn't, and Why.* 1998. Oxford University Press for the World Bank, Washington, DC.	Qualitative and quantitative analysis explaining the interaction of government policies and the quality of governance.	The impact of aid on growth and infant mortality depends on "sound economic management," as measured by an index of economic policies and institutional quality.
Evans, Peter B. and James E. Rauch (2000). "Bureaucratic and Growth: A Cross-National Analysis of the Effects of "Weberian" State Structures on Economic Growth." *American Sociological Review,* forthcoming.	Cross-country growth regressions, testing the impact of bureaucratic structure and meritocracy, as measured by a "Weberian State Scale" constructed from expert opinions for 35 developing nations.	Growth is strongly associated with higher values of the Weberian State Scale.
Fischer, Stanley. 1993. "The Role of Macroeconomic Factors in Growth." *Journal of Monetary Economics.* 32:485-512.	Regression analog of growth accounting used to present cross-sectional and panel regressions showing relationship between growth and macroeconomic factors.	Growth is negatively associated with inflation, large budget deficits, and distorted foreign exchange markets. Hence good polices are conducive to faster growth.

Authors	Methodology	Main Findings
Friedman, Eric, Simon Johnson, Daniel Kaufmann, and Pablo Zoido-Lobatón. 1999. "Dodging the Grabbing Hand: The Determinants of Unofficial Activity in 69 Countries." Forthcoming in *Journal of Public Economics*.	Across 69 countries, higher tax rates are associated with less unofficial activity as a percentage of GDP, but corruption is associated with more unofficial activity. Entrepreneurs go underground not to avoid official taxes but to reduce the burden of bureaucracy and corruption. Dodging the "grabbing hand" in this way reduces tax revenues as a percentage of both official and total GDP.	Corrupt governments become small governments and only relatively uncorrupt governments can sustain high taxes.
Grier, Kevin and Gordon Tullock (1989). "An Empirical Analysis of Cross-National Economic Growth: 1951-80," *Journal of Monetary Economics*, 24: 259-276.	Growth regressions for regional groups of countries, using the Freedom House civil liberties index as "a proxy for the political infrastructure" of nations.	Nations with fewer civil liberties grow more slowly in the African and Latin American samples; no relationship is found for the Asian sample.
Hall, Robert and Charles Jones. 1999. "Why Do Some Countries Produce So Much More Output Per Worker Than Others?" *Quarterly Journal of Economics*, 114: 83-116.	Cross-country regressions using two indexes: one of government anti-diversion policies (GADP) constructed by Knack and Keefer (1995) with data from the ICRG, and one from Sachs and Warner (1995) on trade openness.	Differences in capital accumulation, productivity, and therefore output per worker are driven by differences in institutions and government policies.
Helliwell, John. 1994. "Empirical Linkages Between Democracy and Economic Growth." *British Journal of Political Science*, 24: 225-248.	Cross-country regressions exploring the relationships between income levels, democracy, and income growth.	Higher income levels encourage democratization. Any effects of democracy on income growth appear to be through increasing education and investment rates.
Huther, Jeff and Anwar Shah. 1998. "Applying a Simple Measure of Good Governance to the Debate on Fiscal Decentralization." *World Bank Operations Evaluation Department Policy Research Working Paper No. 1894*. World Bank, Washington, DC.	Construction of an index of governance quality. Index includes citizen participation, government orientation, social development, and economic management.	A positive relationship exists between fiscal decentralization and quality of governance.
Isham, Jonathan, Daniel Kaufmann and Lant Pritchett. 1997. "Civil Liberties, Democracy, and the Performance of Government Projects." *The World Bank Economic Review*. 11(2): 219-42.	Cross-national dataset used on the performance of government investment projects financed by the World Bank to examine the link between government efficacy and governance.	Controlling for other determinants of performance, economic rates of return on projects in countries with the strongest civil liberties average 8 to 22 percentage points higher than countries with the weakest civil liberties.
Johnson, Simon, Daniel Kaufmann, and Pablo Zoido-Lobatón. 1998. "Regulatory Discretion and the Unofficial Economy." *American Economic Review*. 88(2): 387-392.	Cross-country regressions from Heritage Foundation, Global Competitiveness Survey, ICRG, Freedom House to explain the size of the unofficial economy in three regions: Latin America, OECD, and the former Soviet bloc.	Countries with more regulation tend to have a higher share of the unofficial economy in total GDP. Higher tax burden leads to more unofficial activity. Countries with more corruption tend to have a larger unofficial economy.
Johnson, Simon, Daniel Kaufmann, John McMillan, and Christopher Woodruff. 1999. Forthcoming. *Journal of Public Economics*.	Firm-level regressions using "unofficial" activity of private manufacturing firms in Eastern European countries: Russia, Ukraine, Poland, Slovakia, and Romania.	A comparison of cross-country averages shows that managers in Russia and Ukraine face higher effective tax rates, worse official corruption, greater incidence of criminal protection, and have less faith in court system. The firm-level regressions for three Eastern European countries find that official corruption is significantly associated with hiding output.

Authors	Methodology	Main Findings
Kauffman, Daniel and Aart Kraay and Pablo Zoido-Lobatón. (1999a). "Governance Matters." *World Bank Policy Working Paper No. 2196.*	Simultaneous model used to isolate the direct effects of differences in governance on three measures of development outcomes: GDP per capita, infant mortality, and adult literacy. They use a very large set of indicators drawn from commercial sources and investor surveys. They allocate these indicators to six clusters and use a latent variable model to estimate a common element in each cluster.	A strong causal relation exists between governance and development outcomes for all six aggregate indicators. They find that their results hold whether or not OECD countries are included in their sample.
Kaufmann, Daniel, Aart Kraay, and Pablo Zoido-Lobatón. (1999b). "Aggregating Governance Indicators." *World Bank Policy Working Paper No. 2195.*	Simple variant of an unobserved components model used on a sample of 160 countries to combine information from different sources into aggregate governance indicators. These include rule of law, graft, and voice and accountability.	Aggregate governance indicators are more informative about the level of governance than any individual indicator, but the standard errors associated with estimates of governance are still large relative to the units in which governance is measured.
Kaufmann, Daniel and Shang-Jin Wei. "Does 'Grease Money' Speed Up the Wheels of Commerce?" 1999. *NBER Working Paper No 7093.*	In a general equilibrium model in which regulatory burden and delay can be endogenously chosen by rent-seeking bureaucrats, red tape and bribery may be positively correlated across firms. Using data from three worldwide firm-level surveys, the relationship is examined between bribe payment, management time wasted with bureaucrats, and cost of capital.	Firms that pay more bribes are also likely to spend more, not less, management time with bureaucrats negotiating regulations, and face higher, not lower, cost of capital.
Knack, Stephen and Gary Anderson. 1999. "Is 'Good Governance' Progressive?" Unpublished manuscript.	Cross-country regressions examining changes in income growth for different income quintiles, and changes in Gini coefficients over time.	Income growth for the poorer quintiles is more sensitive to the quality of governance (measured by ICRG and BERI indexes) than is income growth for richer quintiles. Gini coefficients decline more where the (initial) quality of governance is higher.
Knack, Stephen and Philip Keefer. 1995. "Institutions and Economic Performance: Cross-Country Tests Using Alternative Institutional Measures." *Economics and Politics.* 7(3): 207-227.	Cross-country regressions using two subjective indexes of institutional development from ICRG and BERI. The ICRG index combines quality of the bureaucracy, corruption in government, rule of law, expropriation risk, and repudiation of contracts by government. The BERI index combines bureaucratic delays, nationalization potential, contract enforceability, and infrastructure quality.	Institutions that protect property rights are crucial for economic growth and rates of investment as a share of GDP. The institutional indexes explain economic performance much better than do the Freedom House indexes, or frequencies of coups, revolutions, and assassinations.
Knack, Stephen. 1996. "Institutions and the Convergence Hypothesis: The Cross-National Evidence." *Public Choice,* 87: 207-228.	Cross-country growth regressions testing for convergence effects.	Unconditional convergence in per capita incomes is not found in broad cross-country samples. It is found however for a sample of nations with high-quality institutions as measured by indexes from ICRG and BERI.

Authors	Methodology	Main Findings
Knack, Stephen and Philip Keefer. 1997a. "Why Don't Poor Countries Catch Up? A Cross-National Test of an Institutional Explanation." *Economic Inquiry.* 35:590-602.	Institutional indexes from BERI and ICRG are interacted with initial per capita income in cross-country growth regressions.	Institutions are important determinants of "convergence" —weak institutions prevent poor countries from exploiting "catch up" opportunities.
Knack, Stephen and Philip Keefer. 1997b. "Does Social Capital Have an Economic Payoff? A Cross-Country Investigation." *Quarterly Journal of Economics.* 112: 1251-1288.	Cross-country regressions using indicators from the World Values Surveys on interpersonal trust, civic cooperation, and memberships in groups.	Trust and civic cooperation have significant impacts on economic performance. Group memberships, hypothesized to have positive effects by Putnam (1993) and negative effects by Olson (1982), have no relation to economic performance.
Kormendi, Roger C. and Philip G. Meguire. 1985. "Macroeconomic Determinants of Growth." *Journal of Monetary Economics,* 16: 141-163.	Cross-country growth regressions with 47 countries for the 1950-77 period. Independent variables include the Freedom House civil liberties index, a proxy for "economic rights, such as freedom from expropriation or the enforceability of property rights and private contracts."	Growth and investment rates are higher, other things equal, in countries with greater civil liberties. The effect on growth appears to be entirely through increasing investment.
La Porta, et. al. 1997a. "Legal Determinants of External Finance. " *Journal of Finance.* 52(3):1131-1150.	Cross-country regressions using measures of legal rules protecting investors and the quality of their enforcement (measures include rule of law, shareholder rights, one-share = one-vote, creditor rights). The data on these qualitative, but objective (except for rule of law), variables are presented in La Porta et. al. (1998 [1996]).	Countries with better investor protections have bigger and broader equity and debt markets.
La Porta, et. al. 1997b. "Trust in Large Organizations. " *AEA Papers and Proceedings.* 87(2):333-338.	Cross-country regressions using measures of trust from the World Values Surveys.	Trust has important effects on economic performance.
Levine, Ross. 1997. "Law, Finance, and Economic Growth. " Mimeograph. World Bank, Washington, DC.	Panel regressions using institutional variables (such as creditor rights, enforcement of contracts, and accounting standards) as instrumental variables.	Countries with more developed institutions (legal and regulatory systems) have better-developed financial intermediaries, and consequently grow faster.
Loayza, Norman. 1996. "The Economics of the Informal Sector: A Simple Model and Some Empirical Evidence from Latin America. " Carnegie-Rochester *Conference Series on Public Policy.* 45:129-162.	Endogenous growth model with data on Latin American countries in the early 1990s. Causal variables include corporate income tax rate, labor market restrictions, strength of the enforcement system.	The size of the informal sector is negatively correlated with the rate of economic growth in countries where the statutory tax burden is larger than optimal and the enforcement system is weak.
Mauro, Paolo. 1995. "Corruption and Growth." *Quarterly Journal of Economics* 110(3): 681-712.	Cross-country regressions using subjective indexes of corruption, the amount of red tape, the efficiency of the judicial system, and various categories of political stability.	Corruption is negatively linked with economic growth.
Rauch, James E. and Peter B. Evans (2000). "Bureaucratic Structure and Economic Performance." *Journal of Public Economics,* 74, 49-71.	Cross-country regressions of bureaucratic quality and corruption on indexes of bureaucratic structure and meritocracy, constructed from expert opinions for 35 developing nations.	Subjective ratings of bureaucratic quality and corruption from ICRG and other sources are positively related to the merit-based hiring index, but are unrelated to indexes of compensation and internal promotion and career stability.

Authors	Methodology	Main Findings
Rodrik, Dani. 1997. "TFPG Controversies, Institutions, and Economic Performance in East Asia." *NBER Working Paper No. W5914.*	Cross-country regressions and correlations using index constructed by Easterly and Levine (1996) using data from Knack and Keefer (1995).	Institutional quality, initial income, and initial education do well in rank ordering East Asian countries according to their growth performance.
Scully, Gerald. 1988. "The Institutional Framework and Economic Development." *Journal of Political Economy,* 96(3): 652-662.	Cross-country regressions of income growth for 1960-80 for 115 nations, using the Freedom House indicators as proxies for property rights and the rule of law.	Controlling for changes in the K/L ratio, income growth is higher where countries are rated more highly on the Freedom House indexes.
Tanzi, Vito and Hamid Davoodi. 1997. "Corruption, Public Investment, and Growth. " *IMF Working Paper WP/97/139.*	Cross-country regressions using measures of corruption, government revenue, O&M expenditures, and quality of public investment.	The presence of corruption tends to increase public investment while lowering its productivity.
Wei, Shang-Jin. 1997. "How Taxing Is Corruption on International Investors?" *NBER Working Paper No. 6030.*	Cross-country regressions using measures of two year bilateral flows of FDI. Explanatory variables include tax rates, corruption, GDP, population, distance, wage, and linguistic ties.	Increases in either tax rate on multinational firms or corruption levels in host government reduces inward FDI and corruption is not treated differently in different parts of the world.
World Development Report. 1997. *The State in a Changing World,* Oxford University Press for the World Bank, Washington, DC.	Survey of the importance of the role of the state in development. A specially commissioned survey of 3,600 firms in 69 countries for the publication reported on perceptions of the stability of laws and policies, adequacy of infrastructure, taxes and regulations, and crime and corruption.	The survey showed that entrepreneurs in some parts of the world live in constant fear of policy surprises and that the institutional framework was not well enough entrenched to withstand changes in government without serious disruption. Sound policies by themselves can improve results. Benefits are magnified where institutional capability is also higher.
Zak, Paul and Stephen Knack. 1998. "Trust and Growth." *IRIS Center Working Paper No. 219.*	Cross-country regressions for 40 market economies, using survey measures of interpersonal trust.	Trust is strongly related to growth rates. With data on 11 countries beyond those analyzed by Knack and Keefer (1997), this relationship is found to be robust to variations in specification or period examined, and to the use of religious composition variables as exogenous instruments for trust. Trust is higher in nations with less income inequality and ethnic heterogeneity, and with more reliable legal mechanisms for enforcing contracts.

An Inventory of the Bank's Governance and Institutional Reform Programs, FY98, FY99, and FY00 (1st half)

Since 1996, the Bank has launched a wide range of activities pursuant to its anticorruption agenda, and the Public Sector Board has regularly compiled a running inventory of those activities (in part to fulfill its monitoring obligations under the Strategic Compact). While the decision to target corruption is relatively new, the Bank has had a long history of promoting reforms that effectively improve the management of public resources and reduce opportunities for corruption. Examples of reforms that have an impact on levels of corruption and the quality of governance include:

- Structural adjustment programs that support the liberalization of markets, prices, trade and exchange regimes,

- Public enterprise sector reforms that result in the sale and liquidation of public enterprises,

- Private sector reforms that relax governments controls and cut off rent-seeking opportunities, and

- Reforms in service delivery and infrastructure programs to give greater "voice" and decisionmaking power to local communities (community action programs).

Since most if not all Bank operations contain some components that could be expected to have a positive anticorruption impact, a complete list of Bank operations that are likely to contribute to the reduction of corruption would be unwieldy.

To keep the inventory manageable and targeted, only those programs targeted explicitly at anticorruption, improvements in governance, or institutional reform in the public sector have been included. The list is organized by region and country, with cross-cutting Bank-wide initiatives included at the end. Programs are organized according to the following categories:

- Grant-based assistance to reduce corruption

- ESW and mission reports on corruption

- In-country workshops and surveys on corruption

- Governance related lending

This list focuses on governance programs under implementation or active preparation in fiscal 1998, fiscal 1999, and the first half of fiscal 2000. The extent of Bank activity in this area is increasing rapidly, and thus more recent initiatives may not be reflected in the inventory.

TABLE 9 Countries with Programs to Strengthen Governance

	Grant-Based Technical Assistance	ESW and Mission Reports
AFRICA		
Regional programs		(FY99) Research program on determinants of corruption in Africa. (FY99) Study on Corruption and the Financing of Politics in Africa. (FY00) Sourcebook for community-driven development
Angola		(FY98) CPFA
Benin	(FY99) IDF Grant. Reinforcement of Anticorruption Unit in Presidency.	(FY99) CPAR (FY99) Pilot IGR to assess areas of weak governance and poor public sector performance (FY00-01) CFAA
Burkina Faso		(FY00) CPAR (FY00) Study on the governance underpinnings of service delivery.
Cameroon		(FY98-FY00): Consultant reports on public expenditure and public investment. (FY00) Development of good governance and anti-corruption action plan. (FY01) CFAA (FY01) CPAR
Cape Verde		
Chad	(FY00) IDF Grant to support National Assembly	(FY00) Development of good governance and anti-corruption action plan. (FY00) CFAA (FY00) CPAR (FY01) PER
Côte d'Ivoire		(FY98) CPFA (FY99) Country regulatory framework paper. (FY00-01) CFAA

In-country workshops, Surveys	Governance-related lending (active projects)
(FY98) Corruption Workshop for Bank Staff and Clients (WBI). (FY98-00) Regional Investigative Journalism Workshops—print and radio journalists (West and East Africa—WBI). (FY99) Role of African Parliaments in Curbing Corruption (WBI). (FY99) Anticorruption Core Course for seven African countries (WBI). (FY99) Workshop: The Media's Role in Curbing Corruption (WBI). (FY99) Information for Accountability Workshops: Supporting Accountability and Anticorruption Strategies in Sub-Saharan Africa (International Records Management Trust/Danish Governance Trust Fund). (FY99-00) Support to the African Parliamentarians Network against Corruption (WBI). (FY00) Presentations at Ninth International Anticorruption Conference in Durban, South Africa. (FY00) Investigative Journalism Teleseminar Series: Anglophone and Francophone Africa (WBI)	(FY00-01) Preparation of a regional project to reform the public procurement systems of member countries of the Union Économique et Monétaire Ouest-Africaine in West Africa.
(FY98) Anticorruption seminar (WBI). (FY98) Anticorruption seminar as part of IDF Grant to Anticorruption unit. (FY99-00) Participant in WBI Core Course on Anticorruption. (FY00) Participant in Investigative Journalism Teleseminar Series (WBI).	(FY99) Private sector development and judicial reform project. (FY99) Transport Sector Investment program. (FY00-01) Preparation of Public Expenditure Reform Credit with financial accountability components (FY00-01) Preparation of Legal and Judicial Reform Project.
	(Approved FY92) Public Institutional Development project.
(FY00) Participant in Investigative Journalism Teleseminar Series (WBI).	(FY00-01) Strong transparency components dominate the overall Chad-Cameroon Pipeline package.
	(Approved FY94) Public Sector Reform and Capacity Building project. (FY98) Economic Reforms Support project. (FY99) Privatization and Regulatory Capacity Building project.
Participatory process linked to PRSP	(Approved FY96) Capacity Building project. (FY99) Structural Adjustment Credit III. (FY00) Technical Assistance Credit on Management of Oil Revenue (FY00-01) Strong transparency components dominate the overall Chad-Cameroon Pipeline package.
(FY00) Conference on Good Governance, focusing on corruption (22-24 November 1999). (FY00) Participant in Investigative Journalism Teleseminar Series (WBI).	(Approved FY93) Economic Management Technical Assistance project.

Countries with Programs to Strengthen Governance, continued

	Grant-Based Technical Assistance	ESW and Mission Reports
AFRICA, continued		
Eritrea		(FY99) CPFA (FY00-01) CFAA (FY00-01) CPAR
Ethiopia (New operations are on hold owing to the war with Eritrea)	(FY99) IDF Grant. Civil Service Reform and Capacity Building.	(FY98) Anticorruption mission and report; Follow-up work is based on decision to designate Ethiopia as the pilot country in Africa for introducing the Anti-corruption Clause in Bank procurement. (FY98) CPFA (FY98-01) PER, conducted annually in Ethiopia (FY98) CPAR (FY99-00) Pilot IGR to assess areas of weak governance and poor public performance. (FY00-01) CFAA
Gambia, The		
Ghana		(FY00) CFAA and CPAR underway. (FY00-01) Participatory CAS and CDF process consulting government, donors and civil society. (FY00-01) Study to develop a consistent, cross-sectoral decentralization strategy, following through on anti-corruption survey, the institutional reform of ministries, and the development of measures to monitor and evaluate government performance.
Guinea		(FY98) CPFA (FY99) Mission to respond to request from President for assistance to fight corruption. (FY99-00) CPAR (FY00) Follow-up to mission—assistance to develop anticorruption strategy and action plan.
Guinea-Bissau	(FY98) IDF Grant. Notary and Registration Service.	(FY98) Strengthening Customs Administration.
Kenya	(FY00-01) Preparation and implementation of IDF Grant for support to the Kenyan Anticorruption Authority.	(FY98) CAS. "Best practice." (FY99) CAS. Addressed problem of corruption and public sector management.
Lesotho		(FY99) Policy dialogue on Civil Service Reform is part of Policy Framework Paper process.

In-country workshops, Surveys	Governance-related lending (active projects)
(FY98) Anticorruption Seminar for Parliamentarians (WBI) (FY99) Three Introductory Investigative Journalism Seminars including Radio and Television journalists (WBI). (FY99-00) Governance and Corruption Survey (WBI/Danish Governance Trust Fund). (FY99-00) Participant in WBI Core Course on Anticorruption. (FY00) Participant in Investigative Journalism Teleseminar Series (WBI). (FY00) Support to GOE/CSR Program, development of Investigative Journalism curricula (WBI).	
(FY98) Improving Cabinet decisions on public expenditure management (WBI).	
(FY98-00) Seminar for Public Accounts and Finance Committees (WBI). (FY99) Seminar for Economic and Financial Journalists on Transparency and Integrity (WBI and African Virtual University). (FY99-00) Participant in WBI Core Course on Anticorruption. (FY00-01) Governance and Corruption Survey. (FY00) Participant in Investigative Journalism Teleseminar series (WBI).	(FY98/FY99) Economic Reform Support Operation project I/II. (FY99) Adaptable Program Loan Public Sector Management program.
(FY00-01) Governance and Corruption Survey.	(FY99) Adaptable Program Loan. Capacity Building for Service Delivery.
(FY99-00) WBI Core Course on Anticorruption. (FY00-01) Governance and Corruption Survey.	(Approved FY93) Parastatal Reform and Privatization Technical Assistance project. (Approved FY95) Institutional Development and Civil Service Reform project. (FY99) Institutional Development and Civil Service Reform project. (FY01) Proposed Public Sector Adjustment Credit will focus on accountability and transparency in the use of public resources.

Countries with Programs to Strengthen Governance, continued

	Grant-Based Technical Assistance	ESW and Mission Reports	
AFRICA, continued			
Liberia		(FY00) Collaborating with IMF to remove monopolies on petroleum products and rice imports.	
Madagascar		(FY98) CPFA	
Malawi	(FY00-01) IDF Grant. Reinforcement of Anticorruption Bureau	(FY98) Anticorruption mission and report.	
Mali		(FY99) Anticorruption mission and report. (FY99) CPAR	
Mauritius		(FY98) CPFA	
Mauritania			
Mozambique	(FY00) IDF Grant. Supporting the Technical Group for Public Sector Reform	(FY00-01) CPAR (FY00-01) Governance central to CAS. (FY00-01) Report on accountability and transparency in the delivery of public services.	
Niger		(FY99) CPAR (FY00-01) CFAA	
Nigeria		(FY00) Missions to develop comprehensive approach to anticorruption. (FY00) CFAA and CPAR	

In-country workshops, Surveys	Governance-related lending (active projects)
	(Approved FY97) Public Management Capacity Building project. (FY99) Structural Adjustment Credit II.
(FY99-00) Participant in WBI Core Course on Anticorruption. (FY00-01) Governance and Corruption Survey	(Approved FY94) Institutional Development project II. The five major components include: (i) improving civil service policy and information framework; (ii) strengthening capacity of department of personnel management; (iii) strengthening institutional capacity of the Ministry of Finance; (iv) support the Department of Statutory Bodies; and (v) strengthen the Malawi Institute of Management. (Approved FY96) Fiscal Restructuring and Deregulation Program project (FRDP). (FY99) FRDP II. (FY00) Structural Adjustment Credit will support financial management reform, the office of Auditor General, judicial and legal reform, and decentralization of the administration of the civil service.
(FY98) Seminar for Public Accounts and Finance Committees (WBI). (FY99) Seminar for Economic and Financial Journalists on Transparency and Integrity (WBI and African Virtual University). (FY99) Seminar for Public Accounts and Finance Committees of Parliament (WBI).	(Approved FY96) Economic Management Credit.
(FY98) Household and Private Sector Corruption Surveys (WBI). (FY98) National Integrity Meeting (WBI). (FY98) Support for Anticorruption Legislation (WBI). (FY98) Introductory and Advanced Investigative Journalism Seminars (WBI).	
	(Approved FY96) Public Resource Management Credit.
	Approved FY93) Legal and Public Sector Capacity project. (FY00-01) Preparation of multi-faceted public sector reform project.
	(FY99) Public Finance Reform Credit.
(FY00) Preparation of governance and corruption surveys. (FY00) Initiation of training program for parliamentarians and journalists (WBI).	(FY00) Preparation of Economic Management Capacity Building Project which will have components for strengthening economic and financial management.

Countries with Programs to Strengthen Governance, continued

	Grant-Based Technical Assistance	ESW and Mission Reports
AFRICA, continued		
Rwanda		(FY98) CPFA
Sierra Leone		
Senegal	(FY98) IDF Grant. National Consultation on Civil Service Reform.	
South Africa	(FY99) IDF Grant. Setting up Institute for Public Finance and Auditing.	(FY98) CPFA
Tanzania		(FY98-00) Anticorruption mission and report—follow-up to the mission is the initiation of an accountability and transparency program. (FY00) CPAR
Uganda	(FY00) IDF Grant. Strengthening the capacity of the Ministry of Ethics and Integrity	(FY98) CPFA (FY99) Anticorruption mission and report. (FY99) Study on corruption and the financing of politics. (FY99) Anticorruption report on the agenda of the Consultative Group Meeting and of February meeting of Global Coalition for Africa. (FY00) CPAR
Zambia		(FY99) CAS. Strong anticorruption components.
Zimbabwe		

In-country workshops, Surveys	Governance related lending (active projects)
	(FY99) Economic Recovery Credit.
	(Approved FY93) Public Sector Management Support project: to strengthen capacity to implement adjustment program and longer-term growth strategy, focusing on fiscal management. (FY00) Governance and anticorruption component included in the new Economic Rehabilitation and Recovery Credit.
(FY00) Regional Johannesburg police to improve security and governance.	
(FY98) Introductory and Advanced Investigative Journalism Seminars—Business Journalists (WBI). (FY98) Integrity Workshop for Parliament (WBI). (FY99) Introductory and Advanced Investigative Journalism including Radio and Television (WBI). (FY99) Strengthening of Parliamentary Oversight (WBI) (FY99-00) Participant in WBI Core Course on Anticorruption. (FY00) Participant in Investigative Journalism Teleseminar series (WBI).	(Approved FY93) Financial and Legal Management Upgrading project. (Approved FY93) Private and Public Sector Management project. (Approved FY97) Structural Adjustment Credit I. (FY99) Tax Administration Program project. (FY00) Public Sector Reform Project focuses on service delivery, merit-based public service, performance management and budgeting, pay reform, and ethics.
(FY98) National Integrity Meeting III (WBI). (FY98) 3 Investigative Journalism workshops (WBI). (FY98) National Integrity Survey (WBI). (FY98) Integrity Meeting and Workshops for Parliament and Judiciary (WBI). (FY99) National Integrity Meeting IV, (WBI). (FY99) National and District Media Training Investigative Journalism—TV & Radio (WBI). (FY99) 10 District Integrity Meetings (WBI). (FY99-00) Participant in WBI Core Course on Anticorruption. (FY00) Participant in Investigative Journalism Teleseminar series (WBI).	(Approved FY95) Institutional Capacity Building project. Includes (i) central government capacity building; (ii) local government capacity building; (iii) legal sector reform; (iv) accountancy profession; and (v) training funds. (Approved FY97) Structural Adjustment Credit III. (FY99) Education Adjustment Credit allocates funds directly to communities. (FY00) Preparation of Public Expenditure Reform Credit (PERC) with components to strengthen governance and accountability.
	(FY99) Public Sector Reform and Export Promotion Credit. (FY00) Public Sector Capacity Building Project to make public service delivery more effective and efficient, facilitate economic growth and thence reduce poverty.
(FY98) Workshop on Training of Trainers for Development of Local Integrity (WBI).	

	Grant-Based Technical Assistance	ESW and Mission Reports

EAST ASIA AND PACIFIC

	Grant-Based Technical Assistance	ESW and Mission Reports
Regional programs		(FY98) Regional strategy review and issues note (Klitgaard) (FY99) Regional Strategy & Action Plan. (FY99–00) East Asia Anticorruption Advisory Group. Meetings held with Regional Management Team and Advisory Group (6/99 Washington DC; Singapore 9/99; Bangkok, 2/2000). (FY00) Handbook for Fighting Corruption. (FY00) East Asia: Regional Study 2000 (chapter 6). (EAPVPC/EASPR) (FY00-01) Study: constraints on the media to help curb corruption.
Cambodia	(FY99-00) IDF-financed TA for financial accountability development.	(FY99) Preliminary survey on "the business environment and governance in Cambodia" (Danish Trust Fund). (FY99) PER—Governance, corruption issues discussed up front in the context of estimating the extent of revenue loss (especially from illegal logging) and expenditure leakages/diversions. (FY99-00) IDF grant: has surveyed public officials and private citizens as input for upcoming Action Plan for Enhancing Governance and Fighting Corruption. (FY00) Translation of "Parliamentarians Guide to Curbing Corruption" (WBI).
China	(FY99) Assistance to develop bidding law, procurement regulations, and a National Audit Office with an audit Management Information System. (FY99) IDF Grant. Strengthening of Enabling Environment for China's NGO Development.	(FY98) Accounting Reform and Development Project.
Indonesia	(FY98) IDF Grant. Legal Reform. (FY99-00) Asia-Europe Meeting (ASEM) Grant. Improving Local Government Expenditure Transparency. (FY99-00) ASEM Grants. Social Safety Net Monitoring with Civil Society and NGOs. (FY00) UNDP/WB Partnership on Governance.	(FY99) Anticorruption Strategy Missions. (FY99) Anticorruption Action Plan for Internal Bank Activities. (FY99) Strong anticorruption focus in CAS-PR. (FY99-00) Anticorruption Handbook. (FY99) Civil Service Review (draft). (FY99) PER – focus on budget management. (FY99) Governance Baseline (under purview of Partnership). (FY00) Translation of "Parliamentarians Guide to Curbing Corruption" (WBI).

In-country workshops, Surveys	Governance-related lending (active projects)
(FY99) Democracy and Governance Conference; Seoul, Korea (WBI). (FY00) Manila Social Forum, November 1999, highlighted session on governance and issues linking poverty and corruption. (FY99) Regional Seminar on parliaments role in curbing corruption (WBI). (FY00) Combating Corruption in Asia-Pacific (WBI, ADB).	
(FY00) Parliamentarians Workshop	
(FY99) Program on Corporate Governance and Enterprise Restructuring with State Economic and Trade Commission (WBI).	(Approved FY95) Fiscal Technical Assistance project. (FY93-00) Reform, Institutional Support and Pre-investment Project (feasibility of introducing tax police). (FY95-99) Economic Law Reform Project. (FY95-99) Fiscal TA for improving tax administration. (FY99) Accounting Reform and Development Project to strengthen financial Management for state enterprises and government bodies. (FY99) State-Owned Enterprise Reform Project. (FY99) Technical Cooperation Credit 4 subcomponent supporting the National School of Administration in exploring adequate anticorruption measures and mechanisms.
(FY99) Regular Meetings with Indonesia Corruption Watch, International NGO Forum on Indonesian Development and other NGOs. (FY99) Procurement Complaint Monitoring System. Wide distribution to the Country Team in FY00. (FY99) Seminar series on Public Sector Reforms. (FY00) CFAA (FY00) Integrity Awareness Seminar. (FY00) Parliamentary Workshop (WBI).	(FY99) Policy Reform and Social Safety Net Structural Adjustment Loans including transparency and other anticorruption and collusion conditions.

Countries with Programs to Strengthen Governance, continued

	Grant-Based Technical Assistance	ESW and Mission Reports	

EAST ASIA AND PACIFIC, continued

	Grant-Based Technical Assistance	ESW and Mission Reports	
Korea, Rep. of	(FY99-00) IDF Grant. Financial Accountability & Good Governance. (FY00) Policy and Human Resource Development (PHRD) Grant. Financial Accounting Standards Board. (FY00) PHRD Grant. Transparency of Regulatory Environment.	(FY99) Comprehensive anticorruption program and report. (FY00) Country Economic Memorandum (CEM) with governance component.	
Lao PDR	(FY99) IDF Grant. Civil Service Reform.		
Malaysia		(FY99) Structural Policy Review (FY99) PER. Analyzes public expenditure/public sector management issues. (FY00) CAS. Includes governance and transparency.	
Mongolia			
Papua New Guinea	(FY98-99) IDF Grant. Independent Commission Against Corruption (ICAC). Draft legislation for establishment of ICAC. (FY99) Financial Management Improvement project. (FY00) Informal assistance to TI (funded by Swedish Governance Grant) in proposal to monitor Government's privatization program using the "islands of integrity approach." (FY00) Consultant Trust Fund established to support structural reform related activities, with a small portion of these funds earmarked to support TI in anticorruption activities.	(FY98) CAS. Strong governance focus. (FY99) CEM focused on improving governance (both public sector and corporate) and included an anti-corruption strategy. (FY00) PER included strategies to combat fraud and waste and improve governance.	
Philippines	(FY97) IDF Grant. Results monitoring. (FY98) IDF Grant. Assistance to government accounting system—Public Expenditure Management Improvement. (FY99) Special PHRD Grant. Upgrading the financial framework. (FY99) ASEM Grants. Poverty monitoring, strengthening for financial infrastructure and financial monitoring and reform (FY00) PHRD Grant. Social and environmental assessments.	(FY98) Transparency study. (FY99) PER (FY99-01) CAS. Includes governance and anticorruption agenda. (FY00) Judicial Assessment. (FY00) SSR looks at medium-term challenges in public sector management, judicial system, and corporate governance. (FY00) Rural Development Trends and Study. (FY00) Client Feedback Survey on Special Zone of Peace and Development Social Fund. (FY00) Anticorruption Report and recommendations submitted to government.	

In-country workshops, Surveys	Governance-related lending (active projects)
(FY99) Anticorruption seminar (ROK). (FY00) Establishment of the Korean Financial Accounting Standards Board. (FY00) Comprehensive Package of Anticorruption Measures announced by ROK, Anticorruption Legislation pending before National Assembly. Government target of raising TI ranking from 43 to 20 by 2003 as part of goal to reach "transparent state." (FY00) International Conference on Combating Corruption, Seoul. (FY00) Seminar on the role of audit committees.	(FY99) SAL II Corporate Governance.
	(FY98) Fiscal Technical Assistance project.
	(Approved FY91) Public Sector Training project. (FY00) SAL (under preparation, anticipated Board date FY00—governance focused operation, including public sector reform and institutional support, focus on oversight entities, privatization, and specific elements to combat corruption and support the rule of law.
(FY98) Draft Terms of Reference for Asian Institute of Management. (FY98) Workshop on financial management. (FY99) Policymaker workshops to bring together policymakers concerned with corruption. (FY99) Identification and development of an integrated program of procurement training and TA to prevent/detect fraud and corruption and incorporate program into FY00 projects. (FY00) Integrated TA in financial management to prevent/detect fraud and corruption. (FY99-00) Judicial Assessment: Judicial System Performance in the Philippines. (PRMPS/Danish Governance TF). (FY00) World Bank anticorruption training for Manila based staff.	(FY99) Banking System Reform Loan (FY00) Social Expenditure Management Project, Housing Finance TA, National Roads Improvement Management program. (FY00) Governance component of SSR.

Countries with Programs to Strengthen Governance, continued

	Grant-Based Technical Assistance	ESW and Mission Reports	

EAST ASIA AND PACIFIC, continued

	Grant-Based Technical Assistance	ESW and Mission Reports
Thailand	(FY98) IDF Grant. Financial Accountability and Good Governance. (FY00) PHRD Grant. Financial Accounting Standards Board. (FY00) ASEM Grant. Institute of Directors. (FY99-00) PHRD Grant. Legal Reform. Economic laws and civil society participation. (FY98-00) PHRD Grant. Preparing Public Sector Reform I. (FY99) IDF Grant. Strengthening the National Decentralization Committee. (FY99-00) Australian Trust Fund Grant. Support of Budget Reform. (FY99-00) Danish Trust Fund Grant. Anti-corruption Surveys of Households and Businesses. (FY00) PHRD Grant. Preparing Public Sector Reform II.	(FY99) CAS. Analyzes corruption risks. (FY99-00) Economic Management Assistance Project (technical assistance on civil service reform/public expenditure management /customs reform). (FY99-00) Public Finance Review renamed: Selected Topics in Public Finance (including public expenditure management, fiscal transparency, and decentralization). (FY99-00) Various reports on accounting and auditing program. (FY99) Anticorruption Strategy. (FY99) Anticorruption Staff Handbook. (FY00) Translation of "Parliamentarians' Guide to Curbing Corruption" (WBI).
Vietnam	(FY98) IDF Grant. Improve government accounting system. (FY00) The Bank has been providing TA on strengthening procurement since 1996. An IDF in FY00 will extend this, specifically to assist government formulate and implement a public procurement ordinance. The objective is to match standards required for entry to WTO.	(FY99) Fiscal Transparency Study (jointly with IMF); to increase budgetary transparency (at National, Provincial, and Commune levels) (FY00) PER will address transparency issues further—reviewing progress on fiscal transparency. (FY00) A Bank paper on Anticorruption will be finalized in FY00, and will contribute to a donor paper on governance—to be discussed with Government.

In-country workshops, Surveys	Governance-related lending (active projects)
(FY99) Policymakers' workshop series on public sector reform (including fiscal transparency and corruption). (FY99-00) Workshops for accountants and auditors. (FY00) Establishment of the Thailand Financial Accounting Standards Board. (FY00) Training for auditors in public sector. (FY00) Corruption surveys and review of regulations. Corruption surveys include public officials, business sector and households. Results of the surveys will be used to organize anticorruption workshop with WBI. (FY99-00) Procurement training for Project Implementation Units. Training workshops have been organized regularly by World Bank Office Bangkok procurement cluster. (FY99-00) Workshop series on economic law and civil society participation law reform that have some aspects of corporate good governance and transparency and public participation in policy formulation. (FY00) Establishment of the Institute of Directors. (FY00) Training for directors of listed companies. (FY00) Parliamentary Workshop (WBI)	(FY99) Economic and Financial Adjustment Loan (corporate governance). (FY99-00) Sector Investment Program (NGO governance) (FY00) Public Sector Reform Loan (PSAL) with large transparency and accountability component. (FY00) Public sector reform and debt management chapters of SSR. (FY00) Economic and Financial Adjustment Loan III (corporate governance).
(FY99-00) CDF pilot governance/anticorruption workshops. (FY00) The Bank is strengthening monitoring of Bank-financed contracts. In addition to ex-post reviews for all large Bank-financed contracts, a selection of small contracts is being surveyed. (FY00) Active in donor working group on governance. The Government and National Assembly have identified public administration reform and anticorruption as key themes. (FY00) Technical advice and backup to Swedish-funded diagnostic survey of corruption (WBI). (FY99) Workshop on fiscal transparency for government officials (with IMF). (FY00) Two workshops on Analytical Framework and Methodology of the PER for central and local government officials. (FY00) Conference on Project Management and Implementation with session on transparency and anticorruption.	(FY00) Structural Adjustment Credit II (SAC II) includes measures on governance, including expanding budgetary transparency (at local and central levels) and providing an enabling environment for civil society organizations.

Countries with Programs to Strengthen Governance, continued

	Grant-Based Technical Assistance	ESW and Mission Reports
EUROPE AND CENTRAL ASIA		
Regional programs		(FY99) PREM Note on new frontiers in diagnosing and combating corruption in ECA. (FY98/99) ECA Regional Anticorruption Study. (FY00) Chapter on Parliamentary Oversight in ECA Region (WBI).
Albania	(FY99) TA. Conduct a Unit Cost Comparison Study, donor coordination, tax/customs, and needs assessment to strengthen Judicial Inspection Panel. (FY99) TA. Unit Cost Comparison Study, donor coordination, tax/customs mission. (FY99) TA. Judicial Inspection Panel, consolidate Central Budget Office for courts, advance Alternative Dispute Resolution, plan dissemination of published laws and judicial decisions. (FY99) IDF Grant. Public procurement recommendations of A/C program, including private sector outreach. (FY99) TA. Support for small grants to NGOs. Government/civil society roundtables on corruption.	(FY98) CAS. Considerable discussion of corruption risks. (FY99) Anticorruption mission, report and dissemination. (FY99) Dissemination and monitoring of Government Action Plan, promotion of civil society participation, health services. (FY99) Publication and dissemination of anticorruption conference Report (including Government Action Plan and Survey Results). (FY99) Tax/customs assessment. (FY00) Preparation of anticorruption strategy. (FY00) CAS. Update continues emphasis on governance and anticorruption.
Armenia	(FY00) IDF on governance. (FY97) IDF on public procurement.	(FY99-00) Pilot IGR.
Azerbaijan		(FY99) CAS. Notable attention to governance and corruption.
Bosnia-Herzegovina		

In-country workshops, Surveys	Governance-related lending (active projects)
(FY98) Multi-country surveys of public officials, enterprises, and households and other instruments to diagnose patterns of corruption. (FY99) OECD/Organization for Security and Cooperation in Europe Workshop on Anticorruption in Transition Economies (WBI). (FY99) Council of Europe Workshop on Corruption and Crime. (FY99) USAID/OECD Workshop on Anticorruption in CIS and CEE Countries. (FY98) Joint Bank/EU Seminar on Anticorruption Strategy and Collaboration. (FY99) Anticorruption Monitoring by Civil Society in Latvia, Albania and Georgia (WBI/Danish Governance TF). (FY00) Regional Seminar for Parliamentarians (WBI). (FY00) 2 Investigative Journalism Workshops (WBI, OECD).	
(FY98) Anticorruption seminar (WBI). (FY98) Cofinance diagnostic surveys, support government-NGO working groups, incremental work on administration and judicial reform. (FY98) Diagnostic surveys on education and health. (FY99) Donor/Government Coordination Meetings (every three months).	(FY98) Structural Adjustment Credit to improve public administration, de-politicize civil service, improve competence of judiciary (required testing of judges), and strengthen Judicial Inspection Office. (FY99) Judicial Reform & Public Administration Credit to improve (financial, personnel and performance) accountability; increase professionalism of judiciary and access to up-to-date legal information; improve court administration. (FY99) Support for the Center for Educational Assessment and Evaluation (to reduce corruption in higher education sector).
(FY99) New diagnostic tools to analyze institutional causes of corruption (IGR). (FY99) Measuring Public Sector Performance in Armenia (Danish Governance Trust Fund).	(FY96) Institution-building Technical Assistance Project. (FY01) Public Sector Reform Credit.
(FY00) Survey on businesses and households.	(FY00) Public Sector Reform Adjustment Loan: policy conditions on judicial reform, public administration, civil service reform, licensing and expenditure management and auditing to improve accountability and governance. (FY00) Institutional Building Technical Assistance II: support of the Public Sector Reform Adjustment Loan.
	(FY99) Public Finance Structural Adjustment Credit.

Countries with Programs to Strengthen Governance, continued

	Grant-Based Technical Assistance	ESW and Mission Reports
EUROPE AND CENTRAL ASIA, continued		
Bulgaria		(FY99) CAS. Pays attention to corruption risks. (FY99) CPAR (FY00) Identification mission on public administration reform, governance, anticorruption, and legal and judicial reform.
Croatia		(FY99) CPAR
Georgia	(FY98) IDF Grant. Public Procurement Reform. (FY99) IDF Grant. Approved for Strengthening State Chancellery and Public Service Bureau. (FY99) TA to finance short-term Institutional Reform Adviser for Ministry of Finance to, inter alia, tackle governance-related issues. (FY00) PHRD Grant. Approved for licensing reform for institutional strengthening of the licensing and regulatory framework, analysis of intergovernmental finance, and strengthening the tax administration. (FY00) CFAA proposed to be conducted.	(FY99) Anticorruption mission and report. (FY99) Public Sector Reform Missions report progress in implementing public service reform-related recommendations from June 1998 Workshop. (FY99) Public Sector Reform missions provided technical assistance to simplify licensing regime (new law on licensing passed April 1999), institutional strengthening of tax administration, and civil service reform.
Hungary		
Kazakhstan	(FY00) IDF Grant. Public procurement.	(FY00) Review of Government's anticorruption program.
Latvia	(FY98) IDF Grant. State Audit Office. (FY98/99) IDF Grant. Public Sector Reform. (FY98) TA. Assess corruption vulnerability in tax administration. (FY98) TA. Review system of income and asset declarations. (FY98) TA. Review anticorruption law. (FY99) Foreign Investment Advisory Service "Red Tape" study. (FY99) TA. Regulatory reform. (FY99) TA. Judicial reform. (FY99) TA. Review amendments to anticorruption law. (FY00) TA. Improve regulatory drafting.	(FY98) Preparation of tax administration project. (FY98) CAS. Highlighting governance and anticorruption issues. (FY99) Corruption diagnostic surveys and report. (FY99) Anticorruption mission and report. (FY99) Report on regulatory reform. (FY99) Report on judicial reform. (FY00) Procurement cost study.
Macedonia		(FY00) CAS. Highlighting governance and anticorruption.

In-country workshops, Surveys	Governance-related lending (active projects)
(FY98) Anticorruption seminars run by WBI. (FY98) Diagnostic work on de-licensing, procurement, and state audit, cofinanced diagnostic survey, public workshop. (FY99) Civil Service Reform Workshop. (FY00) Dissemination of Corruption Survey Report.	(FY99) Judicial Reform Program project. (FY99) Transport Ministry Restructuring project. (FY99) Structural Adjustment Credit III addresses licensing and public procurement reform, and action plans for fiscal institutional reform. (FY99) Structural Reform Support project provides for TA to support Structural Adjustment Credit. (FY02) Public Sector Reform Credit (PSRC) in lending program.
	(Approved FY93) Pensions Administration and Health Insurance project. (Approved FY97) Public Financial Management project.
(FY00) Diagnostic work on corruption and delicensing.	(Approved FY94) Technical Assistance loan. Approved FY97) Treasury Modernization project. (FY98) Public Sector Resource Management Adjustment Loan (PSRMAL). (FY99) Legal Reform project. (FY01) PSRMAL II
(FY98) High-level workshop to create Government's anticorruption program, run by School of Public Administration and WB. (FY98) Public conference to discuss Corruption Prevention Council strategy adopted by Cabinet. (FY99) Public conference to disseminate Corruption Diagnostic Report and develop recommendations on 5 most vulnerable areas. (FY00) Competitive Assessment of energy sector and workshop.	(FY99) State Revenue Service Modernization project. (FY00) Governance Structural Adjustment Loan.

Countries with Programs to Strengthen Governance, continued

	Grant-Based Technical Assistance	ESW and Mission Reports
EUROPE AND CENTRAL ASIA, continued		
Moldova		
Poland	(FY00) IDF Grant. Monitoring subnational government performance.	(FY00) Diagnostic research and report, "Corruption in Poland: Review of Priority Areas and Proposals for Action." (FY00) CAS Update. Noting governance and anticorruption issues. (FY00) Country Public Procurement Assessment mission and report. (FY00) Informal Payments in Healthcare, report. (FY00) Participation in KERM (Council of Economic Ministers) Anticorruption Team. (FY00) Assistance to high-level Anticorruption Group.
Romania		(FY99) CPAR (FY00) Corruption surveys continue with USAID funding.
Russia	(FY98) IDF Grant. Legal and Institutional Framework for Development of Public Procurement.	(FY99) Evaluating and strengthening expenditure controls for greater fiscal accountability. (FY98) Introducing "Case-by-Case privatization methods and use of independent, competitively chosen financial advisors to prepare and sell state assets" (published as Bank monograph). (FY99/00) Corruption Diagnostic. (FY00) Procurement Cost Study. (FY02) Preparation of Tax Administration Modernization Project II.
Slovakia		(FY00) Public administration assessment.
Tajikistan	(FY98) IDF Grant. Public Procurement System.	
Turkey		
Ukraine	(FY98/99) CIDA/USAID/TACIS (Technical Assistance for Commonwealth of Independent States) TA project to support economic reform and integrity. (FY99) TA. Project for public feedback on municipal services. (FY99) IDF Grant. Improving public procurement. (FY00) TA. Civil service reform and deregulation.	(FY99) Study on informal economy.
Uzbekistan		

In-country workshops, Surveys	Governance related lending (active projects)
	(FY98) Structural Adjustment Loan II. (FY01) PRSC I.
(FY00) Diagnostics and workshop in Krakow City council. (FY00) Parliamentary conference on corruption and politics. (FY00) Public conference on public procurement (jointly with the Institute for Public Affairs), where CPAR was launched.	(FY00) Rural Development Project component on strengthening subnational government administration.
	(FY00) Anticorruption/ governance/public administration/legal & judicial reform mission with a $50M lending program.
(FY98) Workshop on Enterprise Reform, to foster rules-based competition, greater financial transparency, an independent regulatory regime, and reduced administrative discretion in licensing. (FY00) Diagnostics and workshop in 6 Oblasts.	(Approved FY95) Tax Administration project. (Approved FY96) Legal Reform project. (Approved FY96) Standards Development project. (FY99) State Statistical System project. (FY98/FY99) Structural Adjustment Loans (SAL2 and SAL3) contain conditionality regarding competitive restructuring of infrastructure monopolies, reducing barriers to entry, implementing international accounting and auditing standards for greater transparency. Also contain conditionality in terms of production by Russian Government of strategy for public administration reform/civil service reform.
(FY00) Diagnostics and workshop.	
	(Approved FY96/FY99) Institution-Building Technical Assistance I/II.
	(Approved FY92) Technical Assistance for Treasury Data Systems. (Approved FY96) Public Financial Management Project.
(FY98) Anticorruption seminar (WBI). (FY98) National Integrity Survey (WBI). (FY98) Deregulation, public administration reform workshop. (FY99) Parliamentary workshop on Anticorruption (WBI). (FY99) 4 Regional investigative journalist workshops (WBI). (FY99) Integrity component in the Ministry of Justice judicial training program (MOJ/WBI/ERIS). (FY99) Two service delivery surveys/corruption workshops at Oblast level (WBI). (FY99) People's Voice Conference.	(FY98) Treasury Systems project. (FY99) Public Administration Reform Loan with conditionality regarding transparency and accountability in the civil service and streamlining licensing, registration, business inspections, and customs operations.
	(Approved FY94) Institution-Building Technical Assistance.

Countries with Programs to Strengthen Governance, continued

	Grant-Based Technical Assistance	ESW and Mission Reports
LATIN AMERICA AND THE CARRIBEAN		
Regional programs	(FY99/00) Fighting Corruption in Bank-financed projects—Guide for Task Managers. Publication and Dissemination. (FY99) Workshop for senior staff on mainstreaming anticorruption work in LCR.	(FY98) Work with Latin American Center for Development Administration (CLAD)/OAS/IDB to promote networks and information exchange. (FY99) Paper for the Consultative Group for the Reconstruction of Central America: "The Fight Against Corruption: A World Bank Perspective". (FY99-00) Public Sector Modernization Projects in Latin America and the Caribbean: An Analysis of the Portfolio and Lessons Learned (Danish Governance TF—work under way).
Argentina	(FY99) IDF Grant. Support implementation of the Ethics Code by the Oficina National de Etica Publica. (FY99) Assistance to the Oficina Nacional de Etica Publica in organization of anticorruption conference.	(FY99) CFAA (FY00) Report on various aspects of governance and anti-corruption, based on three consultants' studies.
Brazil		(FY00) Background note on governance and anti-corruption for CAS.

(FY98) Participation in the Eighth International Anticorruption Conference (Lima, Peru). (FY98) International Anticorruption Forum (WBI). Held in Miami with participants from Bolivia, Chile, Colombia, Dominican Republic, Ecuador, Honduras, Mexico, Nicaragua, Panama, Paraguay, Peru, San Salvador. (FY99) Participation in Central America Regional Integrity Workshop (WBI). (FY99) Participation in III Congreso Internacional del CLAD sobre la Reforma del Estado (Madrid, Spain). (FY99) Participation in Symposium on Enhancement of Probity in the Hemisphere (Santiago, Chile). (FY00) Participation in Central America: Fiscal Transparency and Anticorruption Workshop (Tegucigalpa, Honduras). (FY00) Participation in IV Congreso Internacional del CLAD Sobre la Reforma del Estado (Mexico City). (FY00) Participation in Ninth International Anticorruption Conference (Durban, South Africa). (FY00) Participation in IX OLACEFs conference in Asuncion, Paraguay, on collaboration between the World Bank and Supreme Audit Institutions. (FY00) Participation at 14th Annual New Developments in Financial Management Conference in Miami, FL, with 350 participants from 50 countries between MDBs and Supreme Audit Institutions. (FY00-03) Regional Program to raise awareness and promote investigative journalism (WBI, OAS).	
	(Approved FY95) Provincial Development Loan II. (Approved FY96) Public Investment Strengthening Technical Assistance loan. (Approved FY97) Pension Administration Technical Assistance loan. (FY98) Provincial Reform Adjustment loans (Rio Negro, Salta, San Juan, and Tucuman). (FY99) Argentina Year 2000 project. (FY98) Model Court Development project. (FY99) Social and Fiscal National Identification System Program project. (FY99) Special SAL.
	(Approved FY97) Mato Grosso State Privatization project. (FY98) Minas Gerais State Privatization project. (FY98) Pension Reform Learning and Innovation Loan.

Countries with Programs to Strengthen Governance, continued

	Grant-Based Technical Assistance	ESW and Mission Reports
LATIN AMERICA AND THE CARRIBEAN, continued		
Bolivia	(FY99) IDF Grant. Strengthen institutional capacity of the Ministry of Finance's Internal Auditing Department. (FY99) Institutional Reform Project.	(FY99) CAS. "Best practice." (FY00) IGR (FY00) CFAA (FY00) CPAR
Colombia	(FY98) Anticorruption component of IDF Grant. (FY00) Technical support for anticorruption amendments to national procurement law.	(FY99) CFAA (FY00) Anticorruption component of Cali city development strategy study. (FY00) CPAR
Dominican Republic		(FY99) CAS. "Best practice." (FY99-00) CPAR (FY00) CFAA
Ecuador	(FY00) Preparation of IDF proposal for Commission for Civic Control of Corruption.	(FY99) Contributed to publication of *Etica y Corrupción: Estudio de Casos* by Napoleon Saltos Galarza. (FY00) CPAR
El Salvador		
Guatemala		(FY99-00) CPAR
Guyana		(FY99) CPAR
Haiti		(FY99-00) CPAR
Honduras		(FY99-00) CPAR
Jamaica		(FY00) Background note on governance and anticorruption for CAS.
Mexico		(FY99) Background note on governance and anticorruption. (FY99) Government seminar on public sector reform and anticorruption. (FY99) Anticorruption seminar for state comptrollers (Mazatlan).
Nicaragua		

In-country workshops, Surveys	Governance-related lending (active projects)
(FY98) Ministerial Integrity Workshop (WBI). (FY98) Establish a National Integrity Committee and Unit (WBI). (FY98) Household Service Delivery Survey (WBI). (FY98) Private Sector Service Delivery Survey (WBI). (FY99) National Integrity Workshop (WBI).	(Approved FY95) Judicial Reform project. (FY98) Financial Decentralization and Accountability project. (FY99) APL. Institutional Reform.
(FY00) Help Government in Anticorruption initiative.	(FY99) Public Financial Management Project. Corruption vulnerability study of tax and customs administration with preparation of Risk Maps.
(FY99) Survey: A New Approach to Judicial Reform Policy-making: Stakeholders' Views vs. Court Statistics (Danish Governance TF).	
(FY99) Corruption surveys of households, businesses and public servants (WBI). (FY99) Technical Assistance for the preparation of Anticorruption Action Plan (WBI). (FY99) Anticorruption surveys (WBI).	(Approved FY95) Technical Assistance for Modernization of the State. (Approved FY97) Judicial Reform project.
	(Approved FY97) Public Sector Modernization project.
(FY98) Legal Reform Workshop (WBI).	(FY98) Integrated Financial Management II. (FY98) Tax Administration Technical Assistance Loan. (FY99) Judicial Reform project.
	(Approved FY93) Public Administration project.
	(Approved FY96) Public Sector Modernization Structural Adjustment Credit. (Approved FY96) Public Sector Modernization Technical Assistance Credit.
	(Approved FY94) Tax Administration Reform project. (Approved FY97) Public Sector Modernization project.
(FY98-99) Two National Integrity Workshops (WBI). (FY98) Household Service Delivery Survey (WBI). (FY99) Disaster Relief Integrity Project (WBI).	(Approved FY95) Institutional Development Credit. (FY98) Financial Sector Adjustment Credit (FY00) Preparation of anticorruption component of Economic Management Technical Assistance Credit.

Countries with Programs to Strengthen Governance, continued

	Grant-Based Technical Assistance	ESW and Mission Reports	
LATIN AMERICA AND THE CARRIBEAN, continued			
Panama		(FY00) CPAR	
Peru		(FY00) CPAR	
Uruguay	(FY99) IDF Grant. Improve government auditing and financial management.	(FY99-00) CPAR	
Venezuela			
MIDDLE EAST AND NORTH AFRICA			
Regional Programs		(FY00) Anticorruption strategy note. (FY00) MNA Good Governance	
Algeria			
Djibouti			
Egypt, Arab Rep.		(FY00) Preparatory work for note on Public Sector—Private Business relationship.	
Jordan	(FY99) Public Procurement Modernization.	(FY99) Public Sector Review (FY99) CPAR (FY99) CPFA (FY00) CFAA	
Lebanon	(FY98) Procurement Legislation Reform.	(FY99) Public Expenditure notes (sectoral and overview). (FY99) CPFA	
Morocco	(FY99) Public Procurement Reform.	(FY99) Informal background paper on corruption in Morocco. (FY99-00) CPAR (FY00) CDF Governance and Public Sector Reform—draft under discussion. (FY00) CAS. Gives attention to public sector reform and governance issues.	
West Bank/Gaza	(FY99) Government Financial Management Information System.	(FY99) Public Sector Review. (FY99) CPFA (FY00) CDF Governance and Public Sector Reform—draft under discussion. (FY00) PER. Publication and dissemination.	
Tunisia		(FY99) Social and Structural Review—focus on public sector performance.	

In-country workshops, Surveys	Governance-related lending (active projects)
	(FY99) Urban Property Rights project.
(FY99) Municipal Integrity Systems in Latin America (WBI).	(Approved FY90) Technical Assistance project for Pre-investment and Institutional Development. (Approved FY93) Judicial Infrastructure Development project. (FY98) Supreme Court Modernization project. (FY98) Public Sector Modernization project.
(FY99) Tunis workshop on Cabinet-Level Decisionmaking (WBI).	
	(FY01) Budget Systems Modernization Project.
	(Approved FY97) Technical Assistance project. Supports Government decisionmaking related to macroeconomic reforms and the associated policy and programming framework.
	(FY01) Public Sector Reform Loan (in preparation). (FY00) Accountability and Transparency component of Civil Service Reform under preparation.
(FY99) Procurement Financial Management Training.	(FY94) Technical Assistance for Revenue Enhancement.
(FY99) Anticorruption Workshop for government, private sector and civil society to initiate a joint strategy regarding anticorruption activities. (FY00) Follow-up to Workshop, including support to secretariat of steering committee, preparation of action plans and background briefs.	(FY99) Policy Reform Support Loan. (Expenditure management, Procurement, Judicial Reform). (FY00) Preparation of legal and judicial development projects.
(FY98/99) Service Delivery Survey and workshops (WBI). (FY99)Procurement Financial Management Training.	(FY99/00) Preparation of legal and judicial development projects.

Countries with Programs to Strengthen Governance, continued

	Grant-Based Technical Assistance	ESW and Mission Reports	
MIDDLE EAST AND NORTH AFRICA, continued			
Yemen		(FY99) CAS. Pays particular attention to corruption and civil service reform. (FY00/01) PER	
SOUTH ASIA			
Regional programs		(FY99) Corruption issues in South Asia—paper. (FY99) Supervision and Procurement "best practices" paper. (FY00/01) Staff training on corruption.	
Bangladesh	(FY99) IDF Grant. Improve government auditing and financial management. (FY99) TA. Assist Controller and Auditor General to develop ability to conduct project audits.	(FY98) CAS. Strong discussion of governance issues. (FY98) CPFA (FY99) Diagnostic case studies on corruption in government. (FY99) Bangladesh Procurement Assessment Study. (FY99-00) CPAR (FY00) Country paper on Corruption. (FY00) IGR (FY00) CFAA	
Bhutan		(FY98) CPFA	
India	(FY99) IDF Grant. Upgrade institutional capacity of Auditor General of India.	(FY99) Corruption issues—Country paper. (FY99) Governance issues addressed in state studies. (FY00) CDR (FY99) CPFA (FY00) Economic reports with substantial governance component (Rajasthan, Andhra Pradesh)	
Maldives		(FY98) CPFA	
Nepal	(FY99) IDF Grant. Third IDF Grant to upgrade institutional capacity of Auditor General.	(FY98) CPFA (FY99) Corruption Issues—Country paper (FY99) CPAR	
Pakistan		(FY98) CPFA (FY99) Corruption Issues—Background paper. (FY99) PER (FY99) Governance paper for Pakistan 2010. (FY99/00) CPAR	
Sri Lanka		(FY99) Corruption issues—Country paper. (FY99) CPFA (FY00) Governance and Accountability report. (FY00) Report on the media (WBI)	

In-country workshops, Surveys	Governance-related lending (active projects)
(FY99) Procurement and Financial Management Training.	(FY99) Legal and Judicial Development. (FY99) Public Sector Management Adjustment Credit. (FY00) Civil Service Modernization.
(FY99) Anticorruption seminar for parliamentarians (WBI, Canada, TI-Bangladesh). (FY00) Regional Workshop for Editors (WBI).	
(FY98) Anticorruption seminar (WBI). (FY99) Survey on corruption by TI-Bangladesh.	(FY01) Legal and Judicial Reform Project.
(FY98) Anticorruption seminar (WBI).	(FY99/00) Governance and anticorruption components under preparation for Uttar Pradesh Program Loan 1.
(FY00-01) Pakistan Tripartite Baseline Survey.	(Approved FY96) Improvement to Financial Reporting and Auditing project.
(FY00) Anticorruption workshop and Action Plan.	

BANKWIDE ACTIVITIES

(FY99-00) Public Sector Strategy Paper: "The World Bank: Addressing the Challenge of Reforming Public Institutions and Strengthening Governance."

PREM Notes:

(FY98) PREM Note 4: "Corruption and development"

(FY99) PREM Note 7: "New frontiers in diagnosing and combating corruption"

(FY99) PREM Note 19: "Using an ombudsman to oversee public officials"

(FY99) PREM Note 23: "Using surveys for public sector reform"

(FY99) PREM Note 24: "Fostering institutions to contain corruption"

(FY99) PREM Note 25: "Assessing borrower ownership using reform readiness analysis"

(FY00) PREM Note 26: "The law and economics of judicial reform"

(FY00) PREM Note 29: "Assessing political commitment to fighting corruption"

(FY00) PREM Note 30: "Mobilizing civil society to fight corruption in Bangladesh"

(FY00) PREM Note 31: "Rethinking civil service reform"

(FY00) PREM Note 33: "An anticorruption strategy for revenue administration"

(FY00) PREM Note 34: "Reducing court delays: Five lessons from the United States"

WBI Books and Working Papers:

(FY98) "Curbing Corruption" (WBI Development Series)

(FY98) The Importance of Supreme Audit Institutions in Curbing Corruption

(FY98) Social Marketing Strategies to Curb Corruption

(FY99) New Perspectives in Curbing Corruption (WBI with TI)

(FY00) The Role of Media in Curbing Corruption

(FY99-00) DRG and other research (papers in final or draft form):

- "Aggregating Governance Indicators"
- "Governance Matters"
- Review paper on the consequences of corruption.
- "Assessing Political Will and Opportunity for Anti-Corruption"
- "Corruption and Political Finance in Africa"
- "Corruption, Public Finances and the Unofficial Economy"
- "Making Voice Work: The Report Card on Bangalore's Public Service"
- "Moral Hazard and Optimal Corruption"
- "Regulatory Discretion, Corruption and the Unofficial Economy"
- "Decentralization Data Project" (Danish Governance TF)
- "Does 'Grease' Payment Speed Up the Wheels of Commerce?"
- "Corruption, Composition of Capital Flows and Currency Crisis"
- "Rotten Bureaucracy and Endogenous Capital Controls"
- "Who Must Pay Bribes and How Much?", draft—under review for publication
- "The effects of corruption and taxation on growth: Firm level evidence", draft—under review for publication. Joint with Ray Fisman, Columbia University
- "The cost of doing business: Ugandan firms' experiences with corruption"—Africa Region Working Paper Series No. 6 (forthcoming)

"Special Governance Zone" concept development in transition and developing economies

Training Workshops: (FY98) 48 Integrity Awareness Seminars at headquarters and resident missions. (FY99) Anticorruption Diagnostic Tools (PRMPS, WBI). (FY99) Mainstreaming Anticorruption in the CAS (PRMPS, WBI). (FY99) Reducing Corruption: A Search for Lessons of Experience (PRMPS, WBI). (FY99) Regional Orientation Workshops in AFR, EAP, ECA, LAC, MNA (Regions, WBI). Preparation for SAR (FY00). (FY99) New Employee Orientation: Ethics component (OPE).	(FY98-99-00) Observer status at • OECD Working Group on Bribery, • International Chamber of Commerce Standing Committee on Extortion and Bribery, • DAC Experts Group on Monitoring Performance in Good Governance, • United Nations Office of Drug Control, and • Interpol International Groups of Experts on Corruption. (FY98-99-00) Participation on MDB Working Group on Governance, Anticorruption and Capacity Building.
(FY99-00) Procurement Innovations Workshop (Danish Governance TF).	

1   For fiscal 1999 approximately 30 projects were excluded because relevant documentation was not yet available.

2   The significance of each component is not identified. The components vary from being a very small to a major component of the project.

3   Operations Policy and Strategy. "Fixing ESW: Where Are We," July 11, 2000.

4   These toolkits build on earlier diagnostic efforts in the Bank, including:

- preparing a Public Investment Program (Andrew Bird and Mike Stevens, October 1991)

- questionnaire on comprehensiveness and budget unity (Government Expenditure and Financial Management Training Program, November 1994)

- diagnostic on accounting standards in *Financial Accounting Reporting and Auditing Handbook* (Central and Operational Accounting Division, January 1995)

- Financial Accountability Checklist for the public sector (Randolph Andersen, ACTCO 1996)

- diagnostic on weaknesses and possible improvements in budget and financial management in the public sector (part II, Public Expenditure Management Handbook, World Bank, 1998)

- diagnostic questionnaire (Budget institutions and expenditure outcomes, Campos and Pradhan, World Bank, 1996)

- Checklist of budget/financial management practices (Annex B, *Public Expenditure Management Handbook*, World Bank, 1998)

5   See, for example, Report of the Managing Director and the President on Bank-Fund Collaboration, Sec M98-733, Sept. 4, 1998.

6   In 1997/98, the consultation was postponed pending the completion of the broader review of Bank-Fund collaboration that led to the above-mentioned joint report of the two institutions.

7   This annex draws in part from a briefing note prepared for an informal Board discussion on governance indicators on July 1, 1999. The note was prepared by Eric Swanson (DECDG) with input from Shaida Badiee (DECDG), David Cieslikowski (DECDG), Cheryl Gray (PRMPS) and Daniel Kaufmann (WBI).

8   Cukierman, Alex, Steven Webb, and Bilin Neyapti. 1994. "Measuring Central Bank Independence and Its Effect on Policy Outcomes." *International Center for Economic Growth Occasional Paper No. 58:1-62.*